GENETICS - RESEARCH AND ISSUES

RECURRENCE RISK IN AUTISM SPECTRUM DISORDERS

GENETICS - RESEARCH AND ISSUES

Additional books and e-books in this series can be found on Nova's website under the Series tab.

GENETICS - RESEARCH AND ISSUES

RECURRENCE RISK IN AUTISM SPECTRUM DISORDERS

MICHAEL BEENSTOCK

nova
Medicine & Health
New York

DOI: 10.52305/SKDD3567

Library of Congress Cataloging-in-Publication Data

ISBN: 978-1-68507-129-5

Published by Nova Science Publishers, Inc. † New York

CONTENTS

PREFACE

About ten years ago a colleague asked me about the prospects of having a second child on the spectrum of autism. I replied that I didn't know and, in any case, as an economist, it is not a subject with which I was professionally involved. On the other hand, I added that I knew how to find the answer because I was aware that the National Insurance Institute in Jerusalem provided a special benefit to the parents of children on the spectrum. I had been using personal administrative data records at the National Insurance Institute to study unemployment, so I surmised that there might be personal administrative data records on families of children on the spectrum, and that in these records I would find families with more than one child on the spectrum. My surmises were correct. The director of research at the National Insurance Institute, Dr. Daniel Gottlieb, kindly gave me access to these administrative records in a specially dedicated research room to protect confidentiality. By 2013 I started work with the research assistance of Dan Feldman, who had attended some of my econometrics courses.

My natural inclination was to approach these data as an econometrician, but also as a social scientist. As far as I was concerned, it doesn't make a great deal of difference if the subject matter has nothing to do with economics, provided it is amenable to econometric investigation. I hadn't been working very long when Hagai Levine of the School of

Public Health at my university contacted me to find out what I was up to. To be frank I hadn't planned to do more than estimate recurrence risk using data for Israel. I had no idea at the time that these population cohort data are unique. Hagai and Raanan Raz helped me write a paper on recurrence risk, which was published in *Research on Autism Spectrum Disorders* in 2015.

The next thing that happened was the establishment of an interdisciplinary Center for Autism Research at my university, headed by Cory Shulman. I learned a lot through the Center about treatment, genetics, epidemiology and related matters. I was curious to see what happened to children on the spectrum when they became adults. Ofir Pinto at the National Insurance Institute provided me access to the longitudinal records of individuals on the spectrum between the ages of 18 and 31. Together with Arie Rimmerman of Haifa University we published the results of this research on the transition into adulthood in the *Journal of Disability Policy Studies* in 2020.

During the course of this research I grew increasingly uncomfortable with the absence of social science in the study of recurrence risk, as well as with the statistical methodology used. So, in 2018 I returned to my previous work on recurrence risk, this time with the research assistance of Liraz Klausner. I began to find evidence that the diagnosis timing of index children had direct and indirect causal effects on recurrence risk through reproductive stoppage. These results conflicted with the dominant neurodevelopmental paradigm, and were greeted by skepticism at seminars and conferences. Indeed, an editor of a leading journal wrote to me to say that my paper is too controversial for review.

At this point I should declare an intellectual interest. In 2012 I published book on *Heredity, Inequality and Family* (MIT Press), which included an attack on behavioral genetics. When Folstein and Rutter (1978) found that recurrence risk of ASD is greater for identical twins than for fraternal twins, they appealed to behavioral genetics to claim that the etiology of ASD must be genetic. Behavioral genetics is tautological in that it rules out behavioral reasons for why the outcomes of identical twins are more correlated than for fraternal twins. Hence, what Folstein and

Rutter observed may not have had anything to do with genetics. Since then, their neurodevelopmental model has become the dominant and even exclusive paradigm. The results of this third round of research were published in 2021 in *Research on Autism Spectrum Disorders* and elsewhere.

It is always difficult for academics to cross disciplines. We are trained to be hedgehogs rather than foxes in the sense of Isiah Berlin. Hedgehogs are experts in their immediate location. Foxes roam over many locations; they are interdisciplinary. Academic disciplines have their own journals, have different scientific standards, and even have different styles of communication. In the present volume, in the tradition of the fox, I bring together the fruits of almost a decade of research involving theoretical and methodological issues in the study of recurrence risk.

Michael Beenstock

Jerusalem
September, 2021

Chapter 1

RECURRENCE RISK

Since its identification as a separate pathology in the 1940s by Kanner (1944), autism has grown into a major field of scientific study in terms of its etiology, epidemiology and treatment. Here, however, our concern is limited to the specific issue of recurrence risk, which arises when parents have more than one child with autism spectrum disorder (ASD). Although numerous books have been written about autism in general as well as specific topics in autism, there is apparently no comprehensive text on recurrence risk. So, our present purpose it to fill this lacuna.

AUDIENCES

This study is aimed at three audiences. First, parents of children on the spectrum are naturally concerned that they might have another child with ASD. This child might be the immediate younger sibling of their index child (first child with ASD), or it might be a higher order younger sibling. This concern reflects the fact that recurrence risk for ASD is many times larger than the risk of ASD in the general population. Once parents have a child with ASD, they are much more likely to have a further child with ASD than parents who have children without ASD. As we shall see, empirical estimates of recurrence risk vary widely. However, it turns out that much of this variation may be attributed to inference from non-representative samples, which generate biased estimates of recurrence risk.

The second audience comprises health professionals, clinicians and counsellors who advise parents on the prospects of having further children with ASD. This audience derives from the first, although they are quite separate. Hopefully, the contents of the present study will provide this audience with a more sophisticated and critical understanding about how to intermediate between the results of scientific research and the advice that they give to parents. Indeed, a general theme in this study is that counsellors have most probably been too radical in this intermediation process. They have exaggerated the risks of ASD recurrence by uncritically accepting biased estimates of recurrence risk, and they have failed to distinguish between unconditional and conditional recurrence risk. Unconditional recurrence risk refers to the average risk of recurrence regardless of what is known about parents, including their ages, ethnicity, the number of regular children etc. Conditional risk refers to the risk for specific groups of parents. For example, recurrence risk may be smaller for parents who have managed to have several regular children than for parents whose firstborn has ASD.

The third and most important audience comprises the scientific community. We shall contend that the study of recurrence risk is essentially different from the study of ASD in the general population. The main reason for this difference is that whereas parents in the general population are not overly concerned that their next child might have ASD or some other condition, matters are totally different, as we have seen, for parents of index children. Parents in the general population naturally hope that their children will be healthy and develop normally. They understand, however, the risks that these hopes will not be fulfilled because of physical or developmental handicaps of different types. By contrast, having a child with ASD is a game-changer for parents. Not only must they care for their child, they also understand that any further children they might have are at elevated risk for ASD. Having a physically handicapped child is also a game-changer. However, the risk of having further handicapped children is mostly the same as for the general population. For example, recurrence risk for deafness and blindness is not elevated.

Because recurrence risk for ASD is elevated, parents of index children curtail their fertility by engaging in reproductive stoppage whereas parents in the general population do not. Of course, all parents engage in fertility control to some degree because they plan their family size. However, reproductive stoppage refers to the specific elevated limitation of fertility by parents of children with ASD. Reproductive stoppage makes it difficult for epidemiologists to estimate recurrence risk. If all parents of index children engaged in reproductive stoppage, it would of course be impossible to estimate recurrence risk because by definition children with ASD would not have younger siblings. To estimate recurrence risk, at least some parents must refrain from reproductive stoppage. If parents who refrain from reproductive stoppage are a representative sample of the population of parents who have children with ASD, it will be possible to use their data to obtain unbiased estimates of recurrence risk. Their self-selection into reproductive stoppage is unrelated to outcome of interest, which is recurrence risk. Matters, however, will be entirely different if their self-selection happens to be related to recurrence risk. Intuitively, if for example parents who refrain from reproductive stoppage happen to be more likely to have children on the spectrum, their data will exaggerate estimates of recurrence risk, which will be biased upwards.

In summary, because parents are not randomly assigned to reproductive stoppage and instead are self-selected, epidemiologists face issues of inference that do not arise with the incidence and prevalence of ASD risk in the general population. Although this should be obvious, epidemiologists have on the whole ignored the issue of potential selection bias in the study of recurrence risk. By default, they have implicitly assumed that reproductive stoppage is randomly assigned to parents, and that selection bias is ignorable. Hence, a major theme in the present study is to elevate selection bias to its appropriate place in the study of recurrence risk of ASD.

The failure to account of selection bias in the epidemiology of recurrence risk is surprising because epidemiologists have traditionally prioritized the importance of confounding in their research programs. Confounding arises when an outcome, which truly depends on factor X, appears to depend on factor Z simply because Z and X happen to be correlated. Although selection bias and confounding are conceptually different, they share the same result, which in the present context means that estimates of recurrence risk are biased. It is difficult to understand, therefore, why the epidemiological study of recurrence risk has emphasized confounding to the exclusion of selection bias (Infante – Rivard and Cusson 2018).

Apart from highlighting the importance of selection bias in the study of recurrence risk, the present study involves a second general theme that has been overlooked by epidemiologists in the specific study of recurrence risk and perhaps ASD research in general. During the last 30 years or so, epidemiological research into ASD has been dominated by the so-called neurodevelopmental paradigm (Rutter 2010) according to which the etiology of ASD is essentially biological or genetic. According to this paradigm, the etiology of ASD is not behavioral in general, and it has nothing to do with parents in particular. This was not always the case. Indeed, we shall recall that Kanner and other pioneers of autism research, such as Bettelheim, thought that the etiology of ASD was behavioral in general, and resulted from poor parenting in particular. We shall recall how during the 1980s the neurodevelopmental paradigm supplanted the behavioral paradigm to the point that behavioral research ceased altogether. Indeed, behavioral research has even assumed a status of political incorrectness because it is suggestive that recurrence risk might be blamed on parents.

A central purpose in the present study is to restore the balance between biological and behavioral etiologies of ASD. There are two aspects to this. First, behaviorism does not imply that parents are to blame for ASD in their children. Behaviorism, which characterizes the social sciences, including sociology, anthropology, economics and political science, does not mean that parents are to blame for their children's outcomes in life, or that the poor and unemployed are to blame for their own plights. Second, it is unhealthy when scientific disciplines identify themselves with some exclusive paradigm. Therefore, the approach taken in the present study is more pluralistic and interdisciplinary. Specifically, recurrence risk is investigated drawing on behavioral as well as neurodevelopmental thinking.

A third general theme concerns causality, which tends to be vague in epidemiological inquiry. Epidemiological research is based on observational data rather than experimental data. It is obviously easier to attribute causality in experimental data where, for example, a treatment group is randomly administered some intervention (such as Covid-19 vaccination), while the control group does not receive the treatment, i.e., the gold-standard of randomized trials. When the data are observational the treated are self-selected as are the controls, as are parents who engage in reproductive stoppage and parents who refrain from it. If the treated in observational data happen to have superior outcomes than the untreated, this does not mean that the treatment is efficient. It might simply mean that the treated are positively self-selected; they would have had superior outcomes even without the treatment.

It is traditional in epidemiological research is to list ‘reservations’, which might undermine the results. A common reservation is that the reported effect of factor X on some outcome might not be causal; correlation does not establish causality. By contrast, the present study draws on statistical and econometric methodologies that are concerned with identifying causal effects in observational studies. In particular, the role of ‘natural experimentation’ in the identification of causal effects is highlighted. In natural experiments the causal effect of factor X on some outcome is identified by finding some third factor Z, which is correlated with X but which is independent of the outcome. Hence, Z serves to randomize X as in an experiment from real-life. Z is an ‘instrumental variable’ for X. Indeed, natural experiments involving human beings may be more informative than randomized trials because in the former people are randomized naturally without their knowledge, whereas in the latter there arise problems of compliance and Hawthorne effects, which induce experimental bias. For example, participants in the experiment might try to please by providing positive results, or they might not comply by pretending to take the treatment

Suppose we wish to study the effect of behavioral factor X on recurrence risk, where X refers to parents' behavior, such as their 'resilience' (to be defined later). If more resilient parents are less likely to engage in reproductive stoppage a negative correlation between resilience and recurrence risk does not necessarily mean that there is a favorable causal effect of resilience on recurrence risk. It might simply mean that resilient parents self-select into having further children; the observed negative effect is induced by selection bias. To identify the causal effect of resilience on recurrence risk, we suggest as an 'instrumental variable' for resilience the date at which index children are diagnosed with ASD. We shall argue that although these dates are obviously not random, they are independent of the outcome of interest, the risk of ASD in younger siblings. Hence dates of diagnosis for index children are used to represent Z.

In summary, our study of recurrence risk draws on methodological developments from outside the discipline of epidemiology. These developments concern self-selection by parents into reproductive stoppage and the identification of causal effects in observational studies. Our study is not only methodologically interdisciplinary, it is also scientifically interdisciplinary insofar as it integrates behavioral theory drawn from the social sciences into the dominant neurodevelopmental paradigm. The latter might be less important in the study of the incidence and prevalence of ASD in the general population, but it is essential in the study of recurrence risk in which context the behavior of parents in terms of reproductive stoppage and their resilience might be salient.

PLAN OF STUDY

Broadly speaking, theoretical and methodological issues relevant to the study of recurrence risk are addressed first in chapters 2 and 3 respectively. In chapter 2 we focus on conceptual and theoretical issues, which largely concern the juxtaposition between the neurodevelopmental and behavioral paradigms in the study of recurrence risk. Chapter 2 begins by recalling that the founding fathers of autism were behaviorists, heavily influenced by psychoanalysis. Specifically, 'refridgerator mothers' were blamed for the ASD status of their children. It is surprising that this etiology was based on a handful of cases. This behavioral theory was discredited following the so-called Bettelheim scandal in which Bruno Bettelheim, a founding father of autism, was accused by some of his then adult patients of cruelty and abuse.

It was about this time (late 1970s) that Sir Michael Rutter founded the so-called neurodevelopmental paradigm based on a handful of identical and fraternal twins. Recurrence risk was greater among identical twins than among fraternal twins. Rutter appealed to the discipline of behavioral genetics to account for this difference, according to which the common denominator to identical twins is that they are genetically identical whereas fraternal twins are not. Chapter 2 includes, therefore, a critical appraisal of behavioral genetics. The nub of this critique is that despite the reference to behaviorism in 'behavioral genetics', behavioral genetics ironically rules out behavioral explanations for the larger correlation in the outcomes of identical twins. The neurodevelopmental paradigm conveniently ruled out parenting as a factor in the psychopathology of ASD in general, and recurrence risk in particular.

In the age-old dichotomy between 'nature' and 'nurture', ASD and recurrence risk was attributed to 'nature' by the neurodevelopmental paradigm. All that remained to be done was for investigators to identify the aspects of 'nature' that caused ASD, including genetic, biological and neurological phenomena. 'Nurture' was completely off-bounds and side-tracked. After 1980 there are no references to 'nurture' in the study of ASD and recurrence risk.

Chapter 2 concludes with an outline of behavioral theory, which characterizes the social sciences, and draws particularly on Nobel laureate Gary Becker's seminal *Treatise on the Family* (Becker 1992). It has two separate branches, the rational model and the irrational model. In the former people are assumed to make rational decisions. For example, they make rational decisions to engage or not in reproductive stoppage by conducting informal cost-benefit analyses in which they compare the net advantages to them of stoppage versus the alternative. There are rational theories of fertility, consumer behavior, marriage, education and indeed every aspect of life. The rational model forms the axiomatic foundation of economics dating back to Adam Smith and David Hume.

The irrational model also assumes that people make decisions based on cost-benefit comparisons, however, they are not strictly rational. They use rules of thumb and heuristics to make their decisions. They do not think sufficiently far ahead about the consequences of their choices. The irrational behavioral model was originally developed by psychologists (Kahneman and Tversky 1979), but came to be known as 'behavioral economics'. It is easy to see that in economics the irrational model provides a role for governments to intervene to improve matters. Behavioral theory has deep implications for how society should be run and coordinated.

We shall focus particularly on behavioral theories of the family in which the relation between parents and siblings is germane to the study of recurrence risk. Examples include the emotional and physical investments by parents in their children and the intergenerational transmission of outcomes. Do parents invest more in their less-fit children to compensate them for what they lack, or do they invest more in their fitter children where the returns are greater? Do siblings support each other or do they compete as rivals? These outcomes may be economic, social, criminological and epidemiological. The bottom line is that from a behavioral perspective there is no obvious reason why recurrence risk should be excluded.

It is stressed that our purpose is not to demote the neurodevelopmental paradigm in the study of recurrence risk. Rather, it is to integrate behaviorism with neurodevelopmentalism. The neurodevelopmental interpretation of recurrence risk is based on the idea that if parents have a child with ASD, they are genetically or biologically more predisposed to ASD than parents who have regular children. This explains why recurrence risk is many times larger than the risk of ASD in the general population.

The behavioral interpretation of recurrence risk is based on the idea that if parents have a child with ASD it makes them behave differently to parents of regular children. It might make them rear younger siblings in ways, discussed in detail in chapter 7, that are conducive to ASD. The neurodevelopmental paradigm rules out such behavioral influences. Incidentally, it also rules out the possibility of selection bias; if ASD is genetic or biological self-selection and reproductive stoppage should not matter.

Whereas chapter 2 is concerned with theory, chapter 3 is concerned with methodological issues that arise in the study of recurrence risk. They include sampling methodology, the identification of causal effects in observational studies, testing for sample selection bias, and correcting for sample selection if it is present. This material draws on statistical theory and econometrics. Econometrics was originally developed by economists in the 1930s to test for causal effects in observational studies. These ideas constitute the so-called instrumental variables method, which later on in the 20th century became known as the method of 'natural experimentation'. As often happens, statisticians and econometricians worked in parallel with insufficient communication between them. It is compulsory for students of economics to study econometrics at undergraduate and graduate levels. Increasingly, leading graduate schools in political science, sociology and psychology require their students to study econometrics because it provides them with the methodological tools to identify causal effects and to handle selection bias in observational studies. On the other hand, students of epidemiology have not been exposed to these methodological concerns, which is why they are emphasized in the present study.

We also recall the rudiments of sampling theory. As we shall see, estimates of recurrence risk have been based on clinical data gathered by practitioners treating children with ASD. Since these children are unlikely to be representative of the population of children with ASD, estimates of recurrence risk obtained from clinical data are likely to be biased. In this context, investigators have sought to enhance their sample sizes by using 'snowball' methods in which participants in the sample suggest friends and acquaintances to investigators who might be interested in being enlisted into the sample. These and related heterodox sampling methods are critically appraised.

In recent years investigators have increasingly used ‘population cohort data’ to estimate recurrence risk, which comprise the population of children with ASD by birth cohort. Population cohort data have two obvious advantages. First, sampling methodology is no longer relevant because the universe of children with ASD is observed. Second, the number of observations is many times larger than in clinical samples. Population cohort data for ASD are available in California, Sweden, Denmark and Israel. It turns out, not surprisingly, that estimates of recurrence risk from population cohort data are different to their counterparts from clinical data. We ask whether these population cohort data really cover the entire universe of children with ASD.

Selection bias may also arise in population cohort data. This is particularly important in the context of recurrence risk because parents who engage in reproductive stoppage are self - selected. Hence, the data used to estimate recurrence risk and the factors that determine it are generally not a random sample of parents as a whole. Indeed, most empirical studies of recurrence risk implicitly assume by default that parents who do not engage in reproductive stoppage constitute a random sample of parents as a whole. We mention, however, three studies in which selection bias in recurrence risk is explicitly handled using heterodox methods rather than the canonical methods mentioned below.

Like the issue of causality, the methodological literature on selection bias is large and has attracted extensive attention among statisticians and econometricians. In this literature self-selection is hypothesized to depend on observables, such as age, gender and ethnicity as well as unobservables, such as ability, fear and conviction. Statisticians assume that selection bias depends entirely on observables and then test for the sensitivity of results to potential hidden (unobservable) confounders. If the results are not sensitive then all is well. Econometricians assume from the outset that selection bias depends on unobservables as well as observables. Three main econometric traditions have emerged. In the first, although the unobservables are by definition unknown, their distribution is assumed to be known, e.g., they have multivariate normal distributions. In the second, selection depends on instrumental variables (see above), which by definition are independent of what is unobserved. Whereas the first two traditions make strong parametric assumptions, the third nonparametric tradition makes no assumptions at all.

A further methodological issue concerns data censoring, which arises in two separate contexts. First, as explained below, the study period ends on December 31, 2012. Suppose the younger sibling of an index child happened to be 3 years old on this date and had not been diagnosed with ASD. In the data this sibling does not constitute a case of recurrence risk. However, the same sibling might eventually be diagnosed with ASD after 2012; his ASD status is censored. Matters would be different if the sibling was 15 years old at the end of 2012 by which time his non-ASD status would be ascertained. If he was going to be diagnosed with ASD it would already have happened.

Second, the completed fertility of mothers would be censored if they were of child-bearing age at the end of 2012. The censoring of mothers arises in the analysis of reproductive stoppage. Suppose a mother was 35 years old at the end of 2012 and she had no further children after her index child. In the data this mother would appear as if she had engaged in reproductive stoppage. However, she might have had a further child after 2012.

From the current standpoint of 2021 we could, of course, check whether siblings were diagnosed with ASD after 2012 and whether mothers had further children. Unfortunately plans to extend the study period beyond 2012 were disrupted by the Covid-19 epidemic, which prevented access to the research room at the National Insurance Institute. However, there will always be an end to the study period whether it happens to be the end of 2012 or the end of 2020. The problem of data censoring is always present.

A radical solution to the data censoring problem in the case of recurrence risk has been to exclude sibling dyads in which younger siblings were sufficiently old at the end of the study period. One common practice has been to set this age at eight years under the assumption that if siblings are not diagnosed with ASD by the time they are eight years old, they are unlikely to be diagnosed at all. There are two obvious problems with this solution to the censoring problem. First, it involves a large loss in the number of observations; sibling dyads in which younger siblings are younger than eight years at the end of the study period are excluded from the investigation. Second, as we show, children continue to be diagnosed with ASD into their lower teens, so eight years is too young.

This radical solution would exclude mothers who had not completed their fertility by the end of the study period. Since the majority of mothers in the data have not completed their fertility by 2012, this involves a wholesale loss of data. Applying these censoring solutions to younger siblings and mothers, as required in the study of recurrence risk, is simply not feasible.

Chapter 3 concludes, therefore, with a review of more practical solutions to the censoring problem. Since the probability of censoring varies inversely with the ages of younger siblings and mothers in 2012, and since this relation is unlikely to be linear, we solve the censoring problem by estimating the probability of censoring jointly with the statistical model for recurrence risk.

The literature on recurrence risk is reviewed critically in chapter 4. This review distinguishes between studies informed by clinical data, which largely refer to the United States, and studies informed by population cohort data, which refer to California, Sweden, Denmark and Israel. The literature on recurrence risk tends to be rather limited not just in terms of national coverage, but also in terms of content. A key concern is with the scarcity of studies on recurrence risk for specific population sub-groups, or conditional recurrence risk. Hence most studies are concerned with national averages, and do not distinguish between personal characteristics, such as the ages of parents, their ethnicity, the number of children they have etc. We show that the variation in recurrence risk within countries is greater than the variation of recurrence risk between countries. Parents care about their conditional recurrence risk; one size does not fit all.

Chapter 5 introduces the population cohort data for Israel that are used in chapters 6-10. In 1981 the government of Israel passed a law, which provided a special financial benefit for children with ASD to be administered by the National Insurance Institute. Israel remains the only country with this kind of benefit. At first, the take-up rate of benefit was low; perhaps parents were unaware or they felt embarrassed or shy. Before long, however, this benefit became socially acceptable and, as discussed in chapter 4, take-up rates became high if not comprehensive. Since the financial incentive to apply for benefit is large by Israeli standards, perhaps this explains why take-up rates are large. The author is grateful to the National Insurance Institute for allowing him access to these confidential data in its research room in Jerusalem.

At the author's request the National Insurance Institute linked the universe of approximately 10,000 beneficiaries between 1984 and 2013 to their parents and siblings using the National Population Registry at the Ministry of Interior. These links are made possible by personal id numbers. Whereas data protection laws prevent private individuals and organizations merging confidential micro data, the National Insurance Institute is permitted to do so.

Whereas in California, Sweden and Denmark families tend to be small, the opposite is true in Israel. Fertility in California, Sweden and Denmark fall well below replacement (2.1). Matters are entirely different in Israel where fertility exceeds 3. The population cohort data for Israel include unusually large families, many of which have more than six children, and some more than 10. Whereas in California, Sweden and Denmark the index child is typically a firstborn and ASD recurrence refers to the second child, in Israel the index child may be child 3 and recurrence refers to child 5. To make inferences regarding recurrence risk in the general population, we ideally require data on the natural history of fertility. Instead, with the global trend towards lower fertility where fertility rates are less than replacement in all developed countries (excluding Israel) and in many countries such as Japan, Italy and Spain fertility is as low as 1.2, the natural history of fertility has become increasingly obscured. It would become totally obscured if fertility fell to 1 and below as in South Korea.

Therefore, fertility data for Israel are uniquely appropriate for the study of recurrence risk because they are closest to the natural history of fertility. Consequently, the population cohort data for Israel enable the study of the relation between recurrence risk and birth order as well as birth gaps between siblings in a way that is not feasible for California, Sweden and Denmark. Indeed, the empirical study of recurrence risk becomes more hazardous as fertility rates continue to decrease.

Descriptive statistics of Israel's population cohort data are provided in chapter 5. These include the prevalence and incidence of ASD in the general population, rates of recurrence risk over time, age at diagnosis, handicaps of parents and siblings, step parents and half siblings etc.

Chapter 5 also includes a review of empirical studies of the incidence and prevalence of ASD in Israel, which serves as background to the study of recurrence risk. A shortcoming in all studies of ASD and recurrence risk is the absence of data on severity. The data are binary; either ASD was diagnosed or not. It is generally recognized that with successive DSMs diagnostic criteria for ASD have become increasingly liberal. This most probably explains why the incidence of ASD has increased globally. For example, according to the Center for Disease Control (CDC) in the US prevalence for ASD is currently 1 in 57 children whereas 25 years ago it was 1 in 200. Either ASD has reached epidemic proportions, or less severe cases, which would have been excluded in the past, are increasingly diagnosed with ASD. Chapter 5 describes a recent study in which the author was involved, which shows that there is no trend in the prevalence of ASD in Israel, controlling for severity. The increase in measured prevalence is entirely due to more liberal diagnostic standards; the goal posts have widened.

In the present study population cohort data for Israel are used to measure recurrence risk and to test hypotheses about is determinants. These hypotheses draw on neurodevelopmental as well as behavioral paradigms. Using the methods described in chapter 3, we show that recurrence risk is not exclusively neurodevelopmental; it displays behavioral footprints. We have already mentioned that population cohort data are available for California, Sweden and Denmark. These data rely on comprehensive reporting of children diagnosed with ASD. Hence the data are as good as the reporting systems which provide them. By contrast, the population cohort data for Israel are not generated by organized reporting systems. Instead, they are generated diretly by administrative records created when children diagnosed with ASD began to be entitled to benefit from the National Insurance Institute.

Chapters 6, 7 and 8 are related and are based on the population cohort data for Israel that are introduced and described in chapter 5. Chapter 6 is concerned with the determinants of reproductive stoppage among parents in Israel. It begins with a behavioral theory of reproductive stoppage in which fertility control in the general population is differentiated from reproductive stoppage by parents who have a child with ASD. In the theoretical model the key unobservables are pro-natality and what psychologists refer to by 'resilience' which vary between parents. The theoretical model hypothesizes that when index children are born, their parents do not suspect that they might have developmental problems. With the passage of time their innocence is replaced by worry and concern as these developmental problems express themselves. Because of randomness in the age at which index children are diagnosed, some parents have further children before their index child is diagnosed, while other parents have further children after their index child is diagnosed. The former parents could not have engaged in reproductive stoppage because they did not know for sure that their previous child had ASD. By contrast, the latter parents could consciously engage in reproductive stoppage.

What distinguishes the two groups of parents is the timing of diagnosis relative to the timing of conception for younger siblings of index children. Diagnosis timing serves to randomize parents into two groups as in a natural experiment. Population cohort data for Israel are used to test the hypothesis that age at diagnosis of index children is a major determinant in reproductive stoppage. Specifically, the probability of reproductive stoppage varies inversely with age at diagnosis of index children. Two types of reproductive stoppage are considered. Absolute stoppage occurs when parents cease to have further children. Relative stoppage occurs when parents have fewer children rather than no further children.

Note that this study of reproductive stoppage compares parents of ASD children who engaged in reproductive stoppage with parents who refrained from reproductive stoppage. This within-group comparison is quite different from the between-group comparison in which the fertility of parents of ASD children is compared with parents in the general population. There are several studies of the latter, which are reviewed in chapter 4, but there have been no studies of the former. Indeed, the results in chapter 6 are the first of its within-group genre.

In chapter 7 we study recurrence risk and its determinants using the population cohort data for Israel. We distinguish between two types of parents. Parents who had further children before their index child was diagnosed with ASD, and parents who had further children after the index child was diagnosed. The former parents raised their child under a 'veil of ignorance' until their index child was eventually diagnosed. The latter parents raised their child in the 'shadow of ASD' the duration of which equals the date of birth of younger siblings minus the date of diagnosis of index children. For example, if the index child was diagnosed aged five and his younger sibling was born when he was aged two, the veil of ignorance is three years. If the younger sibling was born when the index child was aged nine, the shadow of ASD is four years.

According to the neurodevelopmental paradigm, the shadow of ASD and the veil of ignorance should not matter for recurrence risk. According to the behavioral paradigm parents who raised their younger child in the shadow of ASD differ from parents under the veil of ignorance because they consciously chose to refrain from reproductive stoppage, and because they acquired four years' experience in raising a child with ASD. On the other hand, veil of ignorance parents enjoyed three years of relative calm in raising their younger sibling. If knowledge empowers, shadow of ASD parents might be expected to mitigate recurrence risk. If, instead, knowledge imperils, veil of ignorance parents might be more successful in mitigating recurrence risk.

Phenomena such as the shadow of ASD and the veil of ignorance do not, of course, apply to the prevalence of ASD in the general population. However, matters are different as far as recurrence risk are concerned. This is why the study of recurrence risk is inherently different from the study of ASD in the general population.

In chapter 7 we show that there are three separate behavioral effects on recurrence risk in Israel. First, parents who refrained from reproductive stoppage have superior outcomes in terms of recurrence risk. Second, recurrence risk varies inversely with the duration of the veil of ignorance. Third, it also varies inversely with the shadow of ASD. The important result is that recurrence risk is influenced by behavioral phenomena; it is not exclusively neurodevelopmental.

The treatment of sample selection bias induced by reproductive stoppage was implicit in chapter 7. Chapter 8 addresses the issue of sample selection bias explicitly drawing on the methodologies reviewed in chapter 3. We begin by obtaining the nonparametric bounds for the effect of selection bias on recurrent risk. The bounds tell us that the true estimate of recurrence risk lies within these bounds. This sounds like negative information; it tells us that recurrence risk cannot be greater than the upper bound or less than the lower bound. It tells us what is not, instead of what is. Negative information is important because it rules out rates of recurrence risk above the upper bound and below the lower bound. We might not be able to agree on what is, but at least let us agree on what is not.

Next, attention is turned to what is from what is not. We apply the canonical methods described in chapter 3 for testing for the presence of selection bias, and correct for it where necessary. The population cohort data for Israel suggest that on average the rate of recurrence risk is 4.6 percent. The econometric approach suggests that the unbiased estimate is 3.7 percent, which is statistically significant. If these results applied elsewhere, they would suggest that standard estimates of recurrence risk are biased upwards. This means that parents who refrained from reproductive stoppage by having further children after their index child were negatively selected. They were more likely to have further children with ASD than would have been the case had parents been randomly assigned into reproductive stoppage. In other words, recurrence risk in the general population id 3.7 percent rather than 4.6 percent.

According to the neurodevelopmental paradigm, selection bias should not be relevant for recurrence risk. If the etiology of ASD is exclusively biological or genetic, it should not matter whether parents are more or less pro-natal or resilient. Nor should the veil of ignorance and the shadow of ASD have mattered. Hence, the combined results of chapters 7 and 8 challenge the exclusivity of the neurodevelopment paradigm, and testify to the role of behavioral phenomena in the etiology of recurrence risk.

It turns out that statistical methods for correcting for selection bias were not useful in the present context because the results were too sensitive to potential hidden confounders. This negative result implies that the unobservables that influence reproductive stoppage and recurrence risk, such as pro-natality and resilience, matter for selection bias. They are the hidden confounders to which the statistical results are sensitive.

This completes the interdisciplinary study of recurrence risk using population cohort data for Israel. The study is methodologically and theoretically interdisciplinary. It applies research methods drawn from statistics and econometrics to the epidemiological study of recurrence risk, and it draws on behavioral theory from the social sciences to complement neurodevelopmental theory. Chapter 9 summarizes the results of the study for the three audiences, parents, health professionals and epidemiologists.

Chapter 10 does not really belong to the present study because it is not concerned with recurrence risk. It is concerned instead with the transition into adulthood of teenagers with ASD. Nevertheless, it is added as a postscript in two senses. First, it is based on the same population cohort data for Israel that have served as the empirical basis for the current study of recurrence risk. Second, it reports what happened to the children with ASD in the study group when they eventually became young adults. These follow-up data focus on four outcomes: participation in tertiary education, military service or national service, participation in the labor market, and marital status. These outcomes are identified by specific administrative codes at the National Insurance Institute reflecting the fact that national insurance contributions and health insurance contributions are different for students, military conscripts, employees and by matrimonial status.

Moreover, these data are longitudinal; they comprise monthly data for members of the study group aged 19 years and up.

To these ends at the author's request, the National Insurance Institute used personal id's to match children with ASD in the study group, who by definition are 18 years old or younger, to their national insurance records when they were aged 19 to 31. These surely must constitute the most comprehensive population cohort data for studying the transition into young adulthood by individuals with ASD.

These data have a further advantage because when individuals in the study group reach the age of 18 and cease to be eligible for benefits from the National Insurance Institute as children or teenagers with ASD, they undergo assessments by health professionals to determine their eligibility to invalid benefits as adults. They are given separate scores to quantify their social and communication skills as well as ADL (activities and daily living) skills.

Three main results arise from these data. First, a surprisingly large number of young adults with ASD participate in tertiary education, military and national service, and the labor market. Second, individuals with superior skill scores observed at age 18 have better transitions. However, these scores are imperfect predictors of the transition unto young adulthood. Third, individuals who were diagnosed with ASD more recently have more successful transitions. By contrast, individuals diagnosed with ASD in the 1980s and 1990s have less successful transitions. This time trend is attributed to the application of more liberal diagnostic standards; more recent cohorts experienced superior outcomes because their ASD is less severe.

Chapter 2

RECURRENCE RISK THEORY

> "Many people made a mistake in going from a statement which is undoubtedly true – that there is no evidence that autism has been caused by poor parenting – to the statement that it has been disproven. It has not actually been disproven. It has faded away simply because, on the one hand, of a lack of convincing evidence, and on the other hand, an awareness that autism was a neurodevelopmental disorder of some kind." (Rutter 2010)

In the quotation Rutter was referring to the early belief that the etiology of autism was behavioral, induced by 'refridgerator' mothers in particular and poor parenting in general. His reference to 'poor parenting' was intended as a criticism of theories due to Kanner and Bettelheim, who claimed that bad parenting plays a key role in the etiology of autism. Kanner (1943) who identified autism as a separate pathology observed that few of his 11 patients had warm-hearted parents, and subsequently noted (Kanner 1949) that his patients "were exposed from the beginning to parental coldness, obsessiveness and a mechanical type of attention to material needs only." Moreover, it is as if they had been "kept in refridgerators which did not defrost." Bettelheim (1967) took this argument to extremes, and attributed autism exclusively to the behavior of parents in general, and to 'refridgerator mothers' in particular. Indeed, psychoanalytical theory continues to inform the treatment of ASD in some parts of the world, especially in France (Robert 2011), Argentina and South Korea.

Kanner (1968) eventually took exception to Bettelheim's extreme position, noting that "at no time have I pointed to parents as the primary post-natal source of pathogenicity." Subsequently, this developmental psychopathology was discredited especially following the scandal which broke out after Bettelheim's death in 1993 (Sutton 1996, Meyer 2010). Children who had been treated by Bettelheim, but where now adults, complained about abuse and cruelty.

Rutter was also referring to the dominance of the neurodevelopmental model, pioneered by Rimland (1964), in the empirical study of ASD, according to which its etiology is mainly genetic and also environmental. However, environmental factors exclude parents and what occurs within families, and refer instead to exposure to pollution and related factors that might harm brain development (Landrigan 2010). Rutter was also referring to his own research (Folstein and Rutter 1977) in which recurrence risk among 11 identical twins was found to be greater than among 13 fraternal twins. Since identical twins are genetically identical whereas fraternal twins are not, Rutter and Folstein concluded that the etiology of autism must be genetic.

We ignore for the moment how this is the second time that a handful of cases launched paradigmatic change. First, Kanner's 11 patients, and Folstein and Rutter's 11 identical twins and 13 fraternal twins. We focus instead on the fact that this conclusion was based on behavioral genetics (Plomin et al. 2001), which is a discipline originally founded by Francis Galton (1875), but which developed in the 1930s with comparisons between MZ (identical) and DZ (fraternal) twins, and matured into a new discipline during the second half of the 20th century. Behavioral genetics is founded on the idea that identical twins are expected to have more correlated outcomes or phenotypes than other sibling dyads, because they are genetically identical. The theory of behavioral genetics has attracted methodological criticism (Goldberger 1977, 1979, 2005); it essentially attributes to genetics what others might attribute to behaviorism. In the context of recurrence risk behaviorism embraces what happens in families, between parents and their children and between siblings.

Rutter is right that the 'poor parenting' theory faded away for lack of convincing evidence even if it has not been disproven. On the other hand, the neurodevelopmental paradigm has become so dominant that investigators might feel reluctant to engage in research outside the mainstream. This is not the first time that a dominant paradigm has crowded out research from a rival paradigm (Kuhn 1970). The main purpose of this chapter is to place the neurodevelopmental and behavioral paradigms on an equal scientific footing; to level the playing field. To add cogency, the theory of behavioral genetics is used to achieve this objective. An important conclusion is that there is more to the behavioral theory of recurrence risk than 'poor parenting'. This narrow view of parenting was informed by psychoanalytical theory, which was a dominant paradigm in the times of Kanner and Bettelheim.

Behavioral Genetics

This section is heavily based on Beenstock (2012, chapters 3 and 10). The starting point of behavioral genetics is the following simple identity:

$$P_i = G_i + E_i \tag{2.1}$$

where i labels individuals, P refers to phenotypes, G refers to genotypes and E refers to the influence of environment on the phenotypes. The correlation for sibling dyads for phenotype P is defined as:

$$r = \frac{cov(P_1 P_2)}{sd(P_1)sd(P_2)} \tag{2.2}$$

Where P_1 and P_2 refer to the siblings in the dyad, cov( ) denotes covariances and sd( ) denotes standard deviations. From equation (2.1) the numerator in equation (2.2) is:

$$cov(P_1 P_2) = cov(G_1 G_2) + cov(G_1 E_2) + cov(E_1 G_2) + cov(E_1 E_2) \quad (2.3)$$

Notice that $cov(G_1E_2)$ is generally different from $cov(E_1G_2)$. The standard deviations in equation (2.2) are the square roots of their respective variances:

$$var(P_1) = var(G_1) + var(E_1) + 2r_1 sd(G_1) sd(E_1) \quad (2.4)$$

$$var(P_2) = var(G_2) + var(E_2) + 2r_2 sd(G_2) sd(E_2) \quad (2.5)$$

where r_1 denotes the correlation between G_1 and E_1 and r_2 denotes the correlation between G_2 and E_2.

If sibling dyads are MZ twins, $cov(G_1G_2) = var(G)$ because $G_1 = G_2$ for genetically identical siblings. If they are DZ twins $cov(G_1G_2) = \frac{1}{2}var(G)$ because siblings share 50 percent of their genotypes. For biological and adopted dyads $cov(G_1G_2) = 0$; they are genetically unrelated. Behavioral geneticists typically assume that genotypes and environments are unrelated, hence $r_1 = r_2 = cov(G_1E_1) = cov(E_2G_2) = 0$. They also make the 'equal environments assumption' (EEA) according to which $cov(E_1 E_2)$ is the same for MZ and DZ twins. This covariance may be expressed as:

$$cov(E_1 E_2) = \rho sd(E_1) sd(E_2) \quad (2.6)$$

where ρ denotes the correlation between sibling environments. Hence, EEA assumes that the sibling correlation for environments is the same for MZ and DZ twins, and so are the products of standard deviations for environments.

Applying these restrictions to equations (2.3) – (2.5) under the further restriction that var(E) is the same within dyads, and environments are independent within families, implies that the phenotypic sibling correlations for MZ and DZ twins are:

$$r_{MZ} = \frac{var(G)+\rho var(E)}{var(G)+var(E)} \qquad (2.7)$$

$$r_{DZ} = \frac{0.5var(G)+\rho var(E)}{var(G)+var(E)} \qquad (2.8)$$

According to equations (2.7) and (2.8) the only reason why sibling correlations for phenotypes may differ is genetic; because the coefficient of var(G) in the numerator is 1 in equation (2.7) and is 0.5 in equation (2.8). Hence, if MZ sibling correlations are larger than their DZ counterparts, the reason must be genetic.

Of course, this tendentious conclusion has been reached by making numerous assumptions on the way. Their common denominator is that they are designed to exclude behavioral influences on sibling correlations. Thus, by default, only genotypes matter. For example, Folstein and Rutter (1977) attributed the larger sibling correlation for recurrence risk among MZ twins to genetics rather than to behavioral phenomena transmitted through environments.

The dichotomy between G and E in equation (2.1) is directly related to the dichotomy between nature and nurture, where G represents nature and E represents nurture. Behavioral geneticists essentially assume away the role of nurture, which leaves nature as the dominant paradigm by default.

This almost trivial result stems from the fact that not only are environments assumed to be independent of genotypes, sibling environments are dependent according to EEA and the variances of sibling environments are homogeneous. These sweeping assumptions rule out behavioral influences of environmental choice on phenotypes. One can't choose one's genes but one can choose one's environments. For example, hay fever sufferers stay clear of gardens in springtime. Musically gifted children learn in special schools. Environmental choice depends behaviorally on genotypes. Parents who suspect that they have a genotype for ASD may choose to engage in reproductive stoppage rather face the risk of ASD recurrence.

In summary, Folstein and Rutter interpreted their results by assuming that only genetics matters. Just as arbitrarily, they might have interpreted their results behaviorally; recurrence risk among MZ twins is larger because their parents and the world at large treat them more similarly. To decompose the contributions of genetics and environments to phenotypes such as recurrence risk requires structural modelling of sibling interactions, the interactions between parents and their children, and of the dependence of environments on genotypes.

According to equation (2.8) identical twins are correlated for behavioral reasons through $\rho var(E)$ as well as for genetic reasons. For example, society may react to MZ twins more similarly simply because they happen to be identical. Or MZ twins may choose similar environments because they enjoy doing things together. EEA states that $\rho_{MZ} = \rho_{DZ}$. Suppose, however, that MZ twins have more correlated environments than DZ twins (for reasons discussed below) so that $\rho_{MZ} > \rho_{DZ}$. Equations (2.7) and (2.8) imply that just as MZ twins might be more correlated for genetic reasons, they might be more correlated for behavioral reasons. In fact, just because MZ twins happen to be more correlated tells us nothing about the relative roles of nature and nurture. The claim that it does, depends critically on EEA.

Just as behavioral geneticists abstract from the role of environments and attribute the differences between sibling correlations to genotypes, so might behaviorists go to the other extreme by attributing the difference between sibling correlations to environments by abstracting from genotypes. However, they do not do so. Behavioral theorists recognize the role of genetics, but behavioral geneticists deny the role of behavior, despite what might have been surmised from the adjective 'behavioral'.

Thus far we have moved beyond behavioral genetics by assuming that sibling environments might be correlated differentially. More generally, equations (2.3) – (2.5) involve dependence between environments and genotypes, which drive further wedges between behavioral genetics and a more general paradigm in which environments matter as well as genetics.

Behavioral geneticists define 'heritability' by $h^2 = var(G)/var(P)$, which, if the gene-environment correlation is zero, as assumed in behavioral genetics, is the proportion of the phenotypic variance that is explained by the genotypic variance. Hence, 1 – h^2 is the proportion explained by the variance in environments. If the gene-environment correlation is non-zero this adding-up property breaks down. For example, if var(G) and var(E) equal 1 and the gene-environment correlation is -0.5, h^2 equals 1, which creates the misleading impression that only genetics matters. In this case so does var(E)/var(P) equal 1, because the adding-up property no longer applies. Hence, both genes and environments matter, and they matter equally (Beenstock 2012, p 97).

Suppose that phenotypes for identical twins are correlated 0.8 and phenotypes for fraternal twins are correlated 0.5. We assume as before that genotypes for identical twins are correlated 1 and for fraternal twins they are correlated 0.5. The EEA assumption of behavioral genetics requires that the gene-environment correlations for the two types of twins is the same. If this common correlation is 0.5, heritability is 0.5. However, if EEA is violated and the gene-environment correlation for identical twins is 0.8 and for fraternal twins it is 0.5, heritability turns out to be zero! (Beenstock 2012, p 102) The 'results' from behavioral genetics are highly sensitive to the strong assumptions upon which they are arbitrarily founded.

Serious research into the gene – environment decomposition of phenotypes such as recurrence risk, requires structural equation modelling of the interactions between siblings, the interactions between parents and children, and the relationship between environmental choice and genotypes. Essentially, Folstein and Rutter arbitrarily attributed the greater recurrence risk between MZ twins to genes rather than to their parents.

Thus, did the neurodevelopmental paradigm get launched on shaky theoretical and methodological foundations, as well as on a handful of observation. These foundations continue to remain shaky today.

BEHAVIORAL THEORY

Folstein and Rutter's results proved to be a game-changer. Apart from encouraging other behavioral geneticist to study recurrence risk among identical and fraternal twins, investigators began to study familial recurrence risk in general, including half-siblings and cousins (Sandin et al 2014, Hansen et al 2019, Constantino et al 2013, Grønborg et al 2013). More importantly, geneticists proper began to search for the genes responsible for autism using the methodology of genome-wide association studies (GWAS), which is critically appraised in the next chapter.

For the present, this section seeks to recall elements of behavioral theory, which are relevant to the study of recurrence risk, and which may serve as a paradigmatic alternative to the dominant neurodevelopmental theory. We begin with the dependence between siblings.

Sibling Interaction

Consider the following simple sibling interaction model for sibling dyads, where sibling 1 is the elder sibling (Beenstock, 2012 chapter 3):

$$E_1 = \gamma_1 G_1 + \lambda_1 E_2 + e_1 \quad (2.9)$$

$$E_2 = \gamma_2 G_2 + \lambda_2 E_1 + e_2 \quad (2.10)$$

The e's are idiosyncratic (sibling specific) random variables. The gamma coefficients relax the assumptions of behavioral genetics that environments are independent of genotypes. The lambda coefficients relax EEA; they refer to sibling interaction. If sibling interaction depends on birth order, λ_2 may be greater than λ_2. If younger siblings revolt against their elder siblings λ_2 may be negative when λ_1 is positive. If E refers to flower gardens and G refers to the genotype for hay-fever, the gammas would be negative. If siblings enjoy sharing common environments the lambdas are positive. The solutions to equations (2.9) and (2.10) for sibling environments are:

$$E_1 = \frac{\gamma_1 G_1 + e_1 + \lambda_1 \gamma_2 G_2 + \lambda_1 e_2}{1 - \lambda_1 \lambda_2} \tag{2.11}$$

$$E_2 = \frac{\gamma_2 G_2 + e_2 + \lambda_2 \gamma_1 G_1 + \lambda_2 e_1}{1 - \lambda_1 \lambda_2} \tag{2.12}$$

Hence, sibling environments depend indirectly on their mutual genotypes and idiosyncratic components (e). Notice that because the lambdas are fractions, so are the denominators of equations (2.11) and (2.12), hence the total effect of genotypes on environments are multiples of their counterparts in equations (2.9) and (2.10), unless these sibling interaction coefficients have different signs. Equations (2.11) and (2.12) may be used to re-express equation (2.6):

$$cov(E_1 E_2) = \frac{\gamma_1 \gamma_2 (1 + \lambda_1 \lambda_2) \rho_G + \gamma_2 \lambda_1 + \gamma_1 \lambda_2}{(1 - \lambda_1 \lambda_2)^2} var(G) \tag{2.13}$$

where ρ_G denotes the sibling correlation for genotypes, and where for simplicity the genotypic variance for siblings is homogeneous. Equation (2.13) states that the covariance between sibling environments varies directly with the sibling correlation for genotypes, and it varies directly with the sibling interaction coefficients.

EEA implies that the gamma and lambda coefficients are the same for MZ and DZ siblings as well as for other types of siblings. This implies that birth order and birth gaps don't matter for sibling interaction. EEA also implies, surprisingly, that ρ_G is the same for different types of siblings, contradicting a basic axiom of behavioral genetics. Hence, there is an internal contradiction in EEA.

In summary, social science is concerned with the rich tapestry of behavioral interaction within families; between siblings and between children and parents. It is also concerned with the rich tapestry between siblings and their chosen social environments, as well as environments such as compulsory school attendance, which are imposed upon them. In denying the existence of these behavioral phenomena, behavioral genetics reductively turns human beings into hard-wired genetic machines.

Rational Selection

Reproductive stoppage arises when parents decide to have no further children following the arrival of a child with ASD. According to the neurodevelopmental paradigm, recurrence risk does not depend on reproductive stoppage; it makes no difference which parents engage in stoppage and which do not. Suppose, instead, that parents have intuitions about their exposure to recurrence risk, and that on average their intuitions are correct, or at least positively correlated with reality. Given everything else, these parents are more likely to engage in stoppage, and because they are on average correct, the incidence of recurrence decreases.

In chapter 3 we discuss methodological implications that arise out of selection bias induced by reproductive stoppage. Here, we present the behavioral theory upon which rational selection theory is based. We begin by introducing the concept of 'truncation'. Suppose a normally distributed random variable has a mean (μ) and standard deviation σ. If values with less than some threshold (a) are dropped (truncated), it is obvious that the truncated mean for the remaining values must be more than μ. It is also obvious that the truncated variance is smaller because values below a have been omitted. For example, if students ignore their weakest grades, their mean grade increases and the variance decreases.

The mean of the truncated normal distribution is:

$$\tilde{\mu} = \mu + \frac{\sigma\phi(\alpha)}{1-\Phi(\alpha)} \tag{2.14}$$

$$\alpha = \frac{a-\mu}{\sigma} < 0 \tag{2.15}$$

where $\phi(\ )$ and $\Phi(\ )$ are the density and the cumulative density of the standard normal distribution. If $\mu = 5$, $\sigma = 2$ and $a = 2$, equation (2.14) implies that the truncated mean is 5.277, which is greater than 5. The truncated mean would be larger if σ was greater and a was larger. The basic intuition is simple; creaming raises the mean. If large values are dropped instead of small values (truncation is from above because $a > \mu$ instead of from below) equation (2.14) becomes:

$$\tilde{\mu} = \mu - \frac{\sigma\phi(\alpha)}{\Phi(\alpha)} \tag{2.16}$$

The truncated mean is less than the original mean; skimming reduces the mean.

Let $Y_{1i} = \mu_1 + u_{1i}$ and $Y_{2i} = \mu_2 + u_{2i}$ be bivariate normal random variables where σ_{12} denotes the covariance between u_1 and u_2. Individuals choose between Y_1 and Y_2. Individuals know their own u_1 and u_2, but these random variables are unknown to scientific investigators studying their behavior. Individuals choose rationally between Y_1 and Y_2. They choose Y_1 if it makes them better-off, i.e., $Y_{1i} > Y_{2i}$. Hence, $\mu_1 + u_1 > \mu_2 + u_2$., or, $\mu_1 - \mu_2 > u_2 - u_1$. Define $z = (\mu_1 - \mu_2)/\sigma$, $u = (u_2 - u_1)/\sigma$, $\sigma^2 = \text{var}(u_1 - u_2)$ and r_{12} denotes the correlation between Y_1 and Y_2 for the individuals. The truncated means for Y_1 and Y_2 are (Maddala 1983 pp 257-8):

$$\tilde{\mu}_1 = \mu_1 - \frac{\sigma_1(r_{12}\sigma_2 - \sigma_1)}{\sigma}\frac{\phi(z)}{\Phi(z)} \tag{2.17}$$

$$\tilde{\mu}_2 = \mu_2 + \frac{\sigma_2(\sigma_2 - r_{12}\sigma_1)}{\sigma}\frac{\phi(z)}{1-\Phi(z)} \tag{2.18}$$

Notice that if $r_{12}\sigma_2 < \sigma_1$ the coefficient of $\phi(z)/\Phi(z)$ in equation (2.17) is positive, and if $\sigma_2 > r_{12}\sigma_1$ the coefficient of $\phi(z)/[1-\Phi(z)]$ in equation (2.18) is positive. Hence, the truncated means exceed their original counterparts because individuals have chosen what is best for them.

For example, if $\mu_1 = 5$, $\mu_2 = 6$, $\sigma_1 = 2$, $\sigma_2 = 2.5$, and $r_{12} = -0.3$. The truncated means, according to equations (2.17) and (2.18), are $\tilde{\mu}_1 = 6.479$ and $\tilde{\mu}_2 = 7.345$, which are considerably larger, as expected, than μ_1 and μ_2. In this example, we have assumed that u_1 and u_2 are negatively correlated, i.e., individuals with Y_1 who are on average better-off with Y_1 are worse off with Y_2. The gains from freedom of choice are always positive, but they may be larger or smaller. Notice that the gains are zero when $r_{12} = 1$ and $\sigma_1 = \sigma_2$ because outcomes are perfectly positively correlated and because Y_1 and Y_2 have the same standard deviation. In general, the gains vary inversely with r_{12} and the difference between the standard deviation.

If Y_1 and Y_2 referred to pay from two occupations, rational selection increases wage inequality relative to random allocation or selection. This inequality arises from two sources. First, random allocation implicitly assumes that $u_1 = u_2 = 0$. Under rational selection individuals improve on this by exploiting their information on u_{1i} and u_{2i} Hence, if $\mu_1 = \mu_2$ each individual is better-off by $u_{1i} - u_{2i}$.. The second source arises from the fact that the proportion choosing Y_1 is $\Phi(z)$, which equals 0.5 if $z = 0$ ($\mu_1 = \mu_2$). In the numerical example $z = -1/3.64 = -0.27$ and $\Phi(-0.27) = 0.3936$. Hence almost 40 percent choose Y_1. The migration of workers to occupations where earnings are higher tends to increases inequality relative to random allocation. Since $\mu_1 = 5$ and $\mu_2 = 6$, random allocation would have generated a mean income of 5.5. Under rational selection the mean increases to 7.002, or by 27.3 percent. In summary, rational choice makes everyone better-off, but it increases inequality.

The same applies if Y_1 refers to reproductive stoppage and Y_2 refers to non-stoppage. Or if Y_1 refers to parents' investment in child 1 and Y_2 refers to parental investments in child 2. Some parents engage in reproductive stoppage because they think it s better for them, while the parents who refrain from reproductive stoppage think it is better for them. Observationally identical parents make different choices because they differ in terms of their pro-natality and resilience, which is unknown to scientific investigators, but known, of course, to parents.

Equations (2.17) and (2.18) involve parameters such as r_{12}, which may be estimated from observational data on individual choices between Y_1 and Y_2. Other parameters are σ_1 and σ_2. In chapter 3 we discuss how these parameters might be estimated (by the method of maximum likelihood).

Reproductive Stoppage

Let C_{it}^* denote a latent or index variable, which measures parents' desire in family i in the general population to have a further child when their previous child is aged t. C_{it}^* is hypothesized to depend on a vector of observable covariates (X_i) including the existing number of children, their gender mix, the age of mothers and perhaps fathers, their ethnicity, schooling and economic status etc. Parents have unobserved pro-natality preferences for children denoted by c_i. Parents may penalize small birth gaps in the interest of birth-spacing, but the penalty, denoted by $g_i(t)$, tends naturally to zero with the birth gap (t).

The latent variable model for the general population may be written as:

$$C_{it}^* = X_i\beta + c_i - g_i(t) \tag{2.19}$$

where β is a vector of parameters to be estimated. Let C_{it} denote a zero-one dummy variable, which equals 1 if parents conceive their next child when their previous child is aged t. This event occurs when C_{it}^* turns positive as illustrated in Figure 2.1 where C* is measured on the vertical and the age of the previous child (t) is measured on the horizontal axis. Schedule A plots the relation between C* and t in Equation (2.19), and is drawn for positive c and Xβ = 0. Schedule A is naturally negative at the origin unless parents wish to conceive straight away, and it tends to c as the birth gap (t) increases. Parents conceive when C* turns positive, when their child is aged t_0, which varies inversely with their preference for children (c) and directly with g(t). If c is negative they won't conceive at all because C* remains negative; they have no further children.

This is an application of optimal stopping theory, or rather optimal starting theory, since conception starts when C* turns positive.

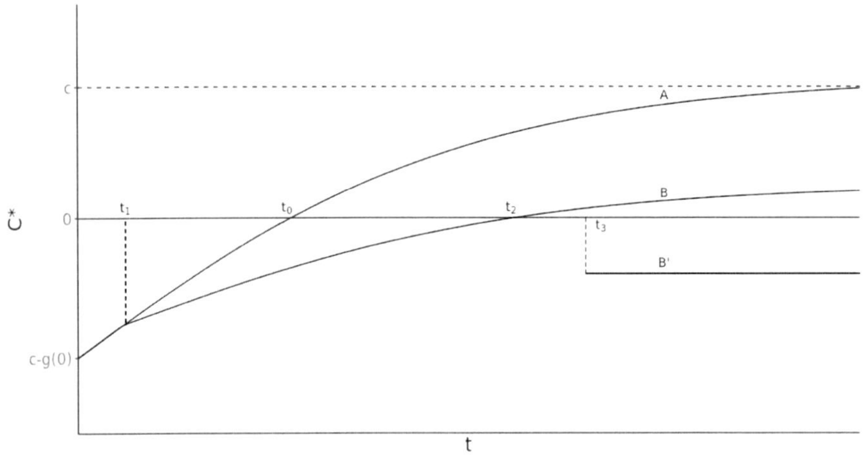

Figure 2.1. Conception Timing for Younger Siblings.

Equation (2.19) applies to the general population, which we adapt for parents of children with ASD. We introduce two new unobservable phenomena in addition to c and g, which apply specifically to parents of ASD children. When their index child is born, parents are unaware that they are no longer part of the general population. However, they gradually realize that their child has developmental difficulties, denoted by d(t), which varies directly with age (t). Even before their child is diagnosed with ASD, they might consider reproductive stoppage. Parents also vary by their resilience (Egeland, Carlson and Sroufe 1993, Yates, Egeland and Sroufe 2002, Richardson 2002, Kumar 2020), denoted by r, which may be positive or negative. Henceforth, we refer to 'resilience' as in the psychological sense. Resilient people cope better with life's adverse events, their healthy coping skills do not allow such events to overwhelm them, they remain calm during crises, and move forward from the event without adverse long-term consequences.

We add to equation (2.19) $r_i - d_i(t)$, which may be positive for resilient parents. Schedule B in Figure 2.1 refers to parents of ASD children. At first, it is congruent with schedule A, but after their child is aged t_1, at which parents begin to worry about their child's developmental problems, it lies below schedule A, where the vertical difference between the schedules equals r – d(t). This distance naturally increases with t. In Figure 2.1 schedule B becomes positive at t_2, so the parents of children with developmental difficulties will tend to delay conception relative to the general population. Of course, schedule B might never become positive, in which case parents decide to have no further children; they engage in reproductive stoppage.

Suppose that the child is diagnosed with ASD when he or she is aged t_3. This would induce a discontinuous increase in d, which lowers schedule B as in schedule B'. The parents depicted in schedule B, who conceived when their index child was aged t_2, regret their decision. However, it is too late and they could not have known. Matters would have been different had their child been diagnosed prior to t_2. Note that if parents are sufficiently resilient and their desire for children is sufficiently strong, schedule B' may lie above zero but below schedule B, in which case parents conceive further children despite the ASD status of their child.

Figure 2.1 may be used to distinguish between four combinations of informed/uninformed and stopped/did not stop, which are presented in Table 2.1. Case 1 is depicted in Figure 2.1. When parents decided to have further children when their index child was t_2 years of age, his/her ASD status was not yet ascertained because he/she was diagnosed at t_3 years of age. Hence case 1 parents were uninformed. Nor did they engage in reproductive stoppage. Geometrically, schedule B was positive before the age of diagnosis (t_3). As already discussed, because B' is negative, case 1 parents eventually regret their decision; if they could turn the clock back they would have engaged in reproductive stoppage. In case 2 the index child was diagnosed before his/her younger was conceived, i.e., t_3 is less than t_2. In this case B' must be positive after the age of diagnosis. Case 3 refers to classic stoppage; parents are informed and decide to have no further children. This will happen if B' is negative. Case 4 is subtler.

Parents stop without knowing whether their index child has ASD or not. This will happen if schedule B does not become positive; they would not have wanted further children in any event. In this contingency, parents do not know for sure that their child has ASD, but they understand that he/she has serious developmental difficulties. Geometrically, d increases sufficiently rapidly so that schedule B' never turns positive regardless of when their index child is diagnosed.

Table 2.1. Taxonomy of reproductive stoppage

Case	Informed?	Stopped?	B'
1	no	no	negative
2	yes	no	positive
3	yes	yes	negative
4	no	yes	negative

The counterpart to equation (2.19) for the parents of children with ASD is:

$$C_{it}^{*} = X_i\beta - \delta D_i + c_i - g_i(t) + r_i - d(t) \tag{2.19A}$$

where $D_i = 1$ if parents happen to be informed when they conceive their next child and $D_i = 0$ otherwise (uninformed). $D_i = 1$ when index children are diagnosed before their younger siblings are conceived ($t_{3i} < t_{2i}$). The parameter δ is the discrete decrease in schedule B in Figure 2.1 when $t = t_3$.

This theory implies that observationally similar parents (with the same X) in the general population will have different probabilities of natural stoppage. It also implies that observationally similar ASD parents will have larger probabilities of reproductive stoppage than in the general population. Finally, it implies that observationally similar parents of ASD children have different probabilities of non-stoppage because they differ by their resilience (r), their desire for children (c), their reaction to developmental difficulties and to diagnoses of ASD (d). It also means that observationally similar parents in the general population cannot be compared with the parents of ASD children, because β in the general population may differ, and because r and d do not apply to the general population. Finally, the probability of non-stoppage varies directly with the age at which ASD is diagnosed, and informed non-stoppage is less probable than uninformed non-stoppage.

In summary, the probability of non-stoppage is predicted to depend through β upon the observable covariates (X) including age at diagnosis.

Relative Stoppage

If C equals one (non-stoppage), the number of children may be larger or smaller. Just as observationally similar families might stop or not depending on what is not observed (u), so might they choose to have different numbers of children if they do not stop absolutely. Since the number of younger siblings of index children has the character of count data, which take discrete but limited values such as 0, 1, 2, etc. we suggest the use of count data methods (Cameron and Trivedi 1998) to test hypotheses about relative stoppage in which the dependent variable is C_i = 0, 1, 2, etc. Specifically, in 'zero-inflated' Poisson regression (ZIP) the probability of absolute stoppage (C = 0) is enlarged according to a complementary log log (CLL) model for the probability of absolute stoppage, and where u is assumed to have a Poisson distribution. ZIP embodies the intuition that to have any further children is a harder decision than to have more or fewer further children. It is hard to break the ice, but once the ice is broken the rest is easier. This specification combines absolute and relative stoppage, where the former is expressed through zero inflation, and the latter by count data regression.

According to ZIP, the probability of having no further children is:

$$P_i(0) = \lambda_i + (1 - \lambda_i)exp(-\mu_i) \qquad (2.20)$$
$$\lambda_i = 1 - exp[-exp(X_i\gamma)]$$
$$\mu_i = exp(Z_i\theta)$$

where λ denotes the CLL probability of having no further children, X are covariates in the CLL model, exp(-μ) is the Poisson probability of having no further children, and Z are covariates in the Poisson model. Since P(0) is the probability of absolute stoppage, it varies directly with λ and inversely with μ. CLL is a nonlinear transform of the logit model since exp(Xγ) equals the log odds ratio.

Relative stoppage occurs when parents who refrain from stoppage have fewer further children. The ZIP probability of having positive numbers of children (C > 0) is:

$$P_i(C > 0) = (1 - \lambda_i)\mu_i{}^C exp(-\mu_i)\frac{1}{C!} \quad (2.21)$$

Suppose for family i the CLL and Poisson probabilities of absolute stoppage are 0.305 (= λ) and 0.223 (= exp(-μ)) respectively so that the probability of absolute stoppage, P(0), is 0.46. These probabilities imply that μ = 1.5, i.e., family i is expected to have 1.5 further children. The ZIP probability of having one further child is 0.232 and having two further children is 0.174. Hence, ZIP has inflated the probability of having no further children from 0.223 to 0.46, and it has deflated the Poisson probability of having positive numbers of further children by a factor of 1 - λ.

The expected value of the number of further children given that it is positive equals:

$$E(C > 0) = \frac{(1-\lambda)\mu}{1-P(0)} = \frac{\mu}{1-exp(-\mu)} \quad (2.22)$$

which varies directly with μ and does not depend on λ. In summary, absolute stoppage varies directly with λ and inversely with μ, and relative stoppage varies inversely with μ.

Parenting

No doubt parents are the most important environmental phenomenon for children. This is reflected, of course, in various social science disciplines such as developmental psychology as well as Becker's monumental *Treatise on the Family* (Becker 1992). In this subsection we recall some of Becker's basic ideas, starting with his theory of marriage, his theory of fertility, and his theory of parenting, which is concerned with the allocation of scarce parenting time between rival siblings. These ideas are far removed from EEA of behavioral genetics. We do not cover Becker's theory of divorce and inheritance or his 'rotten kid theorem' and other aspects of the family that are not directly pertinent.

Beckers' point of departure is that family units are formed to produce children, to provide them and their parents with income and fulfillment over the life-cycle, under the constraint that there are only 24 hours in a day. Becker's theory of assortative mating is based on the idea that men and women choose each other as spouses to form a team, which will expedite this existential purpose. Time is the ultimate constraint, busy parents have to squeeze a lot into their 24 hours including work, leisure and child rearing. Here we simplify greatly by assuming that there are h hours per day available for parenting, which are allocated between two children A and B. Child A may be fitter than child B in the sense that irrespective of parental attention A has superior outcomes to B. Also, children differ by their responsiveness to parenting; fitter children are not necessarily more responsive. The outcomes of the siblings are generated by the following simple model in which f refers to fitness, α refers to responsiveness and τ is the proportion of parent-time allocated to child A:

$$Y_A = f_A \tau^{\alpha_A} \tag{2.23}$$

$$Y_B = f_B (1 - \tau)^{\alpha_B} \tag{2.24}$$

Parents are egalitarian in the sense seek that they seek to maximize Y_AY_B; they attach equal weight to their children's outcomes. The optimal allocation of parenting time for A is:

$$\tau = \frac{\alpha_A/\alpha_B}{1+\alpha_A/\alpha_B} \tag{2.25}$$

Equation (2.25) states that if $\alpha_A = \alpha_B$ parents allocate half their time to each child. It also states that τ varies directly, as expected, with α_A / α_B, and that parents do not take fitness into account.

This parenting policy implies that the relative sibling outcome is:

$$R = \frac{f_A\left(\frac{\alpha_A}{\alpha_B}\right)^{\alpha_A}}{f_B\left(1+\frac{\alpha_A}{\alpha_B}\right)^{\alpha_A-\alpha_B}} \tag{2.26}$$

If fitness and sensitivity to parenting are positively correlated, equation (2.26) implies that egalitarian parenting increases sibling inequality.

Suppose, instead, parents practice aggressive reverse discrimination where they choose τ such that R = 1; complete sibling equality. Without loss of generality, if $\alpha_A = \alpha_B = \alpha$, the critical value of τ, which guarantees equality between siblings is:

$$\tau = \frac{\left(\frac{f_B}{f_A}\right)^{1/\alpha}}{1+\left(\frac{f_B}{f_A}\right)^{1/\alpha}} \tag{2.27}$$

Equation (2.27) states that the allocation of parenting to child A varies inversely with A's relative fitness. If, for example, A is twice as fit as B, $\tau = 0.2$ when $\alpha = 0.5$, i.e., 80 percent of parenting is devoted to the less fit sibling (B). If instead $\alpha = 1$, equation (2.27) states that 2/3 of parenting are devoted to the weaker sibling. If sibling B is 50 percent fitter than A, parents devote 69 percent of their parenting to sibling A when $\alpha = 0.5$, and 60 percent when $\alpha = 1$. The greater the sensitivity of children to parenting (α), the easier it is to achieve equality between siblings.

This simple behavioral model of busy parents has been extended by Lizzeri and Siniscalchi (2008) to take account of the delicate balancing act undertaken by parents in over-protection on the one hand and 'Spartan' exposure on the other. It has also been extended by Akabayashi (2006) to take account of the tension between parents' investment in parenting (τ) and their children's motivation to benefit from this attention (α), and especially when α is not directly observable.

The main purpose here is not to prefer one model to another, but to establish two important principles. The first is that parents are not passive. On the contrary, they are proactive and seek to rear their children to the best of their ability. The second is that siblings are rivals for their parents' attention. The implications of these principles are far-reaching and far-removed from EEA of behavioral genetics. Indeed, behavioral genetics has swept under the carpet the role of behaviorism as a matter of ideology rather than as a matter of orthodox, unbiased science.

A Natural Experiment

The age at which children with ASD are diagnosed serves to randomize their parents' state of mind at the time they decided to have further children. Some parents had further children before their previous child was diagnosed with ASD, while other parents had further children after diagnosis. The former parents could not have engaged in reproductive stoppage because they did not know (for sure) that their child had ASD. The latter parents, by contrast, consciously refrained from reproductive stoppage.

The two types of parents are different in other ways too. Parents who could not have engaged in reproductive stoppage raised their next child under a 'veil of ignorance', which lasted until their previous child was diagnosed with ASD. By contrast, parents who refrained from stoppage raised their next child in the 'shadow of ASD', which lasted from when previous children were diagnosed until their younger siblings were born. Neurodevelopmental theory attaches no importance to the veil of ignorance and the shadow of ASD, or whether parents conceived younger siblings before or after their previous children had been diagnosed. Parents under the veil of ignorance might be less stressed than other parents. On the other hand, parents in the shadow of ASD gained experience in raising children with ASD. If recurrence risk depends empirically on the durations of the veil of ignorance and the shadow of ASD, this begs a behavioral interpretation in which stressed parents may be more likely to raise children with recurrence risk, when experienced parents are less likely.

The main hypothesis of interest is whether recurrence risk of ASD depends on phenomena such as the veil of ignorance and the shadow of ASD. Since recurrence risk is only observed if parents do not engage in reproductive stoppage, these phenomena are to some degree self-selected. If so, their causal effect on recurrence risk would not be identified. To establish causality an auxiliary hypothesis is proposed in which reproductive stoppage depends on when elder siblings are diagnosed with ASD. If the latter is independent of recurrence risk, it serves to randomize the veil of ignorance and the shadow of ASD, which are related to reproductive stoppage, and thereby identify their causal effects on recurrence risk.

Suppose A and B are two observationally similar families. Their first children have ASD, and their second children were born three years afterwards. The only difference is that ASD was diagnosed in family A at 2 years and in family B at 8 years. This gives rise to three differences between families A and B. First, when family A decided to have their second child, they already knew about the ASD status of their first child. They decided against reproductive stoppage in having their second child. Matters are obviously different in family B; they had their second child without knowing about the ASD status of their first child. Second, the younger sibling in family A was raised in the 'shadow of ASD'. His parents had a year's experience raising a child with ASD before their second child was born. Family B obviously had no such experience before their second child was born. Third, the second child in family B was raised until 5 years under a 'veil of ignorance', which ended when his elder sibling was diagnosed. During the veil of ignorance family B might have been concerned about developmental delays in their child, but they did not know for sure that their child would eventually be diagnosed with ASD. In family A the veil of ignorance is zero and the shadow of ASD is a year. In family B the veil of ignorance is 5 years and the shadow of ASD is zero.

According to the neurodevelopmental paradigm of ASD, recurrence risk should be the same for families A and B, because parents' knowledge about the ASD status of their index children plays no role in the neurodevelopmental model. Neuro-developmentalists might argue, however, that family A was more genetically predisposed to ASD recurrence than family B. Family A's child was diagnosed sooner because his ASD were more severe than B's. That is why A's child was diagnosed more quickly. This argument would predict that recurrence risk should be greater in family A than in family B. Suppose, however, that their recurrence risk differs, and that recurrence risk in B- type families is greater than in A-type families. We suggest three behavioral reasons why this might arise. First, family A is positively self-selected because it decided against stoppage. Parents in family A decided to go ahead despite the risk, either because they were more resilient and self-confident of coping with this risk, or because they suspected that the risk of recurrence is relatively low in their family. Either way, this reduces recurrence risk in family A relative to family B. Second, family B had five years to raise its second child under the veil of ignorance, whereas family A raised its second child entirely in the shadow of ASD. If knowledge of ASD empowers family A to mitigate the risk of recurrence, this would further reduce recurrence risk in A-type families relative to B-type families. On the other hand, if knowledge imperils rather than empowers, A-type families who are fearful of ASD might raise their second child less successfully relative to B-type families who are unaware of ASD. This might increase recurrence risk in A-type families relative to B-type families.

The empower-imperil dichotomy is related to self-fulfilling and self-defeating theories in social psychology (Bushman, Baumeister and Stack, 1999), dating back to Thomas' Theorem (Thomas and Swain Thomas, 1928). Family A's knowledge of ASD may become a self-fulfilling expectation if parents believe and fear that ASD will recur in their younger child. If, instead, family A uses its knowledge and experience with ASD to mitigate recurrence risk, the expectation of ASD is self-defeating. During the veil of ignorance, family B has no knowledge of ASD. If knowledge empowers, recurrence risk among B-type families is expected to vary directly with the veil of ignorance. The converse is expected if knowledge imperils.

PARADIGMIC AMBIGUITY

Hopefully, this chapter has gone some way to levelling the playing field between nurture and nature in the way behavioral geneticists have exploited anodyne equation (2.1) to claim that only nature maters. Nature is associated here with the neurodevelopmental paradigm; nurture is associated with behavioral effects on sibling phenotypes. There is a rich corpus of behavioral theory that has been pushed into the sidelines by the neurodevelopmental paradigm. This corpus of theory suggests *a priori* that in equation (2.1) E is just as salient as G.

In epidemiological models for the incidence of ASD as well recurrence risk it has become standard to control for the ages of parents, especially of mothers. The usual interpretation is that ASD risk might be different among older mothers. This phenomenon is usually attributed to genetics or the neurodevelopmental paradigm. Other such variables include birth-spacing. If maturity depends on age, and recurrence risk depends on mother' maturity, given all else, recurrence risk might be expected to be lower among older mothers. The same applies to birth-spacing, which has been given a genetic or biological interpretation (Cheslack-Postava, Lui and Bearman 2011). Recurrence risk may vary inversely with birth-spacing for behavioral reasons; mothers have had a greater chance to get-over their previous birth. Indeed, so-called standard neurodevelopmental controls for recurrence risk are in effect ambiguous; they have behavioral justifications.

Chapter 3

METHODOLOGY FOR RECURRENCE RISK

SAMPLING

Stratified Random Samples

To fix ideas, suppose the population comprises only two types of people e.g., men and women, and that the outcome of interest (y) might differ between types. To obtain an unbiased estimate of the outcome in the population, it is necessarily to obtain random samples of N men (labelled by m) and women (labelled by f), calculate their sample means $(\bar{y}_f, \bar{y}_m)$, and then weight these sample means according to their weights in the population:

$$\hat{y} = w_f \bar{y}_f + (1 - w_f)\bar{y}_m \quad (3.1)$$

In equation (3.1) $\hat{y}$ is an unbiased estimate of the outcome in the population, where w_f denotes the weight of women in the population (equal to 0.51). Its variance is defined by:

$$var(\hat{y}) = w_f^2 var(\bar{y}_f) + (1 - w_f)^2 var(\bar{y}_m) + 2w_f(1 - w_f)cov(\bar{y}_f, \bar{y}_m) \quad (3.2)$$

If men and women are sampled independently, the last term in equation (3.2) is zero. Matters would be different of they were related, e.g., spouses, in which event their outcomes might be correlated.

The sample means in equation (3.1) are averages of the samples for women and men respectively. Their sample variances in equation (3.2) are defined e.g., for women by:

$$var(\hat{y}_f) = \frac{1}{N-1}\sum_{n=1}^{N}(y_{fn} - \bar{y}_f)^2 \quad (3.3)$$

Hence, the variance varies inversely with the sample size, as expected.

In statistical parlance 'types' are referred to as 'strata'. In equation (3.1) $\hat{y}$ is estimated from a 'stratified random sample' in which the strata comprise men and women respectively. It is obvious that $\hat{y}$ will be biased if the sample weights (w_f) are incorrect, except in the unlikely coincidence that $\bar{y}_f = \bar{y}_m$.

What might happen if men and women are not randomly sampled from their strata? The difference between men and women is observable. The same applies to other observable characteristics, which would increase the number of strata, e.g., young women, young men, old women and old men. Indeed, in stratified random samples the number of types or strata may be large, including ethnicity etc. Suppose, however that in each stratum there are two sub-types that are not observable. To revert to men and women, suppose that there are fit and unfit (in the genetic sense) men and women, or resilient and unresilient (in the psychological sense) men and women. In the absence of reliable DNA data, fitness is unobservable, as is resilience. Not only are these phenomena not observable, nor are their shares in the strata. The proportions of fit men and women are unknown.

Random sampling from the strata ensures that fit and unfit men and women will be sampled according to their unknown shares. If the sampling is not random, fit or resilient men and women may be over-represented in the sample in which event $\hat{y}$ will be biased upward if fit and resilient men and women have superior outcomes. Hence, the importance of random sampling.

Human beings are replete with unobserved heterogeneity. Apart from fitness and resilience, people differ by their ability, intelligence, initiative etc. Take, for example, the determinants of wages. Labor economists (Ehrenberg and Smith 2018) find that about 30 percent of inequality in wages is explained by observable heterogeneity, such as schooling, gender, age and ethnicity. The other 70 percent may be attributed to unobserved heterogeneity. Indeed, in the social sciences unobserved heterogeneity is what makes the world go around. Observationally similar people, i.e., who belong to the same statistical stratum are very different in numerous respects. These unobservable differences will play a central methodological role is the present study.

Another example is assortative mating (Becker 1992), which arises when men and women marry people who are observationally similar. For example, spouses are positively correlated for schooling, age, race and religion etc. Although they might be statistically significant, these observable phenomena do not explain much of what happens. The rest is explained by unobservable 'chemistry' or what is referred to here by unobserved heterogeneity.

Clinical Samples

If the outcome of interest is recurrence risk and families are not randomly sampled within strata, estimates of recurrence risk will generally be biased. This arises in clinical samples because the families who attend clinics are unlikely to be randomly selected from the strata to which they belong. They will be 'positively selected' if these families are fitter and more resilient, which might be why they attend clinics in the first place. On the other hand, they will be 'negatively selected' if the families attending clinics do so because their children have severer forms of ASD. There are, of course numerous unobservable reasons why families choose to attend clinics. A further layer of unobserved heterogeneity is added when families choose between different clinics.

To fix ideas suppose that the objective of the clinician is to estimate recurrence risk for some given stratum with a sample size of n out of N families with children on the spectrum. By definition all families in the sample are observationally similar because they share the same covariates; otherwise they would not belong to the stratum. Suppose that recurrence risk happens to be 10 percent. What does this tell us about recurrence risk in the population? To help us answer this question we recall Bayes' Law according to which unconditional probabilities are related to conditional probabilities through the following formula:

$$E(y) = E(y|\, X = 1)P(X = 1) + E(y|\, X = 0)P(X = 0) \qquad (3.4)$$

where X is a binary variable that is either 1 or 0. Equation (3.4) states that the unconditional expectation E(y) equals the probability that X is 1 multiplied by the expected value of y conditional on X being 1 plus the probability that X is 0 multiplied by the expected value of y when X is zero. This simple formula has far reaching implications.

In the clinical example let X = 1 if a family attended the clinic. The clinician observes $E(y|\, X = 1) = 0.1$, i.e., recurrence risk is 10 percent in the sample. Since the sample size is n out of N, $P(X = 1) = n/N$ in which case $P(X = 0) = 1 - n/N$. E(y) is the unconditional recurrence risk in the population. To convince you, suppose in a different context, X = 1 if it is sunny and X = 0 if it is cloudy, and y is temperature. Equation (3.4) states that the weather forecast for temperature is a probability weighted average of the temperature if it is sunny and if it is cloudy. If there is an equal chance that it will be sunny or cloudy, the forecast for temperature will be 25 degrees if it is expected to be 20 degrees if cloudy and 30 degrees if sunny. The weather forecast of 25 degrees is an unconditional expectation. So, does recurrence risk in the population equal its unconditional expectation.

In equation (3.4) the conditional expectation for recurrence risk in the sample is known, but its counterpart outside the sample, $E(y|\, X = 0)$, is not. Suppose the latter happens to be the same as it is in the sample, i.e., $E(y|\, X = 0) = 0.1$. In this case, equation (3.4) states that $\hat{y} = 0.1$; recurrence risk in the population is 10 percent. In this case the clinical sample is a 'quasi random sample'. Obviously, the clinical sample is not random, but it has the properties of a random sample. If this is true the clinical sample may be used to make inferences about recurrence risk in the population.

Of course, we cannot know if it is true and it would be tendentious to assume that it was. If in truth $E(y| X = 0)$ exceeds 0.1 the clinical sample would under-estimate recurrence risk. Suppose that $E(y| X = 0) = 0.15$ and $n/N = 0.1$ because the clinical sample includes 10 percent of the population, equation (3.4) states that $\hat{y} = 0.136$; recurrence risk in the population is 13.6 percent instead of 10 percent. The clinical sample is biased downwards because the families in the sample are positively selected; they are less exposed to recurrence risk for reasons related to unobserved heterogeneity. If $E(y| X = 0)$ is less than 0.1 the opposite applies; the clinical sample is biased upwards because the families in the sample are negatively selected.

The previous discussion refers to clinical estimates of recurrence risk within strata, i.e., conditioning on observables. In chapter 4 we note that in many studies investigators carry out tests to ensure that their clinical samples are representative of the population in terms of observables. For example, in the case of men and women the sample proportions are 0.51 for women and 0.49 for men. Such tests miss the point that what matters is random sampling from strata, i.e., for men and women separately, which is highly unlikely in clinical samples.

Snowball and Recruited Samples

A related issue is 'snowball' sampling in which participants in the sample are asked to recruit their friends to increase the size of the sample. Goodman (1961) assumed that the initial sample is random and each individual in this sample recruits a given number of friends. Recruits are obviously not randomly sampled and are likely to be correlated with the individuals who recruited them. However, this is not helpful in the present context because the initial sample is not random.

Let n_0 denote the original sample size and n_1 denote the recruited sample. If each member of the original sample recruits one friend the combined sample is $2n_0$. Equation (3.4) becomes:

$$E(y)=E(y|X_0=1)P(X_0=1)+E(y|X_1=1)P(X_1=1)+E(y|X=0)P(X=0) \quad (3.5)$$

where subscript 0 refers to the original sample and subscript 1 refers to recruits. Continue to assume that recurrence risk in the original sample is 10 percent, hence $E(y|X_0 = 1) = 0.1$. Let the relation between the outcomes of recruits and their recruiters be:

$$y_{1i} = \alpha + \beta y_{0i} + \varepsilon_i \quad (3.6)$$

where ε is idiosyncratic heterogeneity among recruits. If $\alpha = 0$ and $\beta = 1$ equation (3.6) states that recruits are expected to have the same outcome as their recruiters. This does not, however, mean that the outcomes of recruits and recruiters are perfectly correlated. Equation (3.6) implies that this correlation coefficient equals:

$$r_{01} = \beta \frac{\sigma_0}{\sigma_1} \quad (3.7)$$

where σ_0 denotes the standard deviation of outcomes among recruiters and σ_1 denotes its counterpart among the recruited. Equation (3.6) also implies that the variance of outcomes among the recruited is:

$$\sigma_1^2 = \beta^2 \sigma_0^2 + \sigma_\varepsilon^2 \quad (3.8)$$

If $\beta = 1$ equations (3.7) and (3.8) imply that the correlation squared is:

$$r_{01}^2 = \frac{1}{1+\frac{\sigma_\varepsilon^2}{\sigma_0^2}} < 1 \quad (3.9)$$

Equation (3.9) implies that when $\beta = 1$ the correlation must be less than 1 unless $\sigma_\varepsilon = 0$. This apparent paradox stems from the fact recruits are imperfect copies of their recruiters because of their idiosyncratic heterogeneity (ε).

Equation (3.6) further implies that:

$$\bar{y}_1 = \alpha + \beta \bar{y}_0 \tag{3.10}$$

Hence, $\bar{y}_1 = \bar{y}_0$ when $\alpha = 0$ and $\beta = 1$. In this case recurrence risk among the recruits equals 0.1 in our numerical example, i.e., $E(y/ X_1 = 1) = 0.1$ in equation (3.5).

If α is positive, it means that recurrence risk is systematically larger among the recruits when $\beta = 1$. Although this possibility cannot be ruled out, it is more likely that this will arise when $\beta > 1$. If, e.g., $\beta = 1.2$ and $\alpha = 0$, $E(y/ X_1 = 1) = 0.12$. Suppose the original estimate is biased upwards because the original sample members are positively selected, hence $\hat{y} < 0.1$. The fact that β exceeds 1 makes this bias even larger. The opposite would happen if β is less than 1. The estimate of β (and α) may be obtained by estimating the regression model in equation (3.6).

In summary, because clinical samples are not randomly selected, they must be suspected of delivering biased estimates of recurrence risk. Snowball sampling magnifies the positive bias in estimates of recurrence risk in clinical samples if β exceeds 1 and reduces it if β is less than 1.

Population Cohort Data

If population data happen to be available sampling is no longer necessary. As we shall see, population data are available in some countries for the estimation of recurrence risk as well as other parameters of interest. These data tend to be found in administrative records. Of course, it is necessary to check that these datasets cover the universe of children with ASD, or at least they cover the vast majority. What turns these data into population cohort data is their inclusion of separate birth cohorts. Hence, they may be used to estimate recurrence risk for different birth cohorts, as well as the incidence and prevalence of ASD in the general population. Provided there are sufficient birth cohorts, these data may be used to study time trends in recurrence risk etc.

An important feature of the present study is to emphasize the major advantages of population cohort data over clinical samples and survey data. Unfortunately, population cohort data are scarce for at least two main reasons. First, they have to exist in principle. For example, they exist in Israel because the National Insurance Institute provides benefits to the parents of children with ASD. Or there is a national register of children with ASD for some other administrative reason. Second, since these data are confidential, they have to be made accessible to the research community under restrictions that accord with the laws of confidentiality, e.g., in the research room at the National Insurance Institute. As we shall see in chapter 4, the data in Denmark and California are not strictly population cohort data because the reporting institutions fall short of being comprehensive. In the present study, however, population cohort data for Israel are used. Moreover, these data are longitudinal too because for many outcomes it is possible to follow-up children with ASD over time from the cradle into adulthood and beyond.

CAUSALITY

The Identification Problem

Suppose there is a hypothesis according to which some outcome y (such as recurrence risk) depends causally on two types of variables, denoted by X and Z, where X refers to variables about which individuals have no choice whereas Z refers to variables about which they might exercise some control. For example, age, gender and ethnicity are X variables while schooling, marital status and location are Z variables. The basic hypothesis to be tested using cross-section data on individuals (i) is:

$$y_i = \alpha + \beta x_i + \gamma z_i + u_i \qquad (3.11)$$

where u is a regression disturbance and there is only one X and Z variable for simplicity. The regression disturbance embodies the unobserved heterogeneity discussed in the previous section.

The data used to test the hypothesis in equation (3.11) are observational. If they were experimental it would have been necessary to randomize the Z variables including schooling, marital status and location, which is clearly not feasible. Since the X variables are beyond the control of individual i, they are independent of u_i. Hence, E(xu) = 0 in equation (3.11); x and u are independent. Matters are different for the Z variables. For example, if u embodies unobserved ability and z refers to years of schooling E(zu) would be expected to be positive; abler individuals invest more in education. Since y depends on u in equation (3.11) and z depends on u, reverse causality is implied from y to z. This means that estimates of γ obtained by regression methods might simply be picking-up reverse causality from y to z rather than the causal effect of z on y.

If x and z in equation (3.11) happen to be independent, the ordinary least squares (OLS) estimator for β would be:

$$\hat{\beta} = \frac{cov(yx)}{var(x)} \qquad (3.12)$$

Substituting equation (3.11) for y in equation (3.12) gives;

$$\hat{\beta} = \beta + \frac{\gamma cov(xz) + cov(xu)}{var(x)} \qquad (3.13)$$

Since cov(xz) = cov(xu) = 0, equation (3.13) states that $E(\hat{\beta}) = \beta$, i.e., equation (3.13) delivers the causal effect of x on y because there is no reverse causality from y to x. The counterpart of equation (3.13) for γ is:

$$\hat{\gamma} = \gamma + \frac{\beta cov(xz) + cov(zu)}{var(z)} \tag{3.14}$$

In equation (3.14) cov(xz) is zero but cov(zu) is not. If it is positive $E(\hat{\gamma}) = \gamma + cov(zu)/var(z)$. Hence, the causal effect of z on y is not identified. If cov(zu) > 0 $\hat{\gamma}$ is biased upward for γ. In fact, the true causal effect of z on y might be zero, in which event $\hat{\gamma} > 0$ is entirely an illusion induced by reverse causality. If cov(xz) is not zero (as in the general case) not only is the causal effect of z on y not identified, nor is the causal effect of x on y.

This reminds us that correlation does not establish causality. Since we wish to determine the causes of ASD in general, and the causes of recurrence risk in particular, it is crucial to identify γ in observational studies. In chapter 4 we shall refer to studies in which causality is not clearly established. These studies refer vaguely to 'associations' and 'effects' without establishing causality.

Instrumental Variables and Natural Experiments

The solution to the identification problem is to find instrumental variables for z. Instrumental variables (q) are independent of u but not independent of z. They serve to randomize z as in a natural experiment. Laboratory experiments generate experimental data to test hypotheses by randomizing variables such as z. Natural experiments do the same thing by perturbing z in a way that is unrelated to outcome y. In laboratory experiments investigators perturb z through randomization. In natural experiments z is perturbed by q.

Suppose the auxiliary hypothesis for z is:

$$z_i = \delta x_i + \theta q_i + v_i \tag{3.15}$$

where v embodies unobserved heterogeneity in z. OLS estimates of the parameters in equation (3.15) may be used to decompose $z_i = \hat{z}_i + \hat{v}_i$. Since $\hat{z}$ depends on x and q, which are independent of u, it may be regarded as the experimental or randomized component of z. Substituting $\hat{z}$ for z in equation (3.11) removes the component of z, which depends on u, i.e., it eliminates reverse causality from y to z. Regressing y on x and $\hat{z}$ delivers consistent estimates of β and γ. This is the two stage least squares estimator (2SLS).

Whereas OLS is unbiased and consistent, 2SLS is consistent but biased. Unbiasedness is a preferable property to consistency because it is valid in finite samples, whereas consistency is an asymptotic concept. Parameter estimates are consistent if as the sample size tends to infinity they become infinitesimally close to their true values with probability 1. Consistency may be comforting in large samples, but not in small samples. By contrast, unbiasedness applies in all samples irrespective of their size.

2SLS is a special case of the instrumental variable estimator (IVE). IVE explpoits covariances with respect to q instead of going through two steps in which equation (3.15) is estimated in step 1 and equation (3.11) is estimated in step 2. The IVE for β and γ in equation (3.11) is obtained by taking the moments (covariances) of equation (3.11) with respect to x and q, which feature in equation (3.15):

$$cov(yx) = \beta var(x) + \gamma cov(zx) + cov(xu) \tag{3.16}$$

$$cov(yq) = \beta cov(xq) + \gamma cov(zq) + cov(qu) \tag{3.17}$$

Since cov(xu) and cov(qu) tend to zero asymptotically, equations (3.16) and (3.17) solve for estimates of β and γ in terms of their six sample covariances. Their solutions are:

$$\hat{\beta} = \frac{cov(yx)cov(zq) - cov(zx)cov(yq)}{var(x)cov(zq) - cov(xq)cov(zx)} \tag{3.18}$$

$$\hat{\gamma} = \frac{var(x)cov(yq) - cov(xq)cov(yx)}{var(x)cov(zq) - cov(xq)cov(zx)} \tag{3.19}$$

Notice that moment estimators such as equations (3.18) and (3.19) are obtained by exploiting the fact that moments cov(xu) and cov(qu) are zero.

In equation (3.15) there is only one instrumental variable q because x is specified in equation (3.11). It is obvious that if θ is zero in equation (3.15) $\hat{z}$ would be perfectly colinear with x, in which event it would be impossible to identify β and γ. The fact that θ is not zero ensures that $\hat{z}$ is not perfectly correlated with x. In fact, q 'just identifies' β and γ because there is only one instrumental variable. If there is more than one instrumental variable β and γ would be 'over-identified'. If, for example, there were two instrumental variables, q and w, (where z depends on w but cov(wu) = 0) the job of identification is shared between them. The more instrumental variables the better; there is more natural experimentation.

If y refers to recurrence risk, x refers to demographics and z refers to pollution e.g., recurrence risk is greater in polluted locations, why might z and u be dependent in equation (3.11)? If they are dependent, the causal effect of pollution on recurrence risk would not be identified. Suppose poverty is unobserved and is embodied in u, and recurrence risk is greater among the poor. Suppose further that housing is cheaper where there is more pollution and poorer people are more likely to live in polluted locations, i.e., cov(zu) > 0. Hence, reverse causality is generated from y to z, poorer people who have elevated recurrence risk are more likely to have larger z because they live where there is more pollution.

An instrumental variable would randomize local pollution but it must be entirely independent of recurrence risk. In cross-section data such a variable might be local lockdown policy, which reduces pollution locally. In time series data, such a variable might be gasoline taxation. Since lockdown policy and gasoline taxation have nothing to do with autism, but are relevant to air pollution, these variables might serve as instrumental variables.

The IVE may be used when there are more instrumental variables than there are parameters to be identified. In such over-identified cases there is a more efficient estimator than IVE. It too is a moment estimator and is referred to as the generalized method of moments (GMM). More efficient estimators generate parameter estimates more accurately, i.e., with smaller variances. Since its development in the 1980s, GMM has become the workhorse of identification. However, we do not go into details here because it is conceptually similar to IVE although it is technically different (Greene 2012).

Experiments with Humans

Finally, we mention the issue of experiments involving human beings, which have gained in popularity in recent years (Moffat 2021). Instead of relying on natural experiments to identify causal parameters such as β and γ, these parameters are estimated using experimental data rather than observational data. Randomized trials have been used to evaluate training programs for the unemployed in the US, deworming programs for schoolchildren in Kenya, as well as for medical products, such as vaccines for Covid-19. Randomized trials are popular because they finesse methodological problems involved in sample selectivity and the identification of causality. The treatment group gets the treatment, the control group does not; the difference between the outcomes of the treatment group and the control group identifies the causal effect of the treatment on the general population.

Randomized trials might work for animals, but matters might be different for humans. First, compliance problems arise if members of the treatment group avoid the treatment while members of the control group obtain the treatment by other means. Second, 'Hawthorne effects' arise if members of the treatment group produce positive results hoped for by experimenters. During the 1930s time and motion experiments conducted at the Hawthorne factory near Chicago produced favorable results for efficiency, but which made no difference when they were subsequently implemented. Fourth, experiments are temporary. Participants are likely to behave differently when a treatment is permanent than when it is temporary. By contrast, issues of ethics, compliance, Hawthorne effects and permanence do not arise in natural experiments in which people act spontaneously.

In any case, it is difficult to imagine experimentation in the case of recurrence risk. For example, randomizing reproductive stoppage is not feasible.

SELECTION BIAS

We have already seen how clinical data might induce selection bias in estimates of recurrence risk. Suppose, however, that the data are population cohort data in which this type of selection bias does not arise. Another type of selection bias arises in population cohort data because recurrence risk is estimated for those parents who had further children after their index child with ASD, i.e., for parents who did not engage in reproductive stoppage. If all parents engaged in reproductive stoppage there would of course be no data to estimate recurrence risk. Our objective is to estimate recurrence risk in the general population and not just among those parents who happened to refrain from reproductive stoppage. This includes recurrence risk among parents who engaged in reproductive stoppage, i.e., what would their counterfactual recurrence risk have been had the not engaged in reproductive stoppage?

Whereas the natural histories of fertility for animals are observed, matters are different for humans because they plan their fertility. If humans procreated as animals without planning their fertility, the natural histories of human fertility would be observed too. It would no longer be necessary to be concerned about sample selection bias because parents do not interfere with their fertility. There would still be differences in fertility because parents vary by their natural ability to procreate. What is important is that these differences are unrelated to recurrence risk or other outcomes of interest. As we shall see, methodological solutions for selection bias seek to transform unnatural histories of fertility induced by fertility planning back into their natural histories.

In what follows three canonical methods are described for handling sample selection bias with special reference to recurrence risk.

Manski Bounds: Methodological Minimalism

We appeal once more to Bayes' Law:

$$E(y) = E(y| X = 1)P(X = 1) + E(y| X = 0)P(X = 0) \qquad (3.20)$$

Equation (3.20) repeats equation (3.4) except X = 1 if parents refrain from reproductive stoppage and X = 0 otherwise. E(y) is the expectation of recurrence risk in the population. E(y| X = 1) is the expectation of recurrence rusk among parents who refrained from reproductive stoppage. P(X = 1) is the proportion of parents who did not engage in reproductive stoppage, which is known. So is P(X = 0) = 1 – P(X = 1). What is not known is the counterfactual recurrence risk for parents who engaged in reproductive stoppage, E(y/ X = 0).

Suppose 40 percent of parents engage in reproductive stoppage and recurrence risk is 10 percent among parents who refrained from reproductive stoppage. The unknown counterfactual is naturally bounded between 0 and 1, i.e., ASD might not have recurred among any of the counterfactual younger siblings or it might have recurred among all of them. Plugging the lower bound for the counterfactual values into equation (3.20) states that recurrence risk in the general population cannot be smaller than 0.6x0.1 = 0.06 or 6 percent. Plugging the upper counterfactual bound into equation (3.20) states that recurrence risk in the general population cannot be greater than 0.06 +0.4x1 = 0.46 or 46 percent. So, the data tell us that recurrence risk in the general population is bounded between 6 percent and 46 percent.

The empirical data tell is what is not rather than what is. They reject claims that recurrence risk is less than 6 percent or more than 46 percent. These bounds are admittedly wide. Without data they would be wider; the lower bound would be 0 and the upper bound would be 1. So, the data have removed 60 percent of our ignorance; the cup is more than half full. The fullness of the cup would be even greater if the proportion of parents engaging in reproductive stoppage was smaller. For example, if 20 percent engaged in reproductive stoppage instead of 40 percent the bounds for recurrence risk would narrow to 8 percent to 28 percent, in which event 80 percent of our ignorance would have been removed. Of course, if none of the parents engaged in reproductive stoppage, equation (3.20) implies that all our ignorance would be dispelled, the bounds would narrow to a point estimate for recurrence risk in the population of 10 percent.

We have attributed these bounds to Manski (1995) because he was the first to popularize them. These bounds are informative only in the negative sense (they rule out what is not) because they are based on zero assumptions; as it were, the data speak for themselves. Estimators such as OLS and IVE described in the previous section are based on many assumptions, e.g., the disturbance term u is normally distributed. The precision of estimators depends also on the assumptions upon which they are based. In most cases these assumptions are not testable; they have to be accepted as is. If the assumptions are to one's disliking, find another estimator, which is not. Okkam's Razor implies that the fewer the assumptions the better.

The minimalism in Manski's bounds is attractive because it implies that knowledge is fundamentally ambiguous. For example, recurrence risk is somewhere between 6 percent and 46 percent. These bounds may be narrowed and the ambiguity reduced if we are prepared to make untestable assumptions. For example, the lower counterfactual is not zero but equals the risk of ASD in the general population. Or the upper bound is not one but is no higher than recurrence risk for other medical conditions. The former raises the lower bound to above 6 percent and the latter reduces the upper bound to less than 46 percent. In the next subsection we describe an estimator, which remarkably reduces the bounds to an unambiguous point.

Incidental Truncation Method

Data are 'truncated' when they are completely concealed and 'censored' when they are partially concealed. For example, the younger sibling of a child diagnosed with ASD aged 7 years in 2021, and has not yet been diagnosed with ASD. As of 2021 this younger sibling does not constitute a case of recurrence risk. Of course, this sibling might be diagnosed with ASD subsequently. It would be necessary to wait until about 2030 to ascertain this sibling's recurrence risk status. As of 2021 the sibling's recurrence risk status is censored. Had the sibling been 15 years old in 2021 his recurrence risk status would have been ascertained and consequently uncensored. At least we know that by 2021 there was no recurrence of ASD. Uncensored or ascertained data are always more informative than censored data, but so are censored data informative. It would be a mistake, therefore, to drop censored data from empirical investigations of recurrence risk.

Missing data are truncated as are data, which the statistical authorities do not make publically available on the grounds of confidentiality. These data are completely concealed. Recurrence risk among parents who engaged in reproductive stoppage is by definition concealed; it is 'incidentally truncated'. We know nothing at all about it because it doesn't exist. If data exist but are concealed for some reason, they would be truncated. There are many examples of such data. The fertility of parents who engaged in reproductive stoppage is incidentally truncated rather than just truncated; we know that they had no further children, but we don't know how many children they might have had if they hadn't engaged in reproductive stoppage. Incidentally truncated data tend to be counterfactual data. In what follows we ignore methods to handle truncation bias since they are not relevant to recurrence risk, and focus instead on methods to handle incidental truncation bias, which are clearly relevant to recurrence risk.

On learning that their index child has ASD, parents may engage in reproductive stoppage. As in Figure 2.1 in chapter 2, let C* denote a latent variable, which measures the strength of their desire to have a further child, which is hypothesized to depend on a vector of observable covariates (Z) including the number of children they already have, their gender mix, the age of mothers and perhaps fathers, their ethnicity, schooling and economic status etc. These covariates might also affect fertility in the general population, but their effects on parents of ASD children are likely to be different. C* is also hypothesized to depend on unobservable phenomena such as their psychological resilience (chapter 2) with respect to having another child with ASD, denoted by r in chapter 2. These phenomena do not apply to the general population, and are specific to parents of ASD children. Finally, parents with the same resilience might have different preferences for further children, denoted by c in chapter 2.

In summary, as in equation (2.19) in chapter 2:

$$C_i^* = Z_i\beta + r_i + c_i \tag{3.21}$$

where i labels families, β is a vector of coefficients to be estimated, and r and c are random variables with zero mean (for convenience). Stoppage is hypothesized to occur when C* is less than some threshold (assumed to be zero), otherwise stoppage does not occur.

This simple model implies that observationally similar parents of ASD children (parents with the same Z) may have different rates of stoppage because they differ by r and c, which are unobservable. It also means that observationally similar parents in the general population cannot be compared with their counterparts among the parents of ASD children because β in the general population will differ and because r does not apply in the general population. If r + c = z is assumed to have a logistical distribution, β may be estimated by a logit model in which C is a binary variable, which equals 0 in the event of stoppage and equals 1 otherwise. If z is normally distributed, β may be estimated by a probit model.

Let S* denote a latent variable for recurrence risk, which is hypothesized to depend on observables (X) and unobservable x:

$$S_i^* = X_i\gamma + x_i \tag{3.22}$$

where γ is a vector of coefficients to be estimated. Let S be a binary variable, which equals 1 in the event that ASD recurs among younger siblings and is zero otherwise. S = 1 when S* is positive and is zero otherwise. If z and x are uncorrelated, probit or logit estimates of the probability of ASD recurrence are unbiased. If z and x are correlated with correlation ρ, estimates of recurrence risk may be corrected for selection bias. For example, ρ is positive if more resilient parents are less likely to engage in reproductive stoppage, and if for behavioral reasons discussed in chapter 2 their children are less likely to develop ASD.

The recurrence risk for family i conditional on no stoppage is (Greene 2012, p 732):

$$P(S_i = 1 | \, C_i = 1, X_i, Z_i) = \Phi\left[\frac{X_i\gamma + \rho Z_i\beta}{\sqrt{1-\rho^2}}\right] \tag{3.23}$$

where Φ(.) denotes the standard normal cumulative density, and the correlation between z and x (ρ) is used to correct for self-selection out of stoppage. Note that when ρ = 0 recurrence risk reverts to Φ(Xγ), i.e., sample selectivity is ignorable.

To illustrate, assume that $Z_i\beta = 0.3$ and $X_i\gamma = 1$. If $C_i = 1$ (no stoppage) and $\rho = 0.5$, the expected value of S_i^* is 1.171 and the probability of recurrence is 0.879. If $C_i = 0$ (the counterfactual for stoppers) the expected value of S_i^* is 0.5 and the probability of recurrence is 0.6915. The counterfactual recurrence risk for stoppers is smaller in this example than the observed recurrence risk for observationally similar parents who did not stop. If instead ρ = -0.5 matters are reversed; the counterfactual recurrence risk for stoppers is 0.879 instead of 0.6915.

The counterfactual expected value of S* for family i conditional on stoppage (C = 0) is:

$$E(S_i^* | \, C_i = 0, X_i, Z_i) = X_i\gamma + \rho(2C_i - 1)\frac{\phi[(2C_i-1)Z_i\beta]}{\Phi[(2C_i-1)Z_i\beta]} \tag{3.24}$$

The counterfactual probability of ASD recurrence is

$$P(S_i = 1 \;/\; C_i = 0, X_i, Z_i) = \Phi\left(X_i\gamma + \rho(2C_i - 1)\frac{\phi[(2C_i - 1)Z_i\beta]}{\Phi[(2C_i - 1)Z_i\beta]}\right) \tag{3.25}$$

The unconditional recurrence risk for family i according to Bayes' Law is an average of the two weighted by the probabilities of non-stoppage:

$$P(S_i = 1 | X_i, Z_i) = P(S_i = 1 | C_i = 1, X_i, Z_i)P(C_i = 1 | X_i, Z_i)$$
$$+P(S_i = 1 | C_i = 0, X_i, Z_i)P(C_i = 0 | X_i, Z_i) \qquad (3.26)$$

which is the bias-corrected risk of ASD recurrence for family i. The unconditional recurrence risk in the population is simply the average of these unconditional risks over all families. If $\rho = 0$, there is no selection bias, in which event the unconditional recurrence risk in the population is identified by the recurrence risk in families that did not engage in stoppage.

In summary, equation (3.26) recreates the natural history of recurrence risk for each family by simulating its counterfactual under non-stoppage and by weighting the probabilities of recurrence risk by their respective probabilities of stoppage and non-stoppage.

We have just described the incidental truncation method (ITM) for testing for sample selection bias and dealing with it if it is present. ITM was originally developed by Heckman (1976) for regression models involving sample selection, i.e., sample selection is binary and the variable of interest is continuous. In the case of recurrence risk sample selection is binary, and so is the variable of interest, recurrence risk. Wynand and Van Praag (1981) proposed a maximum likelihood procedure for estimating the ITM parameters, β, γ and ρ. Their procedure, referred to by 'Tobit 2', is available for example in the software of R.

Notice the similarity between ITM and the rational selection model in chapter 2. This is no coincidence. ITM exploits the assumption that individuals make rational decisions.

ITM narrows Manski's bounds down to a point estimate of recurrence risk conditional on the X and Z variables, which define the strata. This remarkable methodological achievement (cited in Heckman's Nobel Prize award in 2000) is achieved at a price. First, individuals choose what is best for them, as discussed in chapter 2; selection is rational. Second, what is not observed about their selection decisions and their outcomes have known distributions (usually bivariate normal). Applying this to recurrence risk means that parents who refrain from stoppage are better-off as far as they are concerned, and that what is not observed about parents of ASD children, represented by z and x are correlated through ρ. ITM involves hypotheses about the observables that determine selectivity into non-stoppage (Z) as well as the observable determinants of recurrence risk (X). ITM has been applied widely in economics, criminology, sociology etc. but it has not been applied to recurrence risk or in epidemiology (Infante-Rivard and Cusson 2018).

The identification of selection bias in ITM has two sources. First, the bivariate distribution of unobserved heterogeneity (z and x) is known. The standard assumption is that this distribution is bivariate normal. In chapter 2 we illustrated rational selection theory under the assumption of bivariate normality. Second, X excludes variables that are specified in Z, i.e., there are observables that affect selection into reproductive stoppage that are not relevant for recurrence risk. These variables serve as instrumental variables for identifying the causal effect of self-selection on recurrence risk. Notice that even in the absence of such instrumental variables, i.e., when Z = X, ITM 'solves' the selection bias problem parametrically through the bivariate distribution for z and x. However, it is advisable that the burden of identification be shared between these two sources.

Although it is not possible to test whether x and z are bivariate normal, it is possible to compare results obtained from other parametric assumptions such as bivariate logistic. If the results are robust with respect to alternative parametric assumptions this would increase confidence in their reliability. In this context copulas are a convenient way to express cumulative density functions (cdf) such as $F_{xz}(x, z/\theta)$ and their marginal cdf's, $F_x(x/\theta)$ and $F_z(z/\theta)$, where θ are parameters (Smith 2003). The marginal cdf's have quantile (inverse) functions $F_x^{-1}(u)$ and $F_z^{-1}(v)$ where u and v take values between 0 and 1. The cdf for x and z equals C(u, v) where C( ) denotes the copula function. The essential point is that marginals do not have to be normal. Hence investigators can specify and analyze the marginals and copulas separately.

Pearson correlation coefficients are not defined for copulas. The Spearman correlation coefficient between x and z may be expressed as:

$$\rho = 12 \iint_0^1 [C(u,v) - uv] dudv \tag{3.27}$$

The Frank copula is:

$$C = \frac{1}{\delta} ln\left[1 + \frac{\exp(\delta u - 1)\exp(\delta v - 1)}{\exp(\delta) - 1}\right] = F_{xz}\left(x, \frac{z}{\theta}\right) \tag{3.28}$$

for which the Spearman correlation lies in the interval of 1 and -1. For most other copulas the correlation is restricted in sign and size.

In summary, robustness tests for parametric assumptions in ITM may be extended to copulas as well as alternative assumptions to the standard case of bivariate normality.

Inverse Probability Weighting (IPW)

Whereas econometricians developed ITM and nonparametric bounds, statisticians developed the method of inverse probability weighting (IPW) for handling sample selection bias (Rosenbaum 2002). Let $\hat{p}_i$ denote the probability that parents from family i refrain from reproductive stoppage according to the selection model. If, for example, the selection model is specified as a probit, based on equation (3.21), this probability is:

$$\hat{p}_i = \Phi(X_i \hat{\beta}) \tag{3.29}$$

IPW maximizes the likelihood function weighted by the inverse of these probabilities:

$$lnL_{IPW} = \sum_{i=1}^{n} \frac{c_i}{\hat{p}_i} lnL_i \tag{3.30}$$

where C = 1 in the event of non-stoppage, and L refers to the likelihood of ASD recurrence, i.e., S = 1. Since $C_i = 1$ for all parents who had further children by refraining from reproductive stoppage, the IPW likelihood attributes more weight to parents who are less likely to have further children, i.e., more likely to stop. The estimator is based on the assumption that P(C = 1| S, X, Z) = P(C = 1| X, Z), i.e., the probability of selection does not depend on recurrence risk once X and Z are taken into account. This is equivalent to assuming that $\rho = 0$, i.e., potential hidden confounders such as z in selection are uncorrelated with randomness (x) in recurrence risk.

In short, IPW involves two steps. In the first, equation (3.21) is estimated as a regular probit model. In the second, equation (3.22) is estimated as a separate probit model by weighting its likelihoods as in equation (3.30) using the estimated probabilities of non-stoppage obtained from step 1. Under its maintained assumptions IPW corrects estimates of γ in equation (3.22) for potential sample selection bias.

Tests have been proposed to determine whether IPW estimates are sensitive to potential hidden confounders (Rosenbaum 2002). Hidden confounders here are variables, which for one reason or another are omitted from Z. Essentially, these sensitivity analyses are based on the idea that if families have the same values for Z their results for recurrence risk should not be significantly different if they also have the same values for X. If the results from IPW are insensitive all is well. However, matters are different if they are sensitive. The trouble is that 'sensitivity' is defined subjectively rather than objectively. There are also different proposals for conducting sensitivity analyses. In chapter 8 we apply the sensitivity analysis proposed by Zhao, Small and Bhattacharya (2019).

Whereas IPW assumes that $\rho = 0$ and carries out sensitivity tests to determine whether this assumption is plausible, ITM does not make this restriction and estimates ρ as a parameter in its own right. This sounds as if IPW is a special case of ITM in which $\rho = 0$. However, this is not so because if $\rho = 0$ ITM implies that equation (3.22) for recurrence risk may be estimated by a regular probit model whereas IPW does not. In short, IPW and ITM are non-nested methods; neither method is a special case of its rival. In principle non-nested tests may be used to determine whether IPW is preferable empirically to ITM (Santos Silva 2001). As is well known, non-nested tests may be inconclusive since neither ITM or IPW may turn out the be mutually preferable.

Confounding

As observed by Infante-Rivard and Cusson (2018) epidemiologists have been exclusively concerned with confounding and have ignored other sources of bias such as selection bias. They also seem to have confounded confounding with causality. Absence of confounding does not imply causality. For example, Weisskopf et al. (2015) assume that if the association between the incidence of ASD and air pollution is not confounded by other variables, the association is causal.

To fix ideas refer back to equation (3.11), which is repeated here for convenience:

$$y_i = \alpha + \beta x_i + \gamma z_i + u_i \tag{3.11}$$

Suppose x and z are independent of u, i.e., they are exogenous, and that equation (3.11) is the true model. OLS estimates of β and γ are causal because x and z are exogenous. If z is omitted from equation (3.11) and z and x are correlated, the estimate of β is biased (see above) in which case it no longer expresses the causal effect of x on y. If, however, x and z are mutually independent, we saw above in the discussion of equation (3.11) that the estimate of β expresses the causal effect of x on y. Of course, a residual confounding test for z will show that u is correlated with z. In fact, the coefficient equals γ. This property is known as the Frisch, Waugh, Lovell theorem. Hence residual tests only establish confounding when z and x happen to be correlated.

Suppose next, that either or both of x and z are endogenous, i.e., they are not independent of u. We concluded above that unless equation (3.11) is estimated by instrumental variables instead of OLS, the estimates of β and γ do not express the causal effects of x and z on y. Suppose the OLS residuals happen to be independent of q. Hence, the OLS estimates of β and γ are not confounded by q. This obviously does not mean that x and z are causal for y because β and γ are not estimated by instrumental variables.

Confounding is about misspecification induced by omitted variables. Causality is about the independence between what is not observed (u) and the covariates (x and z), which are observed, which is an entirely different issue. The so-called Hausman test (Hausman 1978) tests for causality by comparing OLS and IV estimates for β and γ. This is equivalent to regressing the OLS residuals on the instrumental variables. This sounds like a confounding test, but the resemblance is superficial.

Family Metrics

In chapter 4 we report that the empirical investigation of recurrence risk has largely been carried using data on single dyads per family, typically children with ASD and their adjacent younger sibling. This means, for example, that higher order siblings are left out of the study. Suppose child 1 is diagnosed with ASD. Recurrence risk does not arise with child 2 but it arises with child 3. Such a family supplies two opportunities to study recurrence risk; there are two dyads. The number of dyads naturally varies directly with the number of younger siblings.

For present purposes we resort to equation (3.11) but allow repeated observations per family. We continue to label families by i, and label younger siblings by s. Hence, equation (3.11) becomes:

$$y_{is} = \alpha_i + \beta x_{is} + \gamma z_{is} + u_{is} \tag{3.31}$$

where α_i denotes a specific effect for the family; if α_i is positive it means that recurrence risk is greater in family i. The disturbance term u_{is} may be independent between families, but is unlikely to be so within families for two reasons. First, they share the same parents and elder siblings. Second, they share each other. The former correlation is captured by α_i.

Clustering and Sibling Interaction

If there are two younger siblings, let the relation between siblings be (Beenstock 2012, pp 319-324):

$$u_1 = \lambda_1 u_2 + \varepsilon_1 \quad (3.32a)$$

$$u_2 = \lambda_2 u_1 + \varepsilon_2 \quad (3.32b)$$

where ε denotes idiosyncratic heterogeneity with variance σ_s^2. If sibling interaction varies inversely with birth order λ_2 is expected to be larger than λ_1. Positive sibling interaction implies λ is positive. The direction of sibling interaction may depend on birth order. Equations (3.32) imply:

$$u_1 = \frac{\varepsilon_1 + \lambda_1 \varepsilon_2}{1 - \lambda_1 \lambda_2} \quad (3.33)$$

$$u_2 = \frac{\varepsilon_2 + \lambda_2 \varepsilon_1}{1 - \lambda_1 \lambda_2} \quad (3.34)$$

Equations (3.33) and (3.34) imply that the sibling covariances for u depend on birth order:

$$cov(u_1 u_2) = \frac{\lambda_1 \sigma_2^2}{(1 - \lambda_1 \lambda_2)^2} \quad (3.35)$$

$$cov(u_2 u_1) = \frac{\lambda_2 \sigma_1^2}{(1 - \lambda_1 \lambda_2)^2} \quad (3.36)$$

Apart from anything else, equations (3.33) and (3.34) establish that u in equation (3.31) are not independent within families. They also imply that sibling variances for u are heteroscedastic unless $\lambda_1 = \lambda_2$ and $\sigma_1 = \sigma_2$:

$$var(u_1) = \frac{\sigma_1^2 + \lambda_1^2 \sigma_2^2}{(1-\lambda_1\lambda_2)^2} \quad (3.37)$$

$$var(u_2) = \frac{\sigma_2^2 + \lambda_2^2 \sigma_1^2}{(1-\lambda_1\lambda_2)^2} \quad (3.38)$$

The sibling interaction coefficients are naturally fractions in absolute value to ensure the stationarity of u_1 and u_2. Otherwise, if $\lambda_1\lambda_2$ equaled 1, the variance of u would be infinite. Table 3.1 shows that if both sibling interactions are mutually positive or negative, the variances of u_1 and u_2 are magnified. However, if one is positive and the other negative, as in row 3, these variances may be smaller than if siblings were mutually independent.

Table 3.1. The relation between sibling interaction and residual variances

λ_1	λ_2	**Var(u_1)**	**Var(u_2)**	**Cov(u_1u_2)**	**Cov(u_2u_1)**	**det**
0	0	1	1	0	0	1
0.5	0.5	2.21	2.21	0.8'	0.8'	4.03
-0.5	-0.5	2.21	2.21	-0.8'	-0.8'	4.03
0.5	-0.5	0.80	0.80	0.32	-0.32	0.73
0.5	0.2	1.54	1.28	0.51	0.20	1.88
0.5	0	1.25	1	0.5	0	1.25

Note: $\sigma_1 = \sigma_2 = 1$.

In short, using repeated observations by family means that u in equation (3.31) is heteroscedastic and asymmetrically correlated within families.

The variances of parameter estimates for β and γ in equation (3.31) naturally vary directly with the residual variance, var(u) and covariances. In standard regression software it is assumed by default that the observations are independent, and that each observation has the same variance such as 1 in Table 3.1, i.e., u is homoscedastic. In equation (3.31) observations within families are dependent, and if they are positively or negatively dependent the variance is larger, and even much larger. Also, the covariances within families is non-zero and may be positive or negative. If there are two younger siblings per family and there are N families the variance covariance matrix of residuals is 2Nx2N matrix $\Omega = I_N \otimes \begin{pmatrix} var(u_1) & cov(u_1u_2) \\ cov(u_2u_1) & var(u_2) \end{pmatrix}$ where elements between families are zero. When there is only one younger sibling per family $\Omega = var(u)I_N$, as in OLS and IV. Consequently, parameter estimates that happened to be statistically significant when the observations are independent, may be not be statistically significant when they are dependent. Furthermore, in standard regression software the variance of u is assumed to be homoscedastic. Sibling dependence may induce heteroscedasticity as in rows 5 and 6 of Table 3.1.

The determinant of the sibling covariance matrix is:

$$det\begin{pmatrix} var(u_1) & cov(u_1u_2) \\ cov(u_2u_1) & var(u_2) \end{pmatrix} = \frac{(1+\lambda_1^2)(1+\lambda_2^2)-\lambda_1\lambda_2}{(1-\lambda_1\lambda_2)^4}\sigma^4 \quad (3.39)$$

which equals σ^4 in the absence of sibling interaction, as in row 1 of Table 3.1. In the illustrations in Table 3.1 the determinant exceeds 1, sometimes by a large margin is in rows 2 and 3. However, in row 4 the negative sibling interaction for younger siblings reduces the determinant to less than 1, and illustrates the contention that negative sibling interaction may increase the statistical significance of estimates of β and γ.

There are two common solutions to these deviations from the standard assumption that the observations are independent. The most common is to cluster the standard errors of the parameter estimates (Greene 2012, pp 392-4, 428-9, 586) where the residuals from equation (3.31) are used to calculate the variances and covariances along the lines in Table 3.1. The standard errors of the estimates of β and γ are referred to as 'cluster-robust' standard errors. This approach is based on the assumption that the estimates of β and γ are consistent but their standard errors need adjusting to take account of the fact that the observations are dependent within families.

The second solution is to estimate the sibling interaction coefficients together with β and γ by using the method of generalized least squares (Greene 2012, pp 414-6) or GLS for short. GLS is more general in that it allows for the possibility that the estimates of β and γ might be biased in finite samples as a result of sibling dependence between observations within families.

In Table 3.1 we assumed that each family has two younger siblings. In practice the number of siblings varies between families. In the data for Israel used to test various hypotheses of recurrence risk in the present study, many families only had one younger sibling but some families had seven or more younger siblings. The cluster-robust and GLS methodologies for handling different family sizes (N_i) are not discussed here.

Specific Effects

Finally, we return to the estimation of family specific effects, α_i in equation (3.31). Repeated observations on younger siblings in families enable the estimation of family specific effects. Families with larger specific effects for recurrence risk face a greater risk of recurrence conditional on x and z in equation (3.31). Had the data been restricted to first-degree younger siblings these effects would have been an unidentifiable residual component; family specific effects would have constituted a component of unobserved heterogeneity. Relaxing this restriction turns heterogeneity that would otherwise have been unobservable into a phenomenon that is observable and subject to measurement (Greene 2012, pp 386-425).

Specific effects may be specified as 'random' or 'fixed'. In the former case α_i is assumed to have a known distribution, e.g., the specific effects are normally distributed. In the latter case the fixed effect for each family is estimated directly from the data by specifying binary dummy variables to identify each (D_i = 1 if observations are for family i and D_i = 0) otherwise. If there are N families there are N – 1 such dummy variables. An advantage of the random effects model is that it saves estimating N – 1 dummy variable coefficients. An advantage of the fixed effects model is that it does not impose arbitrary assumptions on the distribution of the specific effects. If the N families are a random sample of the population, it makes sense to treat their specific effects as being random. If instead the N families constitute the general population, as in population cohort data, it makes sense to treat the specific effects as being fixed.

In linear estimators such as OLS or IV the fixed effect model is simple to apply using the dummy variable method. This applies also to nonlinear estimators, such as logit. However, it doesn't apply to probit and other nonlinear estimators for which odds ratios do not have analytical solutions (Greene 2012, section 18.4.7).

CENSORING

We have already mentioned the issue of data censoring where outcomes cannot be ascertained. For example, the completed fertility of 50-year old women in the data is ascertained, but matters are different for 35-year old women because they sill might have another child. In the case of recurrence risk reproductive stoppage is ascertained for 50-year old women but not for 35 year-old women; their data are censored. It also applies to recurrence risk itself. If ASD has not recurred among younger siblings aged 15, their recurrence risk status has been ascertained for all practical purposes. Matters are different for 8-year old younger siblings because they might be diagnosed with ASD subsequently.

We have already remarked that some investigators solve the censoring problem radically by dropping censored observations. However, this throws out the baby with the bath water because we learn from censored data even if we would learn more from uncensored data. For example, if 35-year old women had no further children, common sense suggests that although we can't be sure that they engaged in reproductive stoppage, nor can we be sure that the did not. However, we can be surer that they engaged in reproductive stoppage than 30-year old women. The same applies to 12-year old younger siblings not diagnosed with ASD relative to 8-year old siblings. We can be more confident that recurrence risk does not apply to the former than to the latter.

Failure Time or Survival Analysis

Here we focus on solutions to the censoring problem when censoring is related to time or age. Indeed, this is the focus of survival or duration analysis (Greene 2012, pp 901 – 912). Since the identity of censored observations is known, the likelihood function for estimating the survival model distinguishes between the censored and the uncensored.

Let f(s) denote the probability of ASD recurrence when younger siblings are s years old. The proportion of recurrences by period t is the cumulative density function $F(t) = \int_0^t f(s)ds$, and the proportion of younger siblings not diagnosed with ASD by period t is therefore S(t) = 1 – F(t). Whereas S(t) is the probability of surviving out of ASD up to period t. The probability of being diagnosed with ASD during period t (conditional of course on not having been diagnosed before period t) is known as the hazard function $\lambda(t) = -dlnS(t)/dt$. Finally, $f(t) = \lambda(t)S(t)$.

In the simplest model the hazard is fixed at λ, so $S(t) = e^{-\lambda t}$ and $f(t) = \lambda e^{-\lambda t}$. This exponential model implies that as time tends to infinity the proportion surviving tends exponentially to zero. Let $\delta_i = 1$ if observation i is uncensored and $\delta_i = 0$ if it is censored. The likelihood function for estimating λ distinguishes observations according to whether they are censored or not:

$$lnL = \sum_{i=1}^{N}[\delta_i lnf(t_i/\lambda) + (1-\delta_i)lnS(t_i/\lambda)] \quad (3.40)$$

The second term in square brackets takes account of the censored observations according to their survival out of ASD recurrence. For example, in the exponential survivor model the contribution of an uncensored younger sibling to the likelihood would be $ln\lambda - \lambda t_i$ and the contribution of a censored younger sibling would be $-lnt_i$. For the uncensored, t refers to the period in which younger siblings were diagnosed, if at all. For the censored, t refers to the age at which younger siblings were censored.

Equation (3.40) adjusts the estimate of λ to maximize the probability of surviving without ASD recurrence until the age of censoring. It is in this way the censored observations are informative about λ. If λ is assumed to depend on covariates such as birth order and gender they may be specified in equation (3.40).

Equation (3.40) refers to the simplest of parametric survivor or failure time models. Parametric alternatives assume in various ways that the hazard rate is not fixed, and may be duration dependent. Non-parametric models allow the data to describe the hazard function empirically for given covariates such as birth order and gender. The most popular method is the product limit estimator of Kaplan and Meier (1958). The proportional hazard model (Cox 1972) is a popular semiparametric estimator; it follows Kaplan and Meier in allowing the basic hazard model to be estimated non-parametrically, but it allows covariates to shift the hazard function proportionately. For example, the hazard is shifted by gender and birth order.

The methods mentioned in the previous paragraph allow for censoring as in equation (3.40). These methods implicitly assume that if people lived forever, sooner or later they would be diagnosed with ASD, go to jail or whatever. For example, in the exponential model the only reason why recurrence risk occurs in a minority of younger siblings is because λ happens to be small. Long term survivor models (Maller and Zhou 1997, Beenstock and Rahav 2004) hypothesize two populations. In the first the event is indeed a matter of time. In the second the population is immune to the event irrespective of how long they live. Perhaps in the case of recurrence risk there are two populations, one in which ASD will never recur and another in which recurrence is a matter of time.

Logit and Probit Models

Failure time analysis is more ambitious than probabilistic models such as logit and probit in that it purports to answer two research questions. The first concerns the timing of the event. The second concerns the probability of the event occurring. No doubt in many contexts timing is crucial. In the case of recurrence risk most probably parents are not concerned with *when* their younger siblings will be diagnosed with ASD, but *whether* they will be diagnosed with ASD.

Statistical methods come at a methodological price. Simpler, minimalistic or parsimonious methods are preferred by Okkam's Razor to methods that require many assumptions that are usually untestable, as we have seen in this chapter. Failure time analysis which provides ambitiously answers to the *when* and the *whether* might deliver less robust results than probit or logit models that are concerned more humbly with the *whether* but not with the *when*. On the other hand, the treatment of data censoring has been a major methodological contribution in failure time analysis.

This subsection discusses how data censoring might be handled in logit and probit models. Suppose y in equation (3.11) happens to be binary; $y_i = 1$ if younger sibling i was diagnosed with ASD otherwise $y_i = 0$. According to the logit model the log odds ratio of recurrence risk is:

$$ln\frac{r_i}{1-r_i} = \alpha + \beta a_i + \gamma z_i \tag{4.41}$$

where r refers here to the probability of recurrence risk and *a* refers to age. If some of the observations are censored, it might be tempting to apply the procedure in equation (4.40) by distinguishing between the contribution to the likelihood of the censored and uncensored observations. The theoretical justification in equation (4.40) stemmed from the fact that censored younger siblings provide information on diagnosis timing; they had not been diagnosed by the time they were censored. Intuitively, the more censoring there is the smaller must be the hazard of diagnosis. If this hazard was high, there should have been less censoring. If the hazard was extremely high perhaps there might be no censoring at all.

The probability of censoring naturally varies inversely with age at the time of censoring. In the case of recurrence risk an 8 year-old at the time of censoring is more likely to be censored than a 13-year old. In the case of completed fertility a 30-year old mother is more likely to be censored than a 40 year-old mother. Suppose p_i denotes the probability of censoring, which is hypothesized to vary inversely with age (*a*) at the time of censoring. Censoring occurs when *a* is less than a^*, the age of ascertainment. The probability of censoring is zero when $a = a^*$, and is assumed to decrease nonlinearly the smaller is *a*:

$$p_i = max\left(\frac{a^* - a_i}{a^*}, 0\right)^\theta \tag{4.42}$$

where $\theta < 1$. Augmenting equation (4.41) with equation (4.42) takes account of censoring. Notice that β is identified in equation (4.41) because equation (4.42) is nonlinear in *a*.

Count Data

When the data are discontinuous, ordinary least squares (OLS) regression is not appropriate. For example, unlike continuous variable such as weight, height and income, the number of children (C) that parents may have is an integer (0, 1, 2 etc.). They can't have 2½ children, nor are they likely to have more than 10 children. The number of children is an example of 'count' data (Cameron and Trivedi 1998). The Poisson regression model is the most popular of regression methods for count data. It assumes rather restrictively that the mean of the dependent variable equals its variance. However, tests for over-dispersion (where the mean differs from the variance) are standard, as are other count data regression methods, such as the negative binomial regression model, which relaxes this restriction.

If C equals 1 (non-stoppage), the number of children may be larger or smaller. Just as observationally similar families might stop or not depending on what is not observed (u), so might they choose to have different numbers of children if they do not stop absolutely. Since the number of younger siblings of index children has the character of count data, which take discrete but limited values such as 0, 1, 2, etc. we suggest the use of count data methods (Cameron and Trivedi 1998) to test hypotheses about relative stoppage in which the dependent variable is C_i = 0, 1, 2, etc. Specifically, we use 'zero-inflated' Poisson regression (ZIP) where the probability of absolute stoppage (C = 0) is enlarged according to a complementary log logistic (CLL) model for the probability of absolute stoppage, and where u is assumed to have a Poisson distribution (Lambert 1992). See the discussion of equations (2.20) – (2.22) in chapter 2.

Chapter 4

Empirical Estimates of Recurrence Risk

Studies of recurrence risk of ASD have lagged behind studies of the incidence and prevalence of ASD. The earliest studies of recurrence risk date back to the 1990s. However, studies of recurrence risk among twins date back to the influential study of Folstein and Rutter (1977), which played a major role in establishing the neurodevelopmental paradigm of ASD as discussed in chapter 2. Their study was based on twelve pairs of MZ twins and ten pairs of same-sex DZ twins aged 5 to 23 years. Four of the MZ twins were concordant or recurrent for autism, whereas none of the DZ twins were concordant. The authors concluded that because MZ twins are genetically identical whereas DZ twins are not, there must be a genetic etiology to autism.

We shall not repeat here the critique of behavioral genetics in chapter 2 upon which their conclusion was based. Although the sample size is very small, a chi square test (χ^2 = 18.21) easily exceeds its critical value ($\chi^2_{0.05,1} = 3.841$) and rejects the null hypothesis that the rate of concordance among DZ twins is the same as among MZ twins. However, this test does not control for the ages of twins; it is obvious that recurrence is more likely among 23 year old twins than their 5 year old counterparts.

See Tick et al. (2016) for a review of the subsequent literature on twin studies in which the main conclusion continues to be that the etiology of ASD is primarily genetic.

The main concern in this chapter is not with twin studies but with recurrence risk between siblings in general. Rutter (1967) was among the first to notice that recurrence risk is many times larger than the risk of ASD in the general population. Relative recurrence risk (RRR) is defined as the ratio of recurrence risk to the risk of ASD in the general populations. In Rutter's case RRR was 50! As we shall see, all studies of recurrence risk suggest unanimously that RRR exceeds one by a large margin. This result has been given a genetic interpretation; a diagnosis of ASD among index children 'establishes' that the genes for ASD are present within the family. Hence, recurrence risk among younger sibling is elevated because the genotype for ASD is larger than in the general population. In chapter 2 we pointed out that there are also behavioral interpretations for elevated recurrence risk. If ASD has a behavioral etiology related to parenting, recurrence risk might be elevated through positive selection into reproductive stoppage as well as Thomas' theory of self-fulfilling expectations (chapter 2).

Estimates of recurrence risk have been informed by two types of data, clinical or ad hoc samples and population cohort data. The former are usually generated by clinicians who record data on their patients. The latter are usually obtained from national registers of children with ASD. In the nature of things, the sample sizes of the former tend to be relatively small, whereas the sample sizes of the latter tend to be very large. Another difference is that clinical data are not necessarily representative of the population of children with ASD, whereas matters are different for population cohort data because they are close to representing the universe of children with ASD. Indeed, in some cases such as in Israel, as described in chapter 5, the population cohort data come very close to representing the universe of children with ASD. Population cohort data are obviously more informative than clinical data; they are the gold standard for investigating recurrence risk.

Population cohort data have become increasingly available during the last decade thanks to advances in digital technology and the development of 'big data'. Prior to that, the data were exclusively clinical or generated by ad hoc surveys. On the whole estimates of recurrence risk obtained from population cohort data tend to be smaller than their counterparts from clinical data or survey data. Most probably this trend is related to the sampling theory discussed in chapter 3; clinical samples are unlikely to be representative of their populations whereas matters are obviously different for population cohort data.

Whereas estimates of recurrence risk based on clinical data referred exclusively to the United States, estimates derived from population cohort data refer exclusively to countries other than the United States (with the exception of California).

There are also two types of definition of recurrence risk. The first refers to the risk of recurrence among the younger siblings of index children. The second refers to the risk of parents having two children with ASD. The former takes sibling seniority into account; the older index child is diagnosed with ASD, and subsequently younger siblings are diagnosed with ASD. The latter does not attach importance to seniority. Parents might have two children with ASD because elder siblings were diagnosed after their younger siblings. To avoid confusion, we refer to seniority-based measures of recurrence risk by 'net recurrence risk' and the alternative by 'gross recurrence risk'. Inevitably gross recurrence risk is expected to exceed net recurrence risk because the former excludes elder siblings diagnosed out of turn.

What matters for parents of ASD children, concerned about the risk of recurrence if they refrain from reproductive stoppage is net recurrence risk. Perhaps this explains why most studies (including the present) refer to net recurrence risk. Gross recurrence risk is arguably of greater epidemiological interest because if the etiology of ASD is genetic or behavioral, seniority should not matter. If the genotype for ASD is present in families, there is no particular reason why older siblings should be diagnosed before their younger counterparts. The same applies if the etiology of ASD is behavioral.

Finally, we distinguish between conditional and unconditional recurrence risk. The latter refers to the average rate of recurrence risk in the population. The former refers to recurrence risk for specific groups in the population. For example, recurrence risk for younger Arab mothers whose index child was diagnosed with ASD after the birth of their next child. Conditional recurrence risk is calculated by estimating a multivariate model for recurrence risk in which the controls include e.g., age of mothers, ethnicity and age at diagnosis of index children. What matters for parents is conditional recurrence risk, which may vary quite widely. In the present study, unconditional recurrence risk in Israel is estimated at 3.7 percent. For some parents, conditional recurrence risk is as small as 1 percent, while for others it approaches 10 percent. Since unconditional recurrence risk is an average across groups, conditional recurrence risk naturally varies above and below this population average.

DATA

The studies included in Table 4.1 are comprehensive. They refer to an assortment of countries, different time periods, net and gross measures of recurrence risk, relative recurrence risk, small samples and large samples, as well as differences in data sources.

Population Cohort Data

Table 4.1 distinguishes between population cohort data and 'virtual population cohort data'. Conceptually, population cohort data cover the universe of children with ASD. In the next chapter we describe in detail why the data for Israel may be considered as population cohort data. Here we explain why data for counties such as Denmark and Sweden, categorized in Table 4.1 as 'virtual population cohort data', might fall short of population cohort data.

Table 4.1. Studies of recurrence risk

Study	Type	Data	N	Location	Period	RR%	RRR
Beenstock et al. 2015	net	PC	9117	Israel	1985-2013d	4.5	9
Beenstock 2021	net	PC	9117	Israel	1985-2013d	3.7	7.4
Bolton et al. 1994	gross	clin	99	England	na	5.8	
Chakrabarty et al. 2005	gross	clin	51	Stafford		3.94	
Chudley et al. 1998	gross	clin	51	Winnipeg	1991-1996d	8.0	
Constantino et al. 2010	net	rec	1235	US	1989–2003b	10.9	16
Constantino et al. 2013	gross	rec	5237	US	1989-2006b	10.4	
Grønborg et al. 2013	net	PC	13164	Denmark	1980-2004b	6.1	6.9
Hansen et al. 2019	gross	VPC	29998	Total	1998-2007b		
Hansen et al. 2019	gross	VPC		Denmark	1998-2007b		5.6
Hansen et al. 2019	gross	VPC		Finland	1998-2007b		8.9
Hansen et al. 2019	gross	EPC		Sweden	1998-2007b		7.9
Hansen et al. 2019	gross	VPC		W Australia	1998-2007b		15.6
Hansen et al. 2019	gross	VPC		Israel	1998-2007b		9.0
Hoffmann et al. 2014	net	VPC	19710	California	1990-2003b	10.1	
Hoffmann et al. 2014	gross	VPC	15153	California	1990-2003b	8.7	
Jorde et al. 1991	gross	VPC	185	Utah	1965-1984b	4.5	
Lauritsen et al. 2010	gross	EPC	818	Denmark	1994-2001b	3.0	22
Ozonoff et al. 2011	net	clin	664	US Canada	na	18.7	
Ritvo et al. 1989	net	rec	207	Utah	1960-1984b	8.6	215
Sandin et al. 2014	gross	VPC	1788009	Sweden	1982-2006b	10.0	10.3
Sumi et al. 2006	net	rec	269	Nagoya	1995-1999d	10.0	4.76
Wood et al. 2014	net	rec	81	England		24.7	
Wood et al. 2014	gross	rec	113	England		17.1	

Notes: PC: population cohort data, VPC: virtual population cohort data, Clin: clinical data, Rec: recruited/survey data. $Period_b$ birth cohorts included in study. $Period_d$ diagnostic cohorts included in study.

Ideally, population cohort data require that all diagnoses of ASD be registered nationally or within relevant administrative zones, such as Western Australia in Table 4.1. In many cases national registries arise for administrative reasons. For example, population cohort data are available for car owners, drivers, taxpayers, suicides and numerous other phenomena, which involve the public administration. Increasingly, these big data are made available to investigators in compliance with data protection laws. Censuses constitute another source of population cohort data. Each census provides data on the universe of citizens. It is possible to generate population cohort data through matching the same individuals across censuses.

With the exception of Israel, there are no administrative data records for ASD. Nor are there such records in Denmark. However, the Danish Psychiatric Central Register (DPCR) includes information on all inpatient admissions to psychiatric hospitals and psychiatric wards in general hospitals since April 1969, and all outpatient contacts since January 1995. Children who are suspected of having ASD are referred by general practitioners or school psychologists to a child psychiatric ward, where they are evaluated by a multidisciplinary team and assigned a final diagnosis by a child psychiatrist (Grønborg et al. 2013, p E3).

Unless all child psychiatrists work in hospitals the data will be incomplete. For example, in Israel very few children are diagnosed in hospitals. Indeed, there is no reason why diagnoses must be in hospitals, unless to obtain services and special needs education, or Danish children are required to be diagnosed in hospitals. Hence, it is not obvious that the data generated by DPCR cover the universe of children with ASD. This is why the studies for Denmark in Table 4.1 have been categorized as 'virtual population cohort data'. If the participants in DPCR are unrepresentative of the population of children with ASD, estimates of recurrence risk using these data must be suspected of sample selection bias.

In Sweden, all infants and preschool children regularly undergo routine medical and developmental examinations. At age 4 years, a mandatory developmental assessment is conducted. Children with suspected developmental disorders are referred for further assessment by a specialized team in a child psychiatry unit or habilitation service. Diagnostic information is reported to the National Patient Register (NPR). (Sandin et al. 2014, p 1771). The authors refer to a successful validation study for Stockholm youth. There are at least three data leakages from NPR. The first refers to diagnoses not carried out at child psychiatric units and habilitation services. The second concerns children who develop ASD after they are four years old. The third arises if parents don't comply; by not having their child diagnosed. As in the Danish case, unless to obtain services and special needs education, children with ASD in Sweden are required to be diagnosed in child psychiatry units and habilitation centers.

The Californian Department of Developmental Services (CDDS) manages a system of 21 regional centers, which are responsible for coordinating and providing assessments and services for persons with developmental disabilities (including autism and mental retardation). Hoffmann et al. (2014, p 944) cite a validation study in the range of 85 – 90 percent. The obvious source of leakage involves diagnoses not undertaken at the 21 regional centers.

Although Grønborg et al. (2013), Hoffmann et al. (2014) and Sandin et al. (2014) consider their studies to be population cohort studies, in Table 4.1 they are referred to as VPC studies because their data are not universal by design.

Clinical and Recruited Data

Three of the studies in Table 4.1 are based on clinical samples, which naturally tend to be small because they have been collected by the clinicians themselves. As discussed in chapter 3, there is no reason to expect that these ad hoc data are representative of the population of children with ASD in Stafford (England), Winnipeg and England as a whole.

Recruited data come in a variety of forms. The data in Constantino et al. (2010, 2013) come from a National Volunteer Register in which parents of children with ASD from across the US volunteer information on themselves and their children. Clearly the number of volunteers comprises a tiny fraction of parents of children with ASD. There is no way of checking whether parents who volunteer are representative of the silent majority of parents who did not volunteer.

Another example is the early study by Ritvo et al. (1989) in which the authors surveyed parents in Utah (a small state). They managed to recruit 207 parents of children with ASD. The population during this period averaged about 1.6m. There is, of course, no way of knowing the true number of proband parents in Utah. However, the numbers recruited seem low, even for Utah. Here too, are the parents who participated in the survey representative of the silent majority who did not participate? The same questions arise in Sumi et al. (2006) who conducted an epidemiological survey in Nagoya in Japan, and in the case of Wood et al. (2014) who use volunteered data.

The influential study by Ozonoff et al. (2011) is based on data from twelve sites in the US and Canada of the Baby Siblings Research Consortium (BSRC). These sites are clinics operated by universities which pool their data according to a common protocol. Parents attending these clinics for treatment of their children with ASD are invited to participate in a three-year follow-up study in which an important outcome concerns the recurrence of ASD. Hence, BSRC is prospective and delivers net measures of recurrence risk because it focuses on the younger siblings of children diagnosed with ASD. Participating parents are asked to suggest other parents of children with ASD, who might be interested in participating; secondary recruitment. Hence, the data in BSRC are recruited from clinical data.

A number of sample selectivity issues arise in BSRC. First, the twelve sites are not randomly sampled from the population in the US and Canada. For example, California is over-represented. Second, parents attending BSRC clinics are self-selected. For example, parents attending the clinic at UCLA may not be representative of the population of children with ASD in Los Angeles. Third, the parents who agreed to participate in BSRC are also self-selected; they may not be representative of the parents attending the clinics. A fourth issue concerns secondary recruitment, which as related to snowball sampling discussed in chapter 3.

Ozonoff et al. report that the BSRC delivers a large proband for recurrence risk of 664. Hence, on average each site provided 55 participants, which constitute tiny fractions of children with ASD in the catchment areas of the clinics. Obviously pooling these small samples increases the sample size. However, pooling data from geographically dispersed units is not the same thing as pooling data from units, which refer to homogeneous populations. The clinic operated by Nurit Yirmiya at the Hebrew University of Jerusalem is also a member BSRC. Would it have made sense to pool these data with those of Alberta, as if Jerusalem and Alberta comprise homogeneous populations?

Administrative Records

The study by Hansen et al. (2019) refers to itself as population-based as well as multinational. The data for Denmark and Sweden have already been discussed above. Most probably the same issues apply to the data for Finland and Western Australia. However, a completely different set of issues apply to the data for Israel, which is included in the study. These data refer to one of Israel's four major sick-funds (Meuhedet of which I am a member), which cover by law the entire population of Israel, as discussed in chapter 5. These are administrative data comprising members' entire medical histories. Children with ASD are ascertained with probability one, hence there is no leakage of data and coverage is universal and complete.

As we have seen, matters are different in Sweden and Denmark, where leakages are suspected. The issue with the data for Meuhedet is whether its members are representative of the population as a whole. Surprisingly, I have been unable to find local studies of this issue. What matters in the present context is whether children with ASD are randomly selected as members of Meuhedet.

Recurrence Risk: Absolute, Relative and Conditional

Censoring

The main purpose of Table 4.1 is to report estimates of unconditional recurrence risk, both absolute and relative. Unfortunately, each study uses a different time frame for measuring recurrence risk. It is obvious that rates of recurrence risk vary directly with the duration of the follow-up period. For example, Ozonoff et al. (2011) refer to the risk of recurrence within three years, which is the second largest estimate in Table 4.1. Since it is also the shortest follow-up period, this estimate of recurrence risk is the largest in Table 4.1. The only larger estimate is by Wood et al. (2014), who unfortunately are vague about the follow-up period. The authors report that the database used to estimate recurrence risk was established in 2003. However, they do not provide information on the years in which the probands for recurrence risk are observed. Nor do they report the years in which the recurrences were diagnosed. Since their paper was published in 2014, presumably the latest recurrences were in 2013.

A similar criticism applies to Grønborg et al. (2013), who report that their data refer to children born between 1980 and 2004. They also report the number of probands for each year. For example, out of 139,393 children born in 1994-5 1,864 children were diagnosed with ASD for which there were 33 recurrences. For this cohort recurrence risk was 7.1 percent because only 485 out of 1,864 parents did not engaged in reproductive stoppage. When were these 33 recurrences diagnosed? Since the authors are silent, we can only guess what the follow-up period might be.

In Hoffmann et al. (2014) 30,270 index probands are observed between 1990 and 2003. Since the data are sourced from DDS records in California (see above), presumably the authors had access to data until about 2010. This would leave only 7 years follow-up for probands diagnosed in 2003 and a maximal follow-up of 20 years for probands diagnosed in 1990. Here too readers are left to guess what the follow-up period might be.

The National Volunteer Register used by Constantino et al. (2010) was launched in 2007. Parents of children with ASD aged 4 – 18 years who volunteered began to complete on-line questionnaires about a year later. Presumably, therefore, the data are retrospective and refer to children born between 1989 and 2003. However, the authors do not provide information of when these children were diagnosed with ASD. Nor do they provide information on when the recurrences were diagnosed. Consequently, it is impossible to know the follow-up period to which the estimated rate of recurrence risk of 10.9 percent refers. Nor is it possible to judge the degree of censoring induced by the fact that some younger siblings would have been diagnosed with ASD after parents completed their questionnaires.

Sumi et al. (2006) estimate net recurrence risk using 269 probands observed between 1995-1999. It is unclear whether recurrences occurred by 1999, or whether the authors also had data for recurrences that were diagnosed in the early 2000s. If the former is the case, follow-up could not have been greater than only 5 years (a proband of 1995 whose younger sibling was born in 1995).

Hansen et al. (2019) estimate gross recurrence risk using probands for people born during 1998–2007 and recurrence among firstborns regardless of seniority, as explained. The data are censored from 2015. Follow-up is not strictly relevant to gross measures of recurrence risk. Consider the case of a proband observed in 2006, who happens to be a 3rd-born aged three. His firstborn sibling was born in 1996. If the latter had not been diagnosed with ASD by 2015, his non-ASD status is ascertained because he was almost 20 years old in 2015. If instead he was born in 2004 his ASD status might not be ascertained. Hence, although follow-up may not be strictly relevant, it matters for estimating gross recurrence risk. If, indeed, the cut-off date is 2015 the problem of censoring is unlikely to be important.

By contrast Sandin et al. (2014) are very explicit about the follow-up period. Indeed, they report that the cumulative probability of ASD recurrence increases nonlinearly with follow-up. Until 5 years follow-up recurrence risk is of the order of 2 percent, rising to 4 percent after 5 years, and increasing to 10 percent by 17 years. Indeed, the relationship between cumulative recurrence risk and follow-up is surprisingly concave; the probability of diagnosis measured by the hazard varies directly with age.

Beenstock et al. (2015) had access to administrative data up to the end of 2012 (see next chapter). They excluded from their study younger siblings aged less than four years in 2012 on the grounds that they had insufficient time to be diagnosed with ASD; they are censored. In chapter 3 this radical solution to the censoring problem was heavily criticized. Hence, the follow-up period is at least four years, and on average is much greater. The solution to the censoring problem suggested in chapter 3 is applied by Beenstock (2021), i.e., a separate variable based on age in 2012 is used to control for the probability of censoring. Consequently, the estimate of recurrence risk has an open-ended follow-up period, which in practice is up to 15 years.

This serves to remind us that the duration of follow-up and censoring are inversely related; the less censored the data the longer is the period of follow-up. Just as many studies were vague about follow-up, it comes as no surprise that they were also vague about censoring. Consequently, it is impossible to compare the various estimates of recurrence risk in Table 4.1 regardless of how the data were obtained. Consider, for example, the estimate of Ozonoff et al. (2011), which has been influential among clinicians. If the probability of recurrence within three years is as high as 18.7 percent, presumably it is higher still after ten years because this estimate excludes censored younger siblings diagnosed with ASD after the follow-up period. The only study to address this issue is Sandin et al. (2014), who show that recurrence risk over ten years is more than twice its three-year counterpart. Applying this result to the estimate of Ozonoff et al. would imply rates of recurrence risk that are implausibly large; at least 40 percent.

As mentioned, the estimate of Sandin et al. is based on virtual population cohort data whereas the estimate of Ozonoff et al. is based on volunteered clinical data. The former data are likely to be more representative of the population of children with ASD than the latter because of two sample selection issues (self-selection into clinics and into volunteering). If the data (BSRC) used by Ozonoff et al. are negatively selected, this might explain why their estimate of recurrence risk is so large. The same applies to the estimates of Wood at al. (2014).

The only robust result, which is hardly useful, is that recurrence risk is much larger than it is in the general population, i.e., relative recurrence risk is greater than 1. A number of studies in Table 4.1 report RRR as well as RR. Estimates of RRR range from 5.6 to 215. Note that for methodological reasons, Hansen et al. (2019) report RRR but not RR.

Conditional Recurrence Risk

With the exception of Beenstock et al. (2015), Beenstock (2021) and Sandin et al. (2014) the studies in Table 4.1 refer to unconditional recurrence risk. As noted above what matters to parents and clinicians is conditional recurrence risk. Whereas unconditional recurrence risk refers to the average rate of recurrence risk in the population, conditional recurrence risk refers to the specific rate of recurrence risk controlling for the age and ethnicity of parents, the age at which their child was diagnosed with ASD, the child's birth order, current age and gender etc. To be fair, several studies estimate recurrence risk for various sub-groups, the most popular of which concerns gender combinations where the index and sibling belong to the same sex or different sexes. For example, Hansen et al. (2019) report that recurrence risk for sister dyads is 55 percent larger than for brothers, for brother – sister dyads it is 14 percent greater, and for sister - brother dyads it is 48 percent greater. Also, several studies report rates of recurrence risk by age of mothers and fathers. As explained in chapter 3 these sub-groups are not a substitute for multivariate statistical analyses because variables such the age of parents, the gender mixes of children etc. are subject to mutual confounding except in the unlikely event that these variables happen to be mutually uncorrelated.

Table 4.2 uses results from a multivariate logit model for recurrence risk reported by Beenstock, Raz and Levine (2015) to illustrate heterogeneity in conditional recurrence risk. The baseline estimate for recurrence risk in Table 4.2 is greater than recurrence risk reported in Table 4.1 because the latter does not condition on the variables featured in Table 4.2 whereas the baseline estimate is itself conditional. In the baseline conditional recurrence risk is 6.6 percent whereas in Table 4.1 unconditional recurrence risk is 4.5 percent. In the baseline the index and younger sibling are brothers with birth orders 1 and 2 respectively. Parents are non-ultra-orthodox Jews aged less than 35 years. There are three age gaps. The 'interpregnancy gap' (IPG) refers to the age gap between adjacent siblings when the older sibling has ASD. The 'sibling gap' is the age gap between siblings regardless of their ASD status. The 'birth gap' is the age gap between younger siblings and index children. In a family of four in which the second child has ASD, the sibling gap for the youngest child is the birth gap between the third and fourth child. IPG is not defined for the fourth child because he or she is not adjacent to the index child. The birth gap is the age gap between the index child (second child) and the fourth child. In the baseline these gaps are 0-2 years.

The baseline is reported in the top row of Table 4.2. In row 1 the index child is a girl instead of a boy, which increases conditional recurrence risk from 6.6 percent to 9.57 percent. Although recurrence risk is smaller for girls (row 9), female probands increase recurrence risk because their ASD tends to be more severe, as mentioned. In row 2 the birth order of younger siblings increased from two to three. Comparing row 2 with row 1 shows that recurrence risk decreases from 9.57 percent to 8.8 percent because in the model it varies inversely with the product of the birth order of the index (i) and the birth order of younger siblings (s) minus 1. The odds ratio, which is 0.92, is multiplied by $i(s - 1) = y$. In the base line $y = 1$. In row 2 $y = 2$. In row 3 $y = 6$. This important result means that recurrence risk varies inversely and nonlinearly with the birth orders of index children and their younger siblings. In the next chapter we report families in which the birth order of the index child is 7 and the birth order of the younger sibling is 9 so that $y = 56$. For such families, conditional recurrence risk is almost zero because they have succeeded in bringing into the world six regular

Table 4.2. Estimates of conditional recurrence risk

Case	Index	Sibling	Birth order		Ethnicity	Age (years)		Gap (years)		RR
			Index	Sib		Father	Mother	Sib	Birth	
Baseline	brother	brother	1	2	Jew	<35	< 35	0-2	0-2	6.6
1	sister	brother	1	2	Jew	<35	< 35	0-2	0-2	9.57
2	sister	brother	1	3	Jew	<35	<35	0-2	0-2	8.80
3	sister	brother	2	4	Jew	<35	<35	0-2	0-2	6.30
4	sister	brother	2	4	Jew	<35	35-40	0-2	0-2	4.48
5	sister	brother	2	4	Jew	<35	35-40	>2	0-2	4.17
6	sister	brother	2	4	Jew	<35	35-40	>2	>2	2.92
7	sister	brother	2	4	Jew	35-40	35-40	>2	>2	4.20
8	sister	brother	2	4	Haredi	<35	35-40	>2	>2	2.60
9	sister	brother	2	4	Non-Jew	<35	35-40	>2	>2	0.88
10	brother	sister	2	4	Jew	<35	<35	>2	>2	0.85

Based on Beenstock, Raz and Levine (2015) Model 6 in Table 4.3.

children prior to the birth of the index child as well as an additional regular child afterwards. This explains why in row 3 recurrence risk is 6.3 percent instead of 8.8 percent in row 2.

In row 4 mothers' age is increased to 35 – 40 years, which reduces recurrence risk from 6.3 percent in row 3 to 4.48 percent. In the general population the incidence of ASD tends to vary directly with the age of mothers. However, there is no established consensus on this matter as far as recurrence risk is concerned. A comparison of rows 6 and 7 shows that older fathers increase condition recurrence risk. Indeed, when both parents are aged 35 – 40 conditional recurrence risk remains almost unchanged; older fathers offset the negative effect of older mothers.

In row 6 the birth gap is increased to above 2 years, which reduces recurrence risk from 4.17 percent in row 5 to 2.92 percent. This result is consistent with Cheslack – Postava, Lui and Bearman (2011) who claimed that closely spaced pregnancies are a risk factor for ASD. Rows 8 and 9 in Table 4.2 repeat row 6 for haredi (ultra-orthodox) Jews, which account for about 12 percent of the population and non-Jews (mainly Arabs) who account for about 20 percent of the population. Row 8 shows that for haredi families recurrence risk tends to be smaller for given birth orders. Since haredi families are unusually large and consequently birth orders are high, their y tends to be large, which reduces their exposure to recurrence risk even further.

Recurrence risk is smaller still in Non-Jewish families (row 9). It has been argued that the incidence of ASD among Non-Jews might be smaller due to under-reporting and lack of access to services (Raz et al. 2014). However, this cannot explain why recurrence risk is smaller for Non-Jews because their index child has already been reported.

In summary, estimates of conditional recurrence risk vary widely. It is certainly not the case that one number suits all. The range in Table 4.1 understates the support for conditional recurrence risk; there are instance where conditional recurrence risk exceeds 10 percent, and there are instances where it is negligible, especially for large haredi and Non-Jewish families where the index child is a boy.

Familial Recurrence Risk

We have already mentioned that research into recurrence risk began with twin studies and that the elevated risk for MZ twins led to the belief that ASD had something to do with genetics. Some of the studies in Table 4.1 have followed-up this line of thought by comparing recurrence risk for full siblings and half siblings because the former are more genetically similar than the latter. Some have even compared recurrence risk among siblings with recurrence risk among cousins. The expectation is that recurrence risk between full siblings is greater than among half siblings, and recurrence risk among half siblings is greater than recurrence risk among cousins because half siblings are more genetically similar than cousins, but are less genetically similar than full siblings.

The results for the studies in Table 4.1, which focus on half siblings and cousins, are reported in Table 4.3. Two of the studies report results for relative recurrence risk, and two report results for recurrence risk. All four studies show that recurrence risk is largest for full siblings and smallest for cousins, as expected. They also tend to show that recurrence risk for maternal half siblings is larger than for their paternal counterparts. All authors concerned interpret these results as supporting the hypothesis that the etiology of ASD is genetic.

Table 4.3. Familial recurrence risk

		Full Sibs	**Half Sibs**		**Cousins**
			Maternal	**Paternal**	
Sandin et al. 2014	RRR	10.3	3.3	2.9	2.0
Hansen et al. 2019	RRR	8.4	5.8	3.9	1.7
Constantino et al. 2013	RR%	10.4	5.2	9.5	na
Grønborg et al. 2013	RR%	7.5	2.5	1.5	na

Following the critique of behavioral genetics presented in chapter 2, the results in Table 4.3 have a behavioral interpretation. Full siblings are behaviorally more similar than half siblings because step parents relate differently to their children than biological parents. There is a natural greater closeness and affinity between biological parents and their children than between step parents and their step children. This affinity is even weaker for cousins because they do not share common parents. On the other hand, aunts and uncles shared the same environments of their siblings because they were raised in the same families. Hence, elevated recurrence risk for cousins might have nothing to do with genetics, and might instead be simply to do with the fact that aunts and uncles shared common childhoods and parents.

Since maternal and paternal half siblings are genetically similar, and recurrence risk for the former exceeds the latter, the results in Table 4.3 suggest that mothers have a stronger behavioral influence on their children than fathers. Hansen et al. report that relative recurrence risk for maternal cousins (aunts) is 1.9 whereas for paternal cousins (uncles) relative recurrence risk is 1.4. Since aunts and uncles are genetically similar, these results are consistent with the thesis that mothers have a stronger behavioral influence on their children than fathers.

It is unfortunate that there are no comparisons between biological siblings and adopted siblings. Adoptees have genetically nothing in common with their siblings. Therefore, relative recurrence risk for sibling dyads involving adoptees should be 1 if the etiology of ASD is genetic. By contrast behavioral theory predicts that recurrence risk for such dyads should be elevated because adoptees and their siblings share the same household, the same neighborhoods, and they share each other.

It might be thought that the difference between recurrence risk for full siblings and adoptees identifies the influence of genetics. If, for example, this difference is zero, it suggests that the etiology of ASD is behavioral rather than genetic because adoptees do not share the genes of their siblings. This would be true if parents did not relate differently to their adopted children than to their biological children, and if biological siblings did not relate differently to each other than sibling dyads involving adoptees. If, for example, blood matters so that the affinity between biological siblings and between biological parents and their children is greater, recurrence risk would be greater among biological siblings for behavioral rather than genetic reasons.

There are many examples of comparisons involving adoptees (Beenstock 2012). The key methodological problem concerns selection bias induced by the fact that adoptive parents choose which children to adopt, adoption agencies choose where to place adoptees, and biological parents choose whether to put up their children for adoption. Adoptees are not randomly removed from their biological parents, and then randomly assigned to adoptive parents. If adoptees are positively selected their outcomes will tend to be positively correlated with their siblings'.

The studies reported in Table 4.4 show that sibling dyads involving adoptees are positively correlated, but less so than for biological siblings. In one case (neuroticism) dyads involving adoptees are more correlated than for biological siblings. The results reported by Sacerdote are noteworthy because they refer to Korean adoptees who, it is claimed, were randomly assigned to parents in the US. Consequently, they should be free of sample selection bias.

Table 4.4. Correlations between biological siblings and adoptees

	Outcome	Biological sibs	Adoptees
Bouchard & McGue 1981	IQ	0.47	0.29
Jencks 1972	IQ	0.52	0.26
Loughlin 1992	extroversion	0.2	0.07
Loughlin 1992	neuroticism	0.09	0.11
Sacerdote 2007	smoking	0.29	0.15
Sacerdote 2007	drinking	0.35	0.32
Sacerdote 2007	weight	0.28	0.03
Sacerdote 2007	asthma	0.22	0.08

All studies refer to the United States.

Does the fact that sibling correlations for drinking are similar imply that the etiology of drinking is entirely behavioral as suggested by behavioral genetics? This would be the case if parents and biological siblings interacted with adoptees just as they would with biological children. If blood matters, the correlation for biological siblings is expected to be greater than for adoptees. Does this explain why the correlation for biological siblings is slightly larger (0.35 v 0.32)? Or perhaps blood does not matter in a positive direction, and parents and biological siblings interact more closely with adoptees.

Nor does the fact the biological siblings are generally more correlated than sibling dyads involving adoptees mean that the difference is genetic. For example, biological siblings are more correlated for IQ. Do Jencks' results mean that half the correlation is behavioral and half is genetic (because the biological sibling correlation is twice the correlation involving adoptees)? The answer would be positive if blood did not matter in either direction. However, such arbitrary behavioral restrictions would not be scientific.

In summary, the results in Table 4.4 are not informative about the contributions of genetics and behaviorism to the outcomes in the table. On the other hand, they establish that behaviorism matters, for otherwise the correlations involving adoptees should have been zero.

Chapter 5

POPULATION COHORT DATA FOR ISRAEL

In chapter 3 we praised the virtues of population cohort data in the study of recurrence risk, on the grounds that they are free of sample selectivity, as well as the fact that in population cohort data the number of observations is naturally very large. In chapter 4 we observed that although investigators of recurrence risk have increasingly turned to population cohort data in Sweden, Denmark and California, in practice these data may not be entirely free of sample selectivity, even if they are far superior in these respects to clinical and volunteered data. In Table 4.1 of chapter 4 these data were classified as virtual population cohort data. The only case of population cohort data in Table 5.1 was for Israel. In this chapter we justify this classification and introduce the data, which will be used in chapters 6 to 10.

THE NATIONAL INSURANCE INSTITUTE

Israel's National Insurance Institute (NII), in common with similar institutes elsewhere, receives national insurance contributions from employers and the insured population, who receive benefits such as family income support and unemployment benefit contingent on their eligibility.

NII also provides invalidity benefit to the eligible. In 1981 a new benefit was introduced to assist the parents of children with autism and related disabilities. This included a per capita monthly benefit per child as well as well as national tax concessions and local tax concessions. In 2013 the capita benefit amounted to about 25 percent the average wage. Hence the total benefit is quite generous. Beneficiaries are also entitled to attend special needs schools.

At first, these benefits were means-tested. However, in 1995 they were made universal. Also, families with recurrence ASD received more than twice the benefit of families with a single child with ASD. As with all new benefits the take-up rate was initially low either because the public was unaware or because of stigma. However, by the end of the 1980s the take-up rate had matured in line with other NII benefits. Indeed, an ascertainment study for a major Health Maintenance Organization (HMO) for children born between 1995 and 2010 showed a concordance rate of 97 percent between NII data on children diagnosed with ASD and HMO data (Raz et al. 2014).

A typical diagnosis of ASD in Israel starts with a referral by a pediatrician to a child development center where the child is diagnosed by a multidisciplinary team according to DSM criteria. Parents may also get their child diagnosed independently by a child psychiatrist, a pediatric neurologist or a pediatrician with at least 3 years' experience at a child development center. If the child is diagnosed positive for ASD, parents may apply for benefit from NII. If approved, benefit is backdated to the date of diagnosis provided that no more than 12 months have passed since the diagnosis. If not approved, parents may appeal the decision. Note that NII does not provide diagnostic services. However, an NII medical doctor is involved in internal quality checks of a about 5 percent of applications. Typically, approvals take about two months.

To our best knowledge Israel is the only country in which parents of children with ASD receive such a cash benefit. In some countries, such as the UK, parents of children with ASD may apply for various means tested benefits if, for example, they have suffered a loss of income as a result of their child having ASD. These benefits are not automatic, as they are in Israel, and they are not uniquely targeted at children with ASD.

Beneficiaries remain eligible until aged 18 when they are assessed for invalidity benefit as adults, as discussed in more detail in chapter 10. NII is generous insofar as it continues to provide benefit until age 21 if beneficiaries are in some educational or other framework.

All benefits and contributions are recorded monthly at NII. Electronic records are available from 1984. This means that these records are a source of longitudinal information on insured individuals. For example, an individual aged 30 in 2022 was diagnosed with ASD aged 3 years (in 1995). He ceased to receive benefit aged 19 (in 2011) after which he attended a vocational training course for special needs individuals until 2013. He was unemployed until 2014 after which he worked in various jobs until 2022. These milestones are electronically recorded at NII, including how much he earned up to 2022, and in which economic branches he was employed. If he happened to volunteer for national service (see chapter 10) and marry, these milestones are recorded too.

These data are recorded because national insurance contributions vary by status, e.g., students in tertiary education pay a different rate, which is coded. In Israel all residents are required to have health insurance and to join one of the four major MHOs mentioned above. The premiums they pay are earnings-related and depend on their status, e.g., students in tertiary education pay a different rate. NII is responsible for administering the payment compulsory health insurance premia. Hence, the electronic records at NII include contributions and benefits of NII as well as compulsory health insurance contributions.

At birth each child is assigned a unique id number, which applies until death. Immigrants are also assigned unique id numbers. The Population Register at the Ministry of Interior contains information on familial relationships between parents and children as well as between siblings. These relationships are established through id numbers. It is possible, therefore, to match children with ASD in the electronic records of NII with their parents and with their siblings. This means, for example, that it is possible to identify ASD recurrences in siblings. It is also possible to match information on parents such as their income and NII benefits to their children with ASD. It is also possible to match information between children with ASD and their siblings. For example, siblings might have other handicaps apart from ASD revealed through information on benefits.

Data protection laws prevent such matching between electronic archives. The Population Register is not accessible to the public, but matters are different for official institutions such as at the NII. At my request NII matched children with ASD in their records to their parents and siblings using the Population Register. NII provided access to these data in a dedicated Research Room in Jerusalem on a 'sterile' desktop computer (no internet, no USB, no printer) under a personal confidentiality agreement.

The uniqueness of these data is related to the fact that the universe of children with ASD are included because the NII's ASD benefit is universally available, and its take-up rate is almost 100 percent. This coverage differentiates the database for Israel from databases in Denmark, California and Sweden where there is no benefit specifically targeted at children with ASD. This is why in Table 4.1 in chapter 4, the study for Israel was classified as 'population cohort data' and the studies for Denmark, California and Sweden were classified as 'virtual population cohort data'.

Although there are salient data advantages in Israel, there are also a number of deficiencies. First, the database is silent about the severity of ASD, as indeed are databases elsewhere. However, as pointed out in chapter 10, the database includes IDL assessments and functional assessment at age 18, which are correlates of severity. Second, the database is silent about schooling, and especially different types of special needs schooling. In principle, this deficiency may be solved by matching NII records with records at the Ministry of Education, but in practice there has been no such matching. Third, the database is silent about services provided by the Ministry of Welfare for people on the spectrum, largely because this ministry failed to digitize its data records. These deficiencies apply apparently in other countries as well as in Israel.

The Incidence of ASD

The NII database was used by Raz et al. (2014) to study the incidence of ASD in the Israeli population during 1992 – 2009 using data until the end of 2011. Their study population was restricted to children born in Israel, and excludes immigrant children who came in the great wave of immigration from the former USSR in the 1990s (when a million immigrants increased the population by 20 percent). During 1992 -2009 1,247,552 boys were born of which 7,611 were diagnosed with ASD by 2011, and 1,184,097 girls were born of which 1,498 were diagnosed with ASD. NII decomposes the population into three major subgroups, Non-Jews (mainly Arabs) accounting for 18 percent of births, haredi (ultra-orthodox) Jews accounting for 25 percent of births, and other Jews accounting for 54 percent of births.

Haredi Jews are recognizable by the way they dress (similar to Amish folk) and their observant way of life. Other Jews may be just as observant, but they do not have a particular dress code. Haredi Jews in Israel are different to their counterparts elsewhere in that they have political representation in the Knesset, and are exempted from compulsory military service provided that they attend Talmudical college. During this period, which ends when they are 40 years old, they cannot work but receive a modest stipend from the government. Hence, whereas haredi men in the diaspora earn their living, a large minority of haredi men in Israel do not.

The total fertility rate in Israel is 3.2, which greatly exceeds fertility in other advanced economies, where it has been less than replacement for a number of decades. In a number of countries, such as Japan, Italy and Spain the total fertility rate is about 1.2 and in South Korea it is less than 1. In 2018 total fertility in Sweden, the US and the UK stood at 1.76, 1.73 and 1.68 respectively. Completed fertility for haredi women in Israel is 5 children, which is most probably similar to completed fertility among haredi and observant women elsewhere.

Unlike Jews and non-Jews who are positively identified by their id, there is no official definition of who is haredi. However, the NII has an algorithm to identify haredi Jews, which is used in the present data.

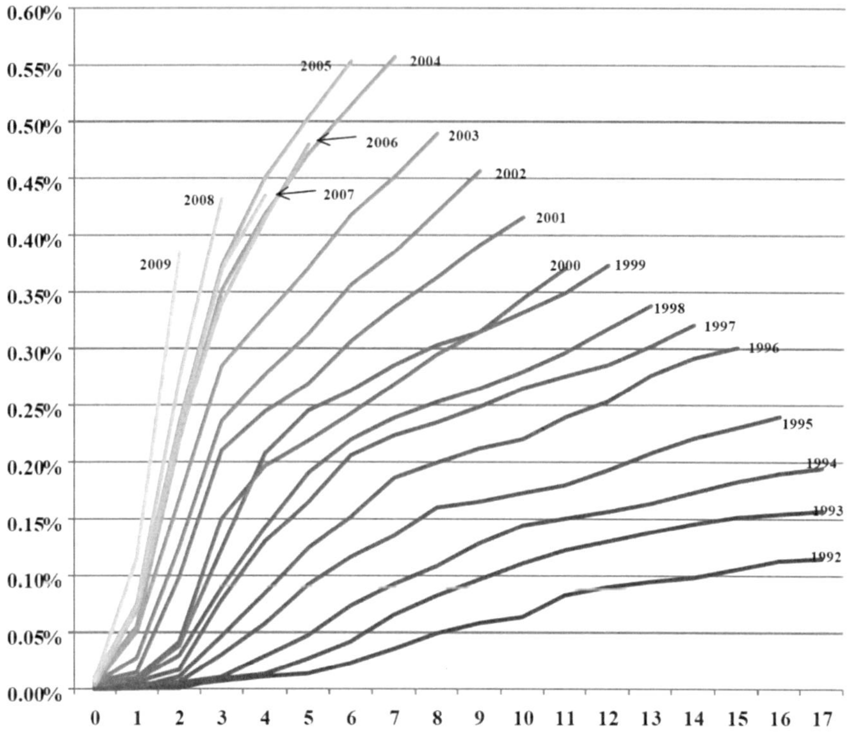

Source: Raz et al. (2014).

Figure 5.1. The Cumulative Incidence (Prevalence) of ASD by Birth Cohort in Israel.

Figures 5.1 and 5.2 plot the cumulative incidence (prevalence) of ASD by birth cohort for the population as a whole and its subgroups. For children born in 1992 the cumulative incidence was 0.05 percent at 8 years, increasing to 0.115 percent at 17 years (Figure 5.1). Notice that the prevalence does not cease to increase; children continue to be diagnosed in their teens. Figures 5.1 and 5.3 show that for successive birth cohorts prevalence increases and children are diagnosed when they are younger. For the birth cohort of 2009 0.375 percent had been diagnosed by the end of 2011. The schedules in Figures 5.1 and 5.2 shorten for successive birth cohorts because the follow-up period ends in 2011. Figure 5.2 shows that prevalence is largest among Jews and smallest among Non-Jews (Arabs). For all sub-groups, prevalence has been increasing.

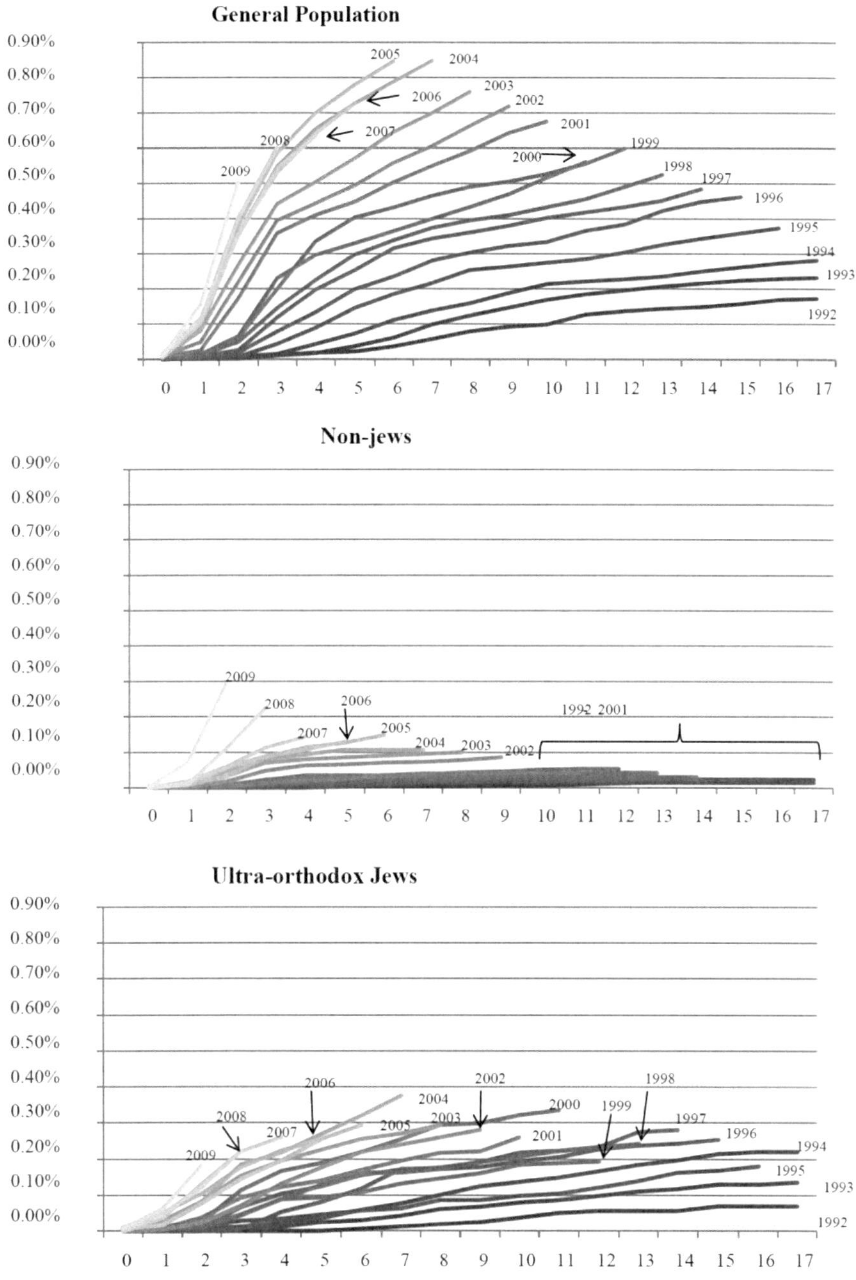

Source: Raz et al. (2014).

Figure 5.2. Ethnic Decomposition of Figure 5.1.

The Trend in ASD Prevalence

Segev et al. (2019) report that the positive time trend in the prevalence (measured at 8 years of age) of ASD in Israel ceased for birth cohorts 2009 – 2012. The trend in prevalence is global even if there are large differences in prevalence between countries. Indeed, national differences in prevalence show no signs of convergence, suggesting that country specific rates of prevalence share a common tend. For example, the country ranking in Table 5.1 below (for 2020) is most probably similar to what it was in 2010 or before.

Broadly speaking there are two hypotheses regarding the global trend in ASD prevalence. The first is that there is a global common factor that is making successive birth cohorts more susceptible to ASD. This has led some investigators to study, for example, the effect of air pollution on the prevalence of ASD. According to the neurodevelopmental paradigm there may be biological reasons why child development may be susceptible to pollutants. The second hypothesis (Eyal et al 2010) is that diagnostic standards have broadened with successive updates between DSM III and DSM V. If this is true, successive birth cohorts should be further up the spectrum (less severe) of ASD.

Unfortunately, in the absence of data on the severity of ASD, and in the absence of neurodevelopmental theory concerning global factors that lie behind the global tend in ASD, it is difficult to explain the global trend in ASD prevalence. If the increase in the incidence of ASD is due to the application of broader diagnostic standards, children diagnosed more recently are likely to have less disability as adults. If the increase in prevalence results from broader diagnostic standards, severity assessments at age 18 should vary inversely with year-of-diagnosis. Fortunately, as explained further in chapter 10, NII has two severity assessment at age 18. The first refers to measures of social severity (SS) and the second refers to measures of functional severity. Both measures are scores on a rising scale between 1 (least severe) to 100 (most severe) undertaken by experts at NII.

We use multiple regression to estimate the determinants of severity assessments at age 18. Results for social (SS) and functional (FS) severity are reported in equations (5.1) and (5.2) respectively, where the covariates are year-of-diagnosis (YOD), age-at-diagnosis (AAD), female (F), born in Israel (BII) and Arab, and p-values are reported in parentheses.

$$SS = \underset{(<0.0001)}{-0.1203}YOD - \underset{(0.0001)}{0.0471}AAD + \underset{(0.0123)}{0.186}\,F + \underset{(0.0006)}{0.6162}Arab$$

$$\underset{(0.0294)}{-0.1912}BII \qquad (5.1)$$

$$\bar{R}^2 = 0.0648\; N = 1599$$

$$FS = \underset{(<0.0001)}{-0.0912}YOD \underset{(0.0001)}{-0.0518}AAD + \underset{(0.0702)}{0.118}\,F$$

$$+\underset{(<0.0001)}{0.8519}\,Arab \underset{(0.0102)}{-0.2038}BII \qquad (5.2)$$

$$\bar{R}^2 = 0.078\; N = 1599$$

Both regression models confirm that severity assessments vary inversely with year-of-diagnosis. They imply that over 20 years, social severity assessments decreased by 12 points out of 100 and functional severity assessments decreased by 9.2 points. These decreases are large and highly statistically significant. Apart from this, ASD was more severe among women and Arabs, and less severe among those born in Israel, and, as expected, was slightly lower for those diagnosed when older.

Obviously, it would have been better if the assessments of severity were made on diagnosis instead of at age 18. However, there are no such data in Israel or elsewhere. Severity may vary over the life-cycle. If severity remains constant over the life-cycle severity at age 18 would be perfectly correlated with severity on diagnosis. If severity is mean reverting so that severity regresses towards the mean, it may be shown (Beenstock 2012, chapter 3) that the correlation is:

$$r = \beta \frac{\sigma_d}{\sigma_{18}} \qquad (5.3)$$

Where β denotes the mean reversion coefficient, σ denotes the standard deviation of severity, and subscipts d and 18 label when severity is measured, on diagnosis d or at age 18. Equation (5.3) states that if the standard deviation of severity does not change over time, then $r = \beta$. It also implies, as expected, that since β is a positive fraction for mean reversion (aka beta convergence, which varies inversely with β), mobility in severity reduces the correlation. Since σ measures inequality in severity, and if treatment of children with ASD succeeds in mitigating the more serious cases, the inequality in severity would be expected to be larger on diagnosis than at age 18 (aka sigma convergence). Given β, equation (5.3) implies that the correlation is larger and exceeds β.

Hence, severity assessments at age 18 are expected to be correlated with their counterparts on diagnosis. The correlation varies inversely with the degree of beta convergence (smaller β) and varies directly with the degree of sigma convergence. In the absence of mobility in severity ($\beta = 1$ and $\sigma_d = \sigma_{18}$), equation (5.3) states, as expected, that $r = 1$. Assessments at age 18 are perfectly correlated with assessments on diagnosis.

International Comparisons of ASD Prevalence

The reported incidence of ASD in Israel is among the lowest in the world (Chiarotti and Venerosi 2020) regardless of the difficulties involved in making international comparisons. If anything, Table 5.1 underestimates the difference between Israel and other countries because the former is based on population cohort data whereas other countries do not have comprehensive reporting systems. It is difficult to evaluate, for example, the estimate for the US, which originates from the US Center for Disease Control. In the light of the critique in chapter 4 of data sources in the US, where there is no national register for ASD, one wonders how CDC generated its estimate for the prevalence of ASD.

Table 5.1. Prevalence rates for ASD in 2020

Hong Kong	3.72
South Korea	2.63
United States	2.22
Japan	1.81
Ireland	1.53
Switzerland	1.45
Canada	1.06
Denmark	0.90
Singapore	0.67
Belgium	0.60
Finland	0.54
Norway	0.51
Israel*	0.50
Netherlands	0.48
Germany	0.38

Source: Statista May 2021. * Own calculation.

THE STUDY GROUP

The ensuing chapters investigate different aspects of recurrence risk, including reproductive stoppage, selection bias in estimates of recurrence risk induced by reproductive stoppage, behavioral effects on recurrence risk, and the transition into adulthood by people with ASD. These related studies use the NII database for which we now describe the characteristics of the study group (Table 5.2).

Demographic Characteristics

The study group comprises all children diagnosed with ASD between January 1984 and December 2012 (Table 5.2). There were 9,572 diagnoses for 9,117 families, hence, there were 455 recurrences. In two families there were two recurrences. The overall gross rate of recurrence was almost 5 percent. However, this rate is censored because recurrences that occurred after 2012 are not included in the data. 4,219 of the 9,117 index children diagnosed with ASD had no younger siblings by the end of 2012. Hence, reproductive stoppage is substantial. Since younger siblings born after 2012 are not included in the data, reproductive stoppage is right-censored. In any case, if the index children have a high birth order their parents might have wanted no further children.

Index children had numerous younger siblings. Some of them had as many as 8 or more younger siblings, each of whom faces a risk of ASD recurrence. It is obvious that families face a greater risk of recurrence the more children they have after their index child. Although index children are most frequently firstborns, Table 5.2 shows that many parents give birth to regular children before having a child with ASD. For example, 131 parents had five regular children before having a child with ASD.

The high birth orders for index children as well as their younger siblings result from the high rate of total fertility in Israel. Since in most other countries where fertility is substantially below replacement, the birth orders of index children are typically 1, and the birth orders of their younger siblings are typically 2. The NII database therefore provides more opportunity to study the natural history of recurrence risk than do databases in Sweden or Denmark where fertility is substantially below replacement. In the limit, if parents had no more than two children and their second child had ASD, or if all parents engaged in reproductive stoppage and their firstborn had ASD, index children would have no younger siblings for the study of recurrence risk. The study of recurrence risk is naturally more fruitful in societies in which fertility is high, and it is correspondingly less fruitful where fertility is low, as it is in many countries.

Finally, Table 5.2 reports the years in which the diagnoses were made, and by ethnicity. The number of diagnoses in Table 5.2 is different to the number in Raz et al. (2014) because the data in Table 5.2 include immigrants, they include cases from before 1992 and for 2012.

Table 5.2. Study group characteristics

Number diagnosed	9572
Number of families	9117
Number of younger siblings	
0	4219
1	2974
2	1222
3	378
4	151
5	91
6	33
7	28
8+	21
Index Year of Diagnosis	
1984-1989	455
1989-1995	217
1996-2001	1622
2002-2006	2534
2007-2012	4744
Index Birth Order	
1	4076
2	2588
3	1336
4	563
5	265
6	131
7	66
8	30
9	23
10	18
11+	21
Ethnicity	
Jews	8539
Ultra-orthodox Jews	935
Non-Jews	500
Mixed-marriages	28

Age at Diagnosis

Figure 5.3 plots the Kaplan Meier survival curve out of ASD based on the diagnoses in Table 5.2. Almost 50 percent are diagnosed by the age of three, and girls are diagnosed slightly faster than boys. However, Figure 5.3 has a long tail and children continue to be diagnosed well into their teens, as is also implied by Figures 5.1 and 5.2. Approximately 20 percent are diagnosed after they are eight years old, which is an age that has been used for ASD ascertainment in several studies. If age at diagnosis elsewhere is similar to what it is in Israel, estimates of ASD prevalence would be biased downwards by approximately 20 percent.

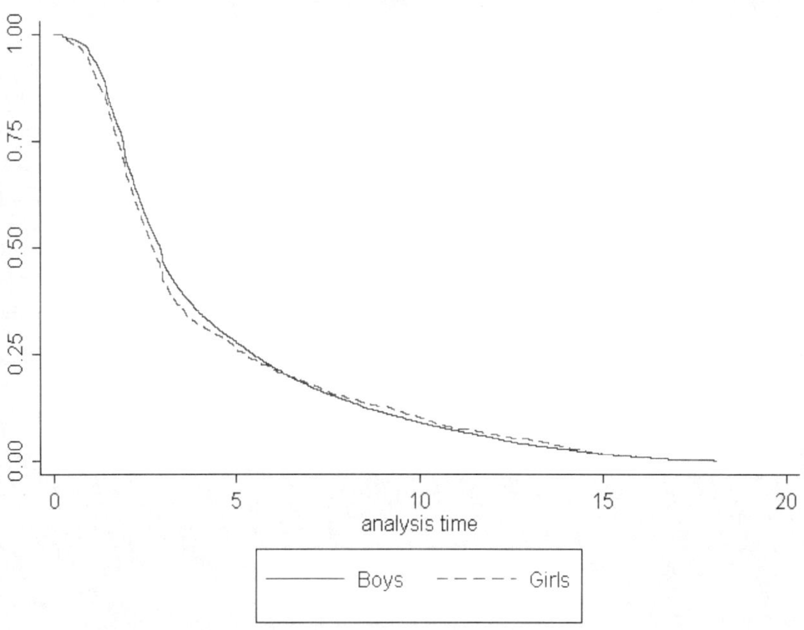

Source: Beenstock et al. (2015).

Figure 5.3. The Age Distribution of ASD Diagnoses in Israel.

Figure 5.4 compares the Kaplan- Meier survival curves for all index children and younger siblings diagnosed with ASD. Instead of comparing boys and girls as in Figure 5.3, Figure 5.4 compares index children (ASD1) with ASD recurrences (ASD2). Cases of ASD recurrence are diagnosed much more rapidly than index children. For example, 75 percent of index children were diagnosed by five years, whereas 90 percent of recurrences were diagnosed by five years. Almost all recurrences were diagnosed by ten years, whereas index children continued to be diagnosed into their teens.

Recurrence risk in the study group is censored because the cut-off date is the end of 2012. Figure 5.4 establishes that recurrence risk is substantially less censored than ASD in the general population. Nevertheless, the fact that recurrent ASD may be diagnosed up to the age of ten years, means that in practice the censoring problem in estimates of recurrence risk remains challenging.

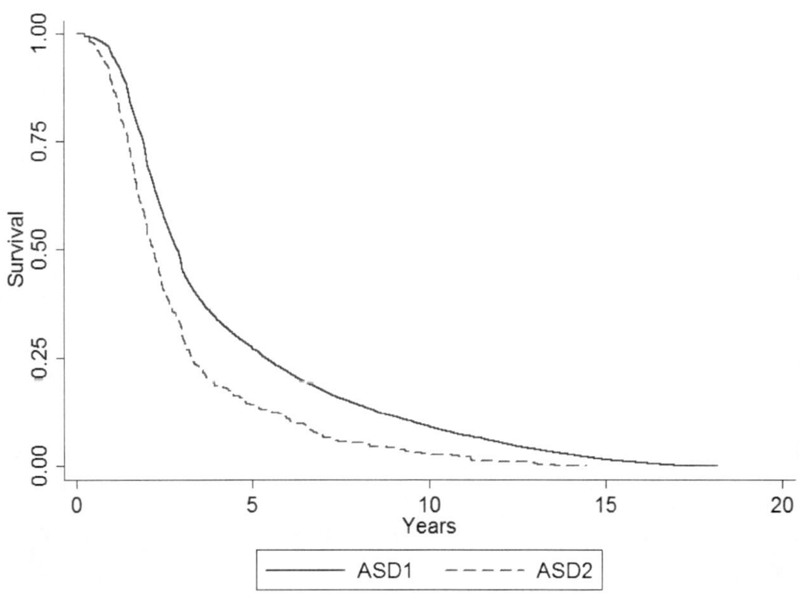

Source: Beenstock et al. (2015).

Figure 5.4. Age Distributions of ASD Diagnoses: Index Children and Younger Siblings.

Reproductive Stoppage

As noted, slightly less than half the parents in the study group had no further children by the end of 2012 (Table 5.3). Stoppage among Non-Jews was similar to stoppage in the general population, which was twice as large as stoppage among haredi Jews. Since fertility is censored, this overstates the true rate of stoppage because parents might have had further children after 2012. In chapter 6 we deal with the censoring problem by applying a proposal suggested in chapter 3 based on the idea that the probability of censoring varies inversely and nonlinearly with the age of mothers in 2012. The ascertainment of completed fertility naturally varies directly with age.

Table 5.3. Stoppage rates for parents (%)

Total	**46.3**
Jews	46.2
Non-Jews, Mixed couples	47.0
Ultra-orthodox Jews	24.5
1989-1995	42.5
1996-2001	37.2
2002-2006	43.6
2007-2012	50.9

In the meanwhile, there is a further issue related to the measurement of reproductive stoppage. Many parents were unaware that their index child had ASD when they conceived their next child. For example, the index child is diagnosed after the younger sibling is conceived or born, so parents did not know about the ASD status of their index child, when their next child was conceived. They might have been concerned about developmental delays, and they might have even suspected that their index child was on the spectrum. However, when parents are informed that their child has ASD after having been diagnosed, this is a major shock for most parents; it is a game-changer.

We therefore distinguish between parents who conceived their next child before their index child was diagnosed, and parents who did not. The latter parents are referred to as 'informed' because they decided to have further children despite the fact that they knew for sure that their index child has ASD. The former parents are referred to as 'uninformed' because they did not know for sure that their index child had ASD when they conceived their next child.

In societies where abortion is common, it might make sense to define 'informed' in terms of birth rather than conception because pregnant women might abort on receiving the diagnosis that their index child has ASD. In the NII database dates of birth are recorded to the day. Dates of conception are unknown, but are estimated by dates of birth of younger siblings minus 9 months.

The decomposition of non-stoppage into 'informed' and 'uninformed' does not necessarily imply that the latter should not be regarded as non-stoppage. Uninformed parents who refrained from reproductive stoppage are most probably different to parents in the general population, whose children are developing normally. On the other hand, they are also different from informed parents who chose to refrain from reproductive stoppage. The difference between the two types of parents will play a major role in investigating (in chapter 7) whether recurrence risk depends on behavioral phenomena. According to the neurodevelopmental paradigm recurrence risk should be the same for informed and uninformed parents, whereas according to the behavioral paradigm, recurrence risk is expected to differ between the two types of parents, as explained in chapter 7.

Table 5.4 decomposes non-stoppage into its informed and uninformed components. The first column reports total non-stoppage (informed plus uninformed) by ethnic group. Not surprisingly, ultra-orthodox (haredi) Jews are over-represented in non-stoppage. Note, however, the non-stoppage rates are the same for Jews and Non-Jews. Whereas column 1 refers to parents, columns 2 and 3 refer to their younger siblings. This explains why the sums of columns 2 and 3 exceed column 1. For example, 4618 Jewish parents engaged in non-stoppage. They had 5508 younger siblings for which they were informed for 2690 younger siblings and uninformed for 2818. All population subgroups in Table 5.4 had more uninformed further siblings than informed.

Table 5.4. Non-stoppage: informed and uninformed

Non-Stoppage	Total		Informed	Uninformed
Jews	4618	54%	2690	2818
Non-Jew + Half	280	53%	174	179
Haredi Jews	706	76%	466	528
Non-Haredi Jews	4192	52%	2398	2469

The previous discussion attaches importance to when index children are diagnosed. A radically different approach is taken by Kuja-Halkola et al. (2019) in their study of reproductive stoppage in Sweden. They "…do not consider the timing of diagnosis meaningful and regard children as having ASD from an early age regardless of when the first diagnosis was registered." There are two criticisms of their approach. First, not all children develop ASD at an early age. Second, the parents of an index child diagnosed at 10 years, who had further children 8 years before their index child was diagnosed, are regarded as having not engaged in reproductive stoppage despite the fact that they were uninformed. Kuja-Halkola et al. assume that these parents were claire-voyants; they knew 8 years in advance that their index child would be diagnosed with ASD. They also assume that parents' stoppage behavior would be the same if parents had further children 1 year before the index child was diagnosed instead of 8 years, and if the index child was diagnosed before younger siblings were conceived or born.

The Veil of Ignorance and Shadow of ASD

Suppose A and B are two observationally similar families. Their first children have ASD, and their second children were born three years afterwards. The only difference is that ASD was diagnosed in family A at 2 years and in family B at 8 years. This gives rise to three differences between families A and B. First, when family A decided to have their second child, they already knew about the ASD status of their first child. They decided against reproductive stoppage in having their second child.

Matters are obviously different in family B; they had their second child without knowing about the ASD status of their first child. Second, the younger sibling in family A was raised in the 'shadow of ASD'. His parents had a year's experience raising a child with ASD before their second child was born. Family B obviously had no such experience before their second

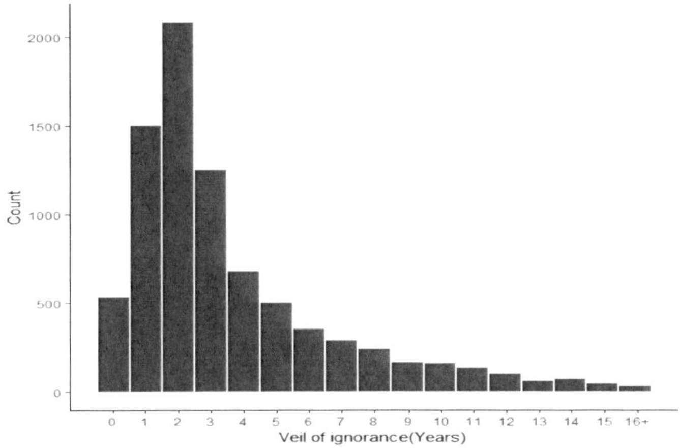

Source: Beenstock (2021a).

Figure 5.5. The Distribution of the 'Veil of Ignorance'.

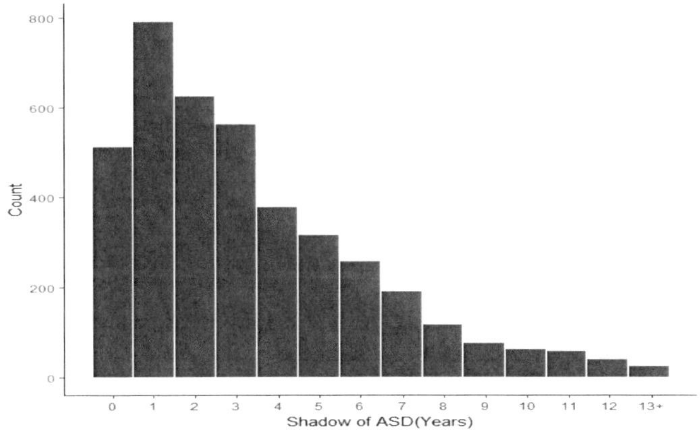

Source: Beenstock (2021a).

Figure 5.6. The Distribution of the 'Shadow of ASD'.

child was born. Third, the second child in family B was raised until 5 years under a 'veil of ignorance', which ended when his elder sibling was diagnosed. During the veil of ignorance family B might have been concerned about developmental delays in their child, but they did not know for sure that their child would eventually be diagnosed with ASD. In family A the veil of ignorance is zero and the shadow of ASD is a year. In family B the veil of ignorance is 5 years and the shadow of ASD is zero.

Figures 5.5 and 5.6 plot the frequency distribution for the veils of ignorance and the shadows of ASD in the study group. Both distributions are skewed to the left and have long tails. The mode for the veil of ignorance is 2 years and the mode for the shadow of ASD is 1 year. Figure 5.5 indicates that many parents raised the younger siblings of their index children for several years before the latter were diagnosed. Figure 5.6 indicates that that many parents raised their younger siblings after acquiring several years' experience in raising their index child, who had already been diagnosed.

Age Gaps

Since importance has been attached to age gaps between index children and their younger siblings (Chestak-Postova, Lui and Bearman 2011, Gunnes et al. 2013 Beenstock, Raz and Levine 2015), Figure 5.7 plots the distribution of the interpregnancy gap (date of birth of adjacent younger siblings minus date of birth of index children), and Figure 5.8 plots the age gap between all younger siblings and index children). Figure 5.8 would be identical to Figure 5.7 had index children only one younger sibling. The difference between them testifies to the high rate of fertility in Israel. Both figures have a natural minimum of nine months.

The model birth gap in Figure 5.7 is 1½ years, and as expected, in Figure 5.8 it is longer (2¼ years) because it includes non-adjacent (higher order) siblings. Although the majority of younger siblings are born before index children are five years old, there is a long tail to the right.

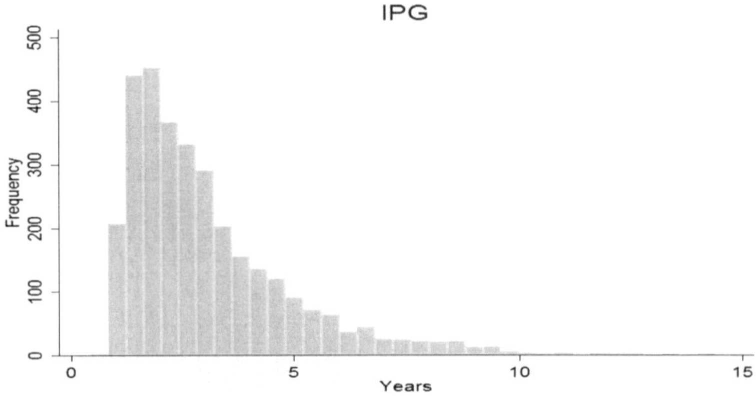

Source: Beenstock, Raz and Levine (2015).

Figure 5.7. Distribution of the Interpregnancy Gap: Index Children and Adjacent Siblings.

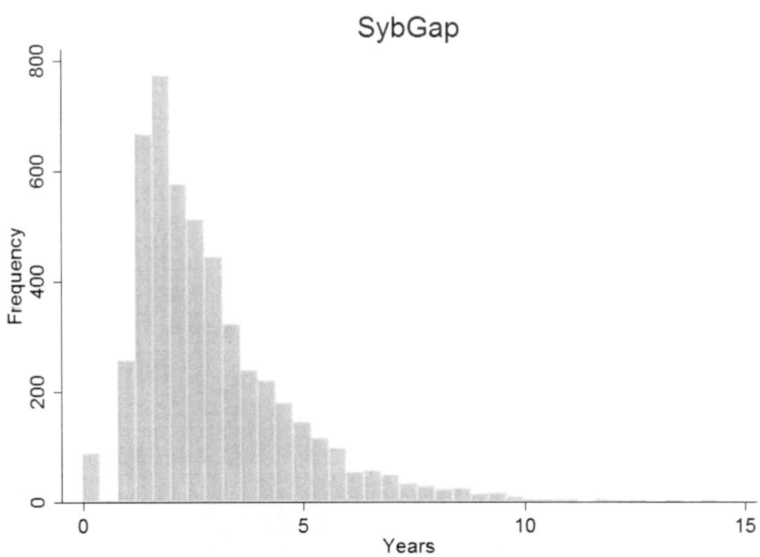

Source: Beenstock, Raz and Levine (2015).

Figure 5.8. Distribution of Birth Gap: Index Children and all Younger Siblings.

Recurrence Risk

Rates of recurrence risk in the study group are reported in Table 5.5. The overall rate of recurrence risk is 4.53 percent, which increased from 3.83 percent prior to 2002. However, this does not mean that the time trend observed in Figures 5.1 and 5.2 regarding the incidence of ASD was also evident in recurrence risk. The increase in recurrence risk may be due to the demographic composition of index children. The same applies to the smaller recurrence risk among ultra-orthodox (haredi) Jews, which later we explain in terms of their larger fertility. Recurrence risk differs according to the sex mix of sibling dyads. It is largest for index sisters and younger brothers (8.62 percent) and smallest for index brothers and younger sisters (1.85 percent).

Table 5.5. Rates of recurrence risk

	Younger siblings	**Recurrence Risk (%)**
All	8205	4.53
Before 2002	1655	3.83
Haredi	1641	3.20
Boy - boy	3296	6.42
Girl –girl	822	3.21
Girl - boy	806	8.62
Boy- girl	3281	1.85
Informed		3.67
Informed – from conception		3.50
Uninformed		4.76
Uniformed – from conception		4.68
Veil of Ignorance		
< 1.25 years		6.69
1.25 – 3.5 years		5.72
> 3.5 years		4.47
Shadow of ASD		
< 1.32 years		4.39
1.32 – 3.33 years		5.72
> 3.33 years		2.78

Recurrence risk is larger for uninformed parents (4.76 percent) than for informed parents (3.67 percent). It makes no difference whether this is measured from conception or birth. Finally, recurrence risk varies inversely with the veil of ignorance and has an inverted U-shaped relation with the shadow of ASD. The fact that recurrence risk varies with these three behavioral variables does not, of course, establish that recurrence risk has a behavioral etiology any more than does the fact that recurrence risk was smaller before 2002 not establish that there is a positive time trend in recurrence risk.

Events of recurrence risk occur when younger siblings are diagnosed after older siblings. In 84 cases older siblings were diagnosed after their younger siblings, suggesting that older siblings may have been diagnosed as a consequence of their younger siblings' diagnosis. These siblings are removed from the study group.

Chapter 6

Within-Group Reproductive Stoppage in Israel

Reproductive stoppage involving children with autism spectrum disorders (ASD) refers to the decision of parents to have no further children on learning that their child has been diagnosed with ASD (Jones and Szatmari 1988). In view of widespread evidence that recurrence risk of ASD is much larger than its incidence in the general population (Beenstock, Raz and Levine 2015, Sandin et al. 2014, Grønborg et al. 2013) parents are understandably concerned about having further children. Indeed, some studies claim that recurrence risk may be as large as 20% or more (Ozonoff et al. 2011, Wood et al. 2014).

The empirical study of stoppage is important for two reasons. First, stoppage conceals the natural history of ASD. Indeed, if all parents stopped, recurrence risk would be unobservable. In practice, estimates of recurrence risk are informed by parents who did not engage in stoppage. The natural history of recurrence risk would be revealed if all parents refrained from stoppage. If recurrence risk happened to differ between families who stopped and families who did not stop, estimates of recurrence risk that ignored stoppage would be biased. Several studies have attempted to adjust estimates of recurrence risk for potential sample selection bias induced by stoppage (Hoffmann et al. 2014, Grønborg et al.

2015, Wood et al. 2014). Second, regardless of its importance for unbiased estimates of recurrence risk, stoppage is of interest in its own right. However, the empirical literature on stoppage is surprisingly thin. Existing studies, including Kuja-Halkola, Lui and Bearman (2019), compare fertility among families in which children have ASD with fertility in the general population.

We are unaware of studies comparing families who stopped with families who did not stop. This within-group comparison is fundamentally different to the between-group comparison featured in the literature. The within-group comparison is concerned with the empirical factors that distinguish parents who stopped with parents who did not. The within-group comparison is important because canonical methods for coping with selection bias such as inverse probability weighting (Rosenbaum 2002) and incidental truncation (Heckman 1976) attach importance to within-group comparisons rather than between-group comparisons (chapter 8).

In this chapter we investigate the within-group comparison using the study group data described in chapter 5. In this context, we emphasize the crucial role played by the age at which index children are diagnosed. We distinguish between cases where younger siblings are conceived before the index child was diagnosed, and where younger siblings are conceived after the index was diagnosed. The latter constitutes 'strong' or 'informed' non-stoppage because parents decided to have further children knowing the ASD status of their index child. The former constitutes 'weak' or 'uninformed' non-stoppage because parents decided to have further children without full knowledge of the ASD status of their index child.

Whereas informed and uninformed non-stoppage are observable, the same does not apply to stoppage. Uninformed stoppage occurs when parents have no further children because they are nevertheless concerned about the developmental problems of their child although they do not yet know that their child has ASD. Parents who stopped might have decided to do so before or after their index child was diagnosed; we shall never know. Conceptually, informed stoppage occurs when parents decide to stop after their index child was diagnosed, and uninformed stoppage occurs when parents decide to stop before their index child was diagnosed. In the absence of data on when parents decided to stop, informed and uninformed stoppage are empirically empty concepts.

We also distinguish between absolute and relative stoppage. The former occurs when parents have no further children. The latter occurs when they have fewer subsequent children as a result of having a child with ASD. The literature has been almost exclusively concerned with absolute stoppage. However, selection bias in recurrence risk may be induced by relative stoppage as well as absolute stoppage. For example, if the index child is firstborn and parents have two children instead of three, they provide only one opportunity to study recurrence risk instead of two. Their unborn third child might have had ASD even if their second child did not. Larger families naturally provide more opportunity for observing recurrence risk. In countries where fertility is low, the difference between absolute and relative stoppage will be less important. It would not be important at all if parents planned to have two children. Matters are different where fertility is high, as in Israel.

Between-Group Stoppage

As mentioned, several studies have investigated between-group stoppage by comparing fertility among parents who have children with ASD and parents in the general population, as in Jones and Szatmari (1988). Most probably family planning is a universal practice, particularly in societies where total fertility is small, such as Denmark and Sweden. In societies in which total fertility is one (on average women have only one child) such as South Korea, the between group comparison is unlikely to be informative. Women typically have only one child who is either on the spectrum or not. Women in the general population typically have no further children as do women whose child has ASD. This phenomenon varies inversely with total fertility; it is more fruitful to study between-group stoppage in Israel where total fertility exceeds 3 than in Sweden and Denmark.

The studies reported in Table 6.1 compare the probability of having a further child within the next ten years with its counterpart for parents in the general population. For example, Grønborg et al. find that 80 percent of parents had a second child within ten years whereas 74 percent of parents of children with ASD had a further child within ten years. Hence, excess stoppage is six percent. Using similar data Kuja-Halkola et al. also find that excess stoppage is of the same order of magnitude (7 percent) but the absolute probabilities of having a further child for the two types of parents are smaller (60 percent in the general population and 53 percent among parents of children with ASD). Excess stoppage in California is considerably larger than it is in Sweden. The excess stoppage from between-group comparisons are statistically significant in all three studies.

Table 6.1. Between-group 10 year non-stoppage rates (%)

Study	Location	General Non-stoppage	ASD Non-stoppage	Excess stoppage	Hazard ratio
Grønborg et al. 2015	Sweden	80	74	6	na
Hoffmann et al. 2014	California	74	52	22	0.655
Kuja-Halkola et al. 2019	Sweden	60	53	7	0.79 0.97

Notes: General non-stoppage – probability of further child in general population. ASD non-stoppage – probability of further child after child with ASD. Excess stoppage – general non-stoppage minus ASD non-stoppage. Hazard ratio – estimated Cox proportional hazard of having a further child among parents of children with ASD relative to parents in the general population.

Two of the studies in Table 6.1 estimate Cox proportional hazard models (chapter 3) in which the dependent variable is the hazard (the probability of an event given that it has not already occurred) of having a further child. The final column of Table 6.1 reports the effect on the hazard of having a child with ASD as a proportion of the hazard in the general population. For example, in California the hazard for parents of children with ASD is only 65.5 percent of its counterpart in the general population.

Hence, conditional on other covariates including birth year, birth weight, maternal age, and race (white, black, Hispanic) having a child with ASD reduces fertility as measured by the hazard by 24.5 percent. Kuja-Halkola et al. report two hazard ratios. The first is estimated using an unconditional Cox proportional hazard model (without covariates), whereas the second conditions on such covariates. The latter implies that having a child with ASD reduces fertility as measured by the hazard by only three percent, once controls such as age of mothers are taken into consideration. It also suggests that evidence of absolute reproductive stoppage as defined in chapter 2) is an artefact induced by confounding.

Grønborg et al. and Kuja-Halkola et al. report multivariate Poisson regression models (chapter 3) for the number of further children born to parents of children with ASD relative to parents in the general population. Both studies find that parents of ASD children have fewer further children than their counterparts in the general population. This result is evidence of relative reproductive stoppage (as defined in chapter 2). In summary, the results of Kuja-Halkola et al. that parents of ASD children in Sweden do not engage in absolute stoppage, but they engage in relative stoppage means that they are just as likely to have further children as in the general population, but they have fewer further children if they do.

The studies in Table 6.1 do not distinguish between informed and uninformed parents, nor do they control for the age at which index children are diagnosed. This obviously does not matter for parents in the general population, but it matters for parents of ASD children for whom the clock of reproductive stoppage is assumed to run from the moment their index child is born, rather than from when he or she is diagnosed or suspected of developmental problems. As we have seen, Kuja-Halkola et al. believe radically that the timing of diagnosis is of no consequence for reproductive stoppage. We show below that their hypothesis is easily rejected using data for Israel.

Poisson regressions assume unreasonably for parents of children with ASD that the decision to have one further child or no further children is essentially similar to the decision to have two further children rather than one (chapter 2). Common sense suggests that there is a natural hierarchy in fertility for parents of children with ASD. The decision to have any further children at all is much harder than it is for parents in the general population. So, might be the decision to have more or fewer children, but this is a lesser dilemma. Absolute stoppage and relative stoppage are not on the same spectrum of fertility. This is why in chapter 2 absolute and relative stoppage were distinguished through 'zero inflation' in count data models. Perhaps failure to zero-inflate accounts for the apparent contradiction in Kuja-Halkola et al. that Swedish parents do not engage in absolute stoppage, but they nevertheless engage in relative stoppage.

WITHIN-GROUP STOPPAGE

In contrast to studies of between-group stoppage, there are no studies of within-group stoppage. It may not be surprising that parents of children with ASD curtail their fertility relative to parents in the general population (between-group), but it is less obvious why some parents of children with ASD engage in reproductive stoppage, while others do not (within-group). Since estimates of recurrence risk may be biased because of self-selection into stoppage by parents of ASD children (within-group), the motivation for comparing the fertility of parents of children with ASD with the fertility of parents in the general population (between-group) is obscure. By contrast, the motivation for studying within-group stoppage is clear.

Observables and Unobservables

In this chapter we break new ground by studying within-group stoppage for the first time for two reasons. First, because it has not been studied before. Second, and more important, because canonical methods for correcting for sample-selection bias in estimates of recurrence risk require an auxiliary model for within-group self-selection into stoppage. In fact, the issue of self-selection does not arise in between-group comparisons. Parents cannot choose to be part of the general population or not. But parents of children with ASD can decide to engage in reproductive stoppage or not. So, it is the within-group comparison that matters for handling selection bias in estimates of recurrence risk, not the between-group comparison as in the studies in Table 6.1.

In chapter 2 we proposed a behavioral theory for within-group stoppage in which there are two types of variables hypothesized to determine stoppage. The first are observable variables such as the number of children they already have (birth order of the index child), their sex mix, and maternal and paternal age. These observables also feature in standard models of fertility in the general population. However, their size effects may differ for parents of ASD children. The second are unobservable variables such as the desire to have further children (pronatality), which also applies to parents in the general population. A crucial unobservable in chapter 2 was specified by 'resilience', which in psychology refers to the ability to cope with stress. More resilient parents of children with ASD are less likely to engage in reproductive stoppage. Another psychological phenomenon discussed in chapter 2 is related to 'Thomas' Theorem' of self-fulfilling expectations according to which parents fear that they will induce ASD in their further children. Such parents are more likely to engage in reproductive stoppage. If instead of imperilment, they feel empowered by the experience of raising children with ASD, they will be more likely to refrain for stoppage. Also, parents might have an intuition about their susceptibility to ASD, which makes stoppage more probable. Finally, parents may respond differently to the formal diagnosis of their children. This is not intended as an exhaustive list of unobservables that might influence reproductive stoppage.

For convenience we recall equation (2.19A) from chapter 2.

$$C_{it}^* = X_i\beta - \delta D_i + c_i - g_i(t) + r_i - \delta_i(t) \quad (6.1)$$

where C* is a latent variable for fertility such that if $C_{it}^* > 0$ parents conceive their next child when their index child is t years old in which event $C_i = 1$ (non-stoppage), and $C_i = 0$ (stoppage) if $C_{it}^* \leq 0$. Recall that D is a dummy variable equal to 1 if parents are informed and D = 0 otherwise. They are informed if the age at diagnosis of their index child (t_3 in Figure 2.1 in chapter 2) occurs before their younger siblings are conceived (t_2 in Figure 2.1 in chapter 2). The parameters of interest are b and d, where the former refer to covariates hypothesized to affect fertility, such as the age of mothers, and d is the shock effect on fertility when parents are informed that their child is diagnosed with ASD.

In many instances unobservables are empirically more salient than the observable covariates. In linear regression models this arises when R^2 is less than 0.5 where the observable covariates explain less of the variance of the dependent variable than do the unobservable variables. The literature in all disciplines is replete with numerous examples. For example, in the recurrence risk model for Israel in Table 4.1 in chapter 4 the pseudo R^2 (R^2 for nonlinear models estimated by maximum likelihood) is only 0.14. However, because the p-value for the model is less than 0.0001, the observable covariates are jointly statistically significant. What matters is not whether R^2 is statistically significantly different from 1, but whether it is significantly greater than 0. These results for Israel suggest that what we don't observe is greatly more salient than what we do.

Bringing Theory to Data

In equation (6.1) there are several unobservables, which may be summed to $z = c - g + r - d$. If the observable covariates happen to be independent of the unobservable variables (z) their parameter estimates (β and δ) are consistent in nonlinear models such as logit and probit, and unbiased in linear models. For example, if resilience is a hard-wired phenomenon it must be independent of z. If, instead, resilience is an acquired phenomenon that grows with life-experiences, age of mothers and resilience might be positively correlated in which event the parameter estimates would not be consistent. Recall from chapter 3 that if the estimates of β and δ are consistent, X and D are causal for stoppage.

$D_i = 1$ when in Figure 2.1 in chapter 2 $t_{3i} < t_{2i}$, i.e., informed parents receive the diagnosis for their index child before they conceive their next child. Let $t_{3i} = t_3 + \tau_i$ where t is a random variable, which expresses the inherent randomness in the timings of diagnoses. If τ is independent of z, estimates of δ are consistent. There is no reason to suspect that τ should be related to resilience etc, but it may be negatively correlated with d if severer cases are diagnosed sooner, and d is positively correlated with severity. Since z varies inversely with d, and D varies inversely with τ, negative correlation is induced indirectly between D and z. Hence, estimates of δ in equation (6.1) might be biased downwards.

The X covariates in equation 6.1 include the existing number of children, their gender mix, the age of mothers and perhaps fathers, their ethnicity, schooling and economic status etc. Dates of diagnosis are observed directly (chapter 5) as are dates of birth. Hence if D is defined by birth it is known exactly. If D is defined by conception, D is proxied using dates of birth minus 9 months. Table 2.1 in chapter 2 summarizes combinations of informed status of parents (yes or no) and their stoppage (yes or no).

Equation (6.1) implies that observationally similar parents of children with ASD (with the same X) have different probabilities of stoppage because they differ by their resilience (r), their desire for children (c), their reaction to developmental problems (d) and birth spacing (g). It also means that observationally similar parents in the general population cannot be compared with the parents of ASD children because β in the general population may differ, and because r, d and δ do not apply to the general population. Finally, the probability of non-stoppage varies directly with the age at which ASD is diagnosed.

Two empirical methodologies are considered for estimating β. If z is assumed to have a logistical distribution, β may be estimated by logit using data for C where C = 1 if parents had further children and C = 0 otherwise. For informed non-stoppage, the relevant population consists of parents who conceived further children after the date of diagnosis of their index child. For uninformed non-stoppage, the relevant population consists of parents who conceived further children before this date of diagnosis. These two populations may be combined by controlling for the age of diagnosis of the index child. Parents are less likely to have further children if their index child is diagnosed sooner rather than later.

The second methodology is based on survival analysis focusing on the age of the index child when and if parents conceived their next child. Specifically, a Cox proportional hazards model may be estimated for these purposes. The second methodology (Hoffmann et al. 2014 and Kuja-Halkola et al. 2019) is more ambitious than the first (used by Grønborg et al. 2015), because it professes to explain the timing of conception and not merely whether stoppage occurred or not. We prefer the first method to the second because more ambitious methods are generally less robust (chapter 3). For example, Hoffmann et al. assume that birth hazards are strictly proportional to all the covariates in their model, even though this assumption is not essential for testing hypotheses about non-stoppage.

Because the data end in December 2012 fertility is right-censored; parents of index children who had no further children by December 2012 might have had children subsequently. Hence, censoring artificially increases the stoppage rate even controlling for age of mothers in December 2012. If mothers' age in December 2012 exceeds 45 years, fertility is ascertained and is not censored. A radical solution to the censoring problem is to ignore diagnoses made after 2004 under the assumption, for example, that if younger siblings are not born within 8 years, parents have stopped. An alternative solution, which avoids discarding data, is to assume that the probability of censoring varies inversely with mothers' age in December 2012 (chapter 3). Since this probability is likely to vary nonlinearly with age in December 2012, we estimate this censoring effect as a spline (Greene 2012, p 199). We also use splines to estimate other potentially nonlinear time related variables, such as mothers' age and the age at diagnosis of index children.

Relative Non-Stoppage

Thus far we have been concerned with absolute non-stoppage or the decision to have no further children. Relative non-stoppage is concerned with the decision to have fewer children as a result of having a child with ASD. If C equals one (non-stoppage), the number of children may be larger or smaller. Just as observationally similar families might stop or not depending on what is not observed (u), so might they choose to have different numbers of children if they do not stop absolutely. Since the number of younger siblings of index children has the character of count data, which take discrete but limited values such as 0, 1, 2, etc. we suggest the use of count data methods described in chapter 3.

The most popular count data method is the Poisson regression which assumes in the context of relative stoppage that parents' decision to have any further children after their child with ASD is essentially similar to their decision to have two further children rather than one. It ignores the phenomenon that the decision to have any further children is essentially different to the decision to have more or fewer children if they refrain from reproductive stoppage. As described in chapter 3 'zero-inflated' count data methods take into account that the decision to refrain from stoppage is a bigger hurdle to overcome than the decision about the number of children having jumped over this hurdle. For example, the zero-inflated Poisson regression (ZIP, Lambert 1992), which recognizes the difference between absolute and relative non-stoppage, is used below to distinguish between relative and absolute stoppage. See further details of ZIP in chapter 3.

Poisson regression has been used before (Kuja-Halkola et al. 2019)) to test hypotheses of relative non-stoppage in a between group context (comparing the number of children in the general population with the number of children of parents with ASD children). As already mentioned, this unreasonably treats the decision of parents whose firstborn has ASD to have a second child as essentially the same as the decision of parents in the general population to have a second child. Therefore, below we make two changes. First, as appropriate, ZIP is used instead of Poisson regression to take account of the existential difference between relative and absolute non-stoppage. Second, the comparison is within-group instead of between-group; the investigation is limited to absolute and relative stoppage among parents of children with ASD. The focus is upon why some parents engage in absolute non-stoppage and not others, and if they do not stop absolutely, why some engage in more relative non-stoppage than others.

Results

The population cohort data for Israel used here to investigate absolute and relative stoppage have been presented in detail in chapter 5 where Table 6.2 provides information on the characteristics of the study group, Table 6.3 reports censored stoppage rates for Jews, Non-Jews and haredi Jews as well as stoppage rates over time, and Table 6.4 distinguishes between non-stoppage rates for 'informed' parents who had further children after their child with ASD was diagnosed and 'uninformed' parents who had further children before their child with ASD was diagnosed.

We focus here on results from multivariate statistical models for absolute and relative non-stoppage within-group.

Absolute Stoppage

The results in Table 6.2 refer to the probability of parents of children with ASD having further children (non-stoppage) by the end of the study period in December 2012. Model 1 refers to all parents regardless of being informed or not. It shows that non-Jews (Arabs) and ultra-orthodox Jews are more likely to engage in non-stoppage than Jews in general, while mixed couples (Jews and Arabs) behave similarly to Jews in general. A number of variables capture the effect of target family size. Non-stoppage varies inversely with the birth order of the index child. If the index child has a twin, the probability of non-stoppage decreases by more than what is implied by birth order. Several studies have shown that there is male preference in Israel (Beenstock 2007, Angrist, Lavy and Shlosser 2012);

Table 6.2. Logit models for absolute non-stoppage

	1 Informed + Uniformed		2 Informed from birth		3 Uninformed from birth		4 Uninformed from conception	
	OR	P-value	OR	P-value	OR	P-value	OR	P-value
Intercept	8.5079	0.0380	0.5022	< 0.0001	0.2999	0.2987	0.6654	0.6901
Mixed	0.5434	0.1742	0.4403	0.1190	0.5861	0.3036	0.7826	0.5832
Non-Jew	1.4855	0.0007	1.3376	0.0107	1.6157	0.0001	1.5044	0.0004
Ultra-Orthodox	4.4353	< 0.0001	2.5784	< 0.0001	3.6689	<0.0001	3.9408	<0.0001
Twins	0.3482	< 0.0001	0.6697	0.0007	0.2470	<0.0001	0.2456	<0.0001
Index birth order	0.7557	< 0.0001	0.8333	< 0.0001	0.8525	<0.0001	0.8176	<0.0001
Disabled sibling	0.7791	0.1420	0.9239	0.6515	0.8296	0.3430	0.8593	0.3987
No males	1.0261	0.7550	1.0280	0.7238	1.0076	0.9329	1.0523	0.5370
year of diagnosis	0.9156	0.1567			1.0165	0.8142	1.0060	0.9228
Mother age at birth of index	Spline -	0.0308	Spline -	< 0.0001	Spline -	<0.0001	Spline -	<0.0001
Mother age in 2012	Spline +	<0.0001	Spline +	< 0.0001	Spline +	0.0217	Spline +	0.0126
Age at diagnosis	Spline +	< 0.0001			Spline +	<0.0001	Spline +	< 0.0001
Log likelihood	-4929.6		-4886.6		-4053.7		-4722.3	
Observations	9087		9087		9087		9087	

Note: OR odds-ratio. Direction of splines indicated by −/-. Source: Beenstock (2021a).

parents are more likely to have further children if their children are all girls. Table 6.2 suggests that male preference does not apply to families with ASD. Finally, the presence of other disabled siblings in the family increases stoppage, but this effect is not statistically significant.

Several time-dependent variables in Table 6.2 have been estimated by splines, all of which are statistically significant. The direction of their effects are indicated by +/- signs in Table 6.2. For example, older mothers are less likely to engage in non-stoppage. Mothers who were older in 2012 were more like to have not stopped, implying that the fertility of younger mothers in December 2012 is right-censored, as expected. Finally, the probability of non-stoppage varies directly with age of diagnosis, implying that ignorance about the ASD status of their children reduces the probability of stoppage.

Models 2 and 3 decompose the non-stoppage models for informed (at birth) and uninformed parents. Model 2 and 3 refer to the probability of informed and uninformed stoppage respectively in the population as a whole. The covariates that are statistically significant (or not) in Model 1 are also statistically significant in Models 2 and 3. However, their odds-ratio (OR) coefficients are different. On the whole, their deviations from unity are larger for the uninformed than the informed. For example, the OR coefficient for non-Jews is 1.62 in Model 3 and 1.34 in Model 2, and the coefficients for twins are 0.67 and 0.25 respectively. Age at diagnosis is omitted from Model 2 because it is not relevant for informed parents, but it is extremely statistically significant in Model 3. This effect ranges between -2 at two years to 1.8 at five years and 2 at ten years. Therefore, the size effect of age at diagnosis on the odds-ratio for stoppage is large and negative, especially over the range of 2 – 5 years.

Model 4 refers to uninformed parents according to age at conception rather than age at birth. The OR coefficients in Model 4 should therefore be compared with their counterparts in Model 3. On the whole, the OR coefficients are similar in terms of their p-values and their size effects. However, because these estimates are precise, the differences between them are statistically significant.

In Table 6.3 we use the results in Table 6.2 to calculate the probability of non-stoppage for observationally similar families, which differ by the age at which their index child was diagnosed, according to various models. According to model 1, the probability of non-stoppage varies directly with age at diagnosis, as expected. The probability of non-stoppage increases from 0.45 when age at diagnosis is 2.5 years to 0.63 at 7 years. For uninformed parents at birth (Model 3) these probabilities are initially much smaller (0.19 instead of 0.45) but are slightly larger at 7 years (0.66 instead of 0.63). For uninformed parents at conception the probabilities of non-stoppage are larger as expected. Model 2 does not feature in Table 6.3 because for informed parents age at diagnosis does not matter.

Table 6.3. Non-stoppage and age at diagnosis

	Probability		
Age at diagnosis	**Model 1**	**Model 3**	**Model 4**
2.5	0.45	0.19	0.29
5	0.55	0.62	0.73
7	0.63	0.66	0.77

Notes: Jews excluding ultra-orthodox, dummies = 0, year of diagnosis 2010, mother age = 30.

Relative Stoppage

We use the zero-inflated Poisson (ZIP) model to distinguish between absolute and relative stoppage (chapter 2). As in Table 6.2, we compare families with ASD children who stopped or not, and who had more or fewer further children if they did not stop. The first column in Table 6.4 refers to the complementary log log (CLL) component of the ZIP model in which 1 refers here to non-stoppage, and the covariates refer to the X variables hypothesized to affect the logit probability of engaging in absolute non- stoppage, i.e., the probability of having further children after the index child. For example, Non-Jews and ultra-orthodox Jews are more likely to engage in absolute non-stoppage (less likely to engage in absolute stoppage). The second column refers to the Poisson probability (m) of having 0, 1, 2, etc. further children after the index child, and the covariates refer to the Z variables hypothesized to affect the number of further children. For example, the ultra-orthodox are likely to have exp(0.8299) = 2.3 further children more than other parents. This means that the ultra-orthodox are less likely to engage in absolute stoppage and less likely to engage in relative stoppage. As in Table 6.2 mothers' age in 2012 specified to control for the censoring of fertility.

In Table 6.4 the X and Z covariates are almost identical. Covariates that are statistically significant, carry the same signs in the CLL and Poisson models (non-Jews, ultra-orthodox, age of mother, age at diagnosis). An exception is birth order of the index, which reduces absolute stoppage, but increases relative stoppage. This means, for example, that parents of second children diagnosed with ASD are more likely to stop than parents of firstborns, but the former are likely to have more further children than the latter. Another exception is twins, which increases absolute stoppage but does not significantly affect relative stoppage.

Table 6.4. Zero-inflated Poisson model for absolute and relative stoppage

	CLL model		Poisson model	
	Estimate	**p-value**	**Estimate**	**p-value**
Intercept	-0.7409	<0.0001	0.0378	0.2791
Non-Jew	0.3889	<0.0001	-0.4153	0.1892
Mixed			0.2787	0.0001
Ultra-orthodox	0.9184	<0.0001	0.8299	<0.0001
Twins	-0.1186	0.2450	-0.7496	<0.0001
Birth order	0.0800	<0.0001	-0.2051	<0.0001
Disability	-0.0778	0.4457	-0.1729	0.1325
Mother age	Spline -	<0.0001	Spline -	<0.0001
Age at diagnosis	Spline +	0.0084	Spline +	<0.0001
Mother age 2012	Spline +	<0.0001	Spline +	<0.0001
Observations	9087			
Log likelihood	-9664			

Source: Beenstock (2021a).

Age at diagnosis is specified in the CLL and Poisson models as is appropriate. The former implies, as in Table 6.2, that the probability of absolute non-stoppage varies directly with age at diagnosis. The latter implies that the probability of having more than one subsequent child also varies directly with age at diagnosis. Hence, both absolute and relative non-stoppage vary directly with age at diagnosis.

In Table 6.5, we use the results in Table 6.4 to calculate the effect of age at diagnosis on the probabilities of absolute and relative non-stoppage, where the former refers to the probability of non-stoppage, and the latter refers to the expected value of the number of further children. As expected, both outcomes vary directly with age at diagnosis. The probability of absolute non-stoppage increases from 0.48 when the age at diagnosis is 2.5 years to 0.61 when the age at diagnosis is 10 years, and relative non-stoppage as measured by the expected value of the additional number of children increases from 0.37 to 0.7. Recall that the latter is defined by the probability of having one further child multiplied by one plus the probability of having a second further child multiplied by two etc. Hence, the expected number of children are weighted probabilities, which may be fractions as in Table 6.5.

Table 6.5. Age at diagnosis and absolute and relative non-stoppage

Age of index at diagnosis	Probability of stoppage	Expected number of children
2.5	0.72	1.44
5	0.71	1.52
7	0.71	1.61
10	0.73	1.69

Notes: See Table 6.3.

DISCUSSION

This is the first study to focus on within-group reproductive stoppage among parents of children with autism spectrum disorders instead of between-group stoppage. Whereas the latter compares fertility in families with ASD to the general population, the former compares families with ASD who stopped to families who did not stop. Although both comparisons are of interest in their own right, canonical methods for dealing with potential sample selection bias in estimating recurrence risk of ASD require within-group models of stoppage rather than their between-group counterparts (chapters 3 and 7).

Much of the literature on reproductive stoppage has ignored whether parents were fully aware that their index child had ASD. Many parents of children with ASD no doubt had further children simply because they were unaware that their index child was on the spectrum. They might have been concerned about their child's developmental deficits, but an important break occurs when parents are informed that their child has been diagnosed positive for ASD. New ground is broken in using data on dates of diagnosis by distinguishing between parents who had further children knowing about the ASD status of their index child, and parents who did not. Not surprisingly, the age at which index children were diagnosed plays a major empirical role in reproductive stoppage.

This is the second study to distinguish between absolute and relative stoppage among families with children on the spectrum where the former refers to parents who have no further children and the latter refers to parents who have fewer children. In societies where fertility is low the difference between relative and absolute stoppage may be unimportant. It would be of no importance if parents had only two children. In Israel the distinction is important because fertility is high. Indeed, the frequency of large families provides a rare opportunity to study relative as well as absolute stoppage. The first study, Kuja-Halkola et al. (2019) distinguish between relative and absolute fertility between families with ASD children and families in the general population. Unlike us, however, they use a standard Poisson regression methodology, which treats having no further children, or absolute stoppage, as being conceptually the same as having two instead one further child, or relative stoppage.

We find that diagnosis timing of index children plays an important role in absolute and relative stoppage, which varies inversely with the age of diagnosis. The older children are when they are diagnosed with ASD, the more likely it is that their parents did not engage in stoppage simply because they were unaware of the ASD status of their index child. The trend to earlier diagnosis will increase the incidence of reproductive stoppage because parents will be better informed about the ASD status of their index children.

Although diagnosis timing is salient for reproductive stoppage, we do not think that lack of data on dates of diagnosis undermines results from previous studies about the determinants of between-group reproductive stoppage. In our case, the covariates that predict stoppage are the same whether or not dates of diagnosis are controlled for, although their size effects are somewhat sensitive.

We have assumed that age at diagnosis is independent of fertility in general and reproductive stoppage in particular. If parents initiate diagnoses before conceiving their next child to discover whether their child has ASD, we will have confused cause and effect. Although we cannot rule this out, it is unlikely that health practitioners would cooperate with such requests. Another potential confounder is that severer cases are diagnosed sooner. If reproductive stoppage varies directly with severity, this might explain the negative relationship between age at diagnosis and stoppage. Ideally, we need data on severity to rule this out, but unfortunately these data are not available in Israel or elsewhere.

The results in Tables 6.2 and 6.4 indicate that the probability of non-stoppage is influenced by fertility censoring. Women did not have further children by the end of December 2012 simply because they had not completed their fertility. Hence, although the data show that 46 percent of parents appear to have engaged in reproductive stoppage, the true rate of stoppage is much smaller. In principle, the models in Tables 6.2 and 6.4 may be simulated to calculate the degree to which fertility censoring exaggerates the rate of reproductive stoppage. This exaggeration is obviously larger the lower is the average age of mothers in 2012 and the more fertile they are. What is methodologically important for the results in Tables 6.2 and 6.4 is that had the probability of fertility censoring not been specified the parameter estimates may have been inconsistent and biased.

Chapter 7

Behavioral Influences on Recurrence Risk

"Many people made a mistake in going from a statement which is undoubtedly true – that there is no evidence that autism has been caused by poor parenting – to the statement that it has been disproven. It has not actually been disproven. It has faded away simply because, on the one hand, of a lack of convincing evidence, and on the other hand, an awareness that autism was a neurodevelopmental disorder of some kind." Sir Michael Rutter. (Feinstein 2010)

In chapter 2 we recalled the etiological history of autism in which the neurodevelopmental model emerged as the dominant paradigm. This chapter responds to Rutter's challenge, repeated from chapter 2, regarding the 'lack of convincing evidence'. However, the behavioral phenomena discussed here do not concern 'poor parenting'. Instead they refer to four behavioral phenomena that have arisen in previous chapters.

First, according the neurodevelopmental paradigm recurrence risk should not depend on whether index children had been diagnosed with ASD before or after parents conceived their next child. By contrast behavioral theory predicts that if younger siblings were born after index siblings were diagnosed, this knowledge might increase recurrence risk if it imperils, and reduce it if it empowers.

Second, according to the neurodevelopmental paradigm recurrence risk should not depend on whether parents gained experience in raising children with ASD, which in chapter 2 is referred to by the 'shadow of ASD', and is measured in chapter 5. By contrast behavioral theory predicts that more experienced parents may be able to mitigate recurrence risk by using this experience in raising their further children.

Third, according to the neurodevelopmental paradigm it should make no difference to recurrence risk when their index children are diagnosed after the birth of their younger siblings, which in chapter 2 is referred to by the 'veil of ignorance', and is measured in chapter 5. By contrast, behavioral theory predicts that if index children are diagnosed when their younger siblings are older, the latter are raised in a more normal environment, which might mitigate recurrence risk.

Fourth, according to the neurodevelopmental paradigm there should be no selection bias in estimates of recurrence risk. Selection bias induced by within-group reproductive stoppage is behavioral rather biological or genetic. If parents knew their genetic predisposition to ASD, they might self-select into reproductive stoppage for neurodevelopmental reasons. However, parents do not have such genetic knowledge, so we are left with behavioral theories of self-selectivity. The empirical presence of selection bias therefore rejects the hypothesis that recurrence risk is exclusively neurodevelopmental.

In this chapter we focus on the first three behavioral phenomena. The next chapter focuses on the fourth.

To investigate the empirical salience of these behavioral hypotheses, we use the population cohort data for Israel described in chapter 5. In doing so, we control for covariates that typically feature in standard neurodevelopmental models of recurrence risk as reviewed in chapter 4. These controls include the age of parents, birth order, birth gaps, ethnicity etc. These 'neurodevelopmental' controls are supplemented by three 'behavioral' controls:

1. A dummy variable (D) equal to 1 if parents were 'informed' (their index child was diagnosed before they conceived their next child) and D = 0 otherwise.
2. The duration of the veil of ignorance.
3. The duration of the shadow of ASD.

If these three controls are partially or jointly statistically significant in models of recurrence risk (such as logit and probit), we may reject the null hypothesis that recurrence risk is exclusively neurodevelopmental, and we cannot reject the null hypothesis that recurrence risk exhibits behavioral footprints.

Table 7.1. Rates of recurrence risk

	Recurrence Risk
All	0.0453
Before 2000	0.0380
Ultra-orthodox	0.0320
Boy - boy	0.0642
Girl -girl	0.0321
Girl - boy	0.0862
Boy - girl	0.0185
Informed	0.0367
Informed - from conception	0.0350
Uninformed	0.0476
Uniformed - from conception	0.0468
Veil of Ignorance	
< 1.25 years	0.0669
1.25 – 3.5 years	0.0572
> 3.5 years	0.0447
Shadow of ASD	
< 1.32 years	0.0439
1.32 – 3.33 years	0.0572
> 3.33 years	0.0278

Notice that it is not our intention to reject the neurodevelopmental paradigm, but merely to question its exclusivity. However, variables such as the age of parents and ethnicity have behavioral interpretations too. For example, older parents are more mature and ethnicity may not be biological or genetic especially where religiosity is concerned. Arabs may be genetically different to Jews, but haredi Jews are genetically identical to other Jews.

Since details of the data have already been provided in chapter 5, we turn directly to the results, which are reported in Table 7.1. For convenience, we begin by repeating Table 5.3 in chapter 5. As explained in chapter 5, the data include all younger siblings of 8,164 index children, the standard errors of the parameter estimates need to be clustered because younger siblings from the same family are unlikely to be independent (chapter 3). This might be less important where the data mainly comprise sibling dyads because fertility is low. Matters are different in Israel because fertility is high; each index child typically has several younger siblings. Indeed, there are almost 30,000 younger siblings in the study.

Model 1 in Table 7.2 clusters the standard errors, which tend to be smaller than, their unclustered counterparts. As explained in chapter 3, this implies that recurrence risk is negatively correlated within families, which arises when sibling interaction is negative (chapter 2).

Model 2 in Table 7.2 specifies family specific effects (chapter 3), which account for the susceptibility of siblings from different families to recurrence risk, and are specified as random effects rather than fixed effects (chapter 3). The empirical distribution of the odd-ratios for these random specific effects is plotted in Figure 7.1. These results suggest that recurrence risk differs widely among families. Figure 7.1 suggests that there are two types of family. The first group has odds-ratios that are slightly less than 1, while the second group, which is smaller, has odds-ratios that are about 1.3.

These random effects are hypothesized to be normally distributed with mean normalized to zero. The standard deviation of these effects is estimated at 0.588, which implies that recurrence risk for families at the lower 95 percentile is 1.47 percent, and it is 13 percent at the upper percentile. Mean recurrence risk is 4.5 percent. The asymmetry stems from the fact that the standard deviation refers to the log odds ratio.

Specific effects and clustering are separate phenomena. The latter arise out of the interaction between siblings, and the former arises out of unobservable family characteristics. In principle, therefore, models estimated with specific effects may also involve clustering. In practice, however, we have been unable to combine clustering with family specific effects (R does not allow for this), which is why there is no Model 3 in Table 7.2, which combines the two.

Table 7.2. Logit Model for Recurrence Risk: Informed at Birth

Model	**1 Common Effects**			**2 Random Effects**	
	Odds Ratio	**SD-cluster**	**P-value (clustered)**	**Odds Ratio**	**P-value**
Intercept	0.1706	0.1661	< 0.0001	0.1693	<0.0001
Female sibling	0.2851	0.1274	< 0.0001	0.2847	<0.0001
Birth order after index	0.8344	0.0704	0.0102	0.8374	0.0226
Index birth order	0.9244	0.0488	0.1077	0.9251	0.0999
Birth gap < 2	1.4297	0.1363	0.0087	1.4350	0.0090
Female index	1.6112	0.1324	0.0003	1.6094	0.0003
Mother disability	1.6995	0.2273	0.0196	1.7016	0.0217
Ultra-Orthodox	0.7682	0.1674	0.1153	0.7675	0.1058
Non-Jew	0.2294	0.4222	0.0005	0.2294	0.0005
Veil of ignorance	*0.8552*	*0.0286*	*< 0.0001*	*0.8547*	*<0.0001*
Shadow of ASD	*0.9300*	*0.0350*	*0.0387*	*0.9830*	*0.0593*
Informed	*0.6364*	*0.1621*	*0.0053*	*0.6355*	*0.0069*
Censor	Spline +		<0.0001	Spline +	0.0024
Observations	8164			8164	
Log likelihood	-1376			-24864	

Source: Beenstock (2021a).

Because most of the variables in Table 7.2 were featured in a previous study (Beenstock, Raz and Levine 2015), we focus here on the three new behavioral variables, which are highlighted in underlined italics. The results of the previous study focused on birth gaps and birth orders of index children and their younger siblings. We reconfirm that short birth gaps (less than 2 years) increase recurrence risk, that recurrence risk varies inversely with the birth orders of younger siblings and the birth orders of index children. Also, recurrence risk is smaller in the non-Jewish population, varies directly with mothers' disability, and younger siblings are censored, as expected, with the probability of censoring tending to zero at 9 years of age. We found no evidence that recurrence risk varies with mothers' age (when her index child was born), nor could we detect a time trend in recurrence risk that might have reflected the positive time trend in the incidence of ASD in the general population, as in Figure 7.1 in chapter 5.

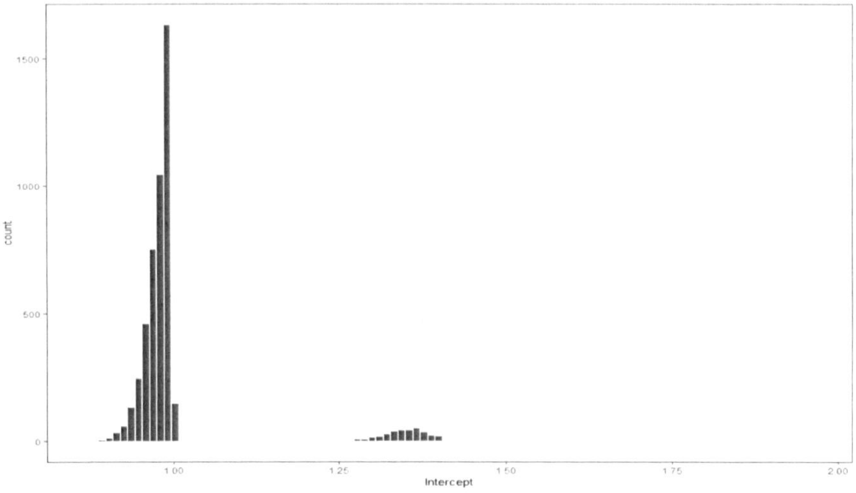

Source: Beenstock (2021a).

Figure 7.1. Distribution of Family Specific Odds Ratios.

We turn now to the three highlighted behavioral variables in Table 7.2. 'Informed' is a dummy variable, which equals 1 if index children were diagnosed before their younger siblings were born and is zero otherwise. The relative risk of ASD recurrence when parents are informed is reduced by slightly more than 30 percent. This effect is statistically significant and its p-value is 0.0053. 'Shadow of ASD' refers to the experience (in years) that informed parents had in raising their children with ASD before their younger siblings were born. The estimated coefficient implies that the relative risk of recurrence decreases by approximately 7 percent for each additional year of experience. This effect is very statistically significant since its p-value is almost zero. Finally, 'veil of ignorance' refers to the period of time (in years) during which uninformed parents raised the younger siblings of index children before the latter were diagnosed. The estimated coefficient implies that the relative risk of recurrence decreases by about 15 percent for each year of ignorance. This effect is very statistically significant too. Indeed, a likelihood ratio test overwhelming supports the retention of all three variables. However, their inclusion does not significantly affect the parameter estimates of the other variables in Table 7.2.

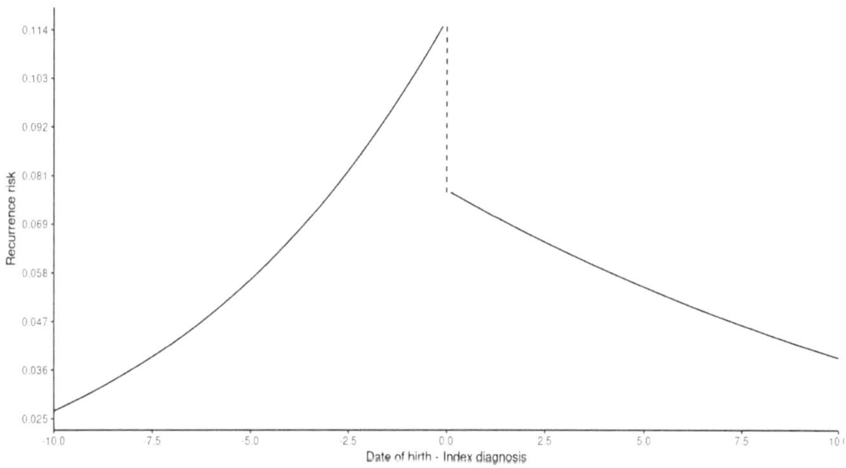

Source: Beenstock (2021a).

Figure 7.2. Recurrence Risk and Shadow of ASD or Veil of Ignorance.

In Figure 7.2 we plot the relationship, implied by Model 1 in Table 7.2, between recurrence risk (on the vertical axis) and the difference between the birth dates of younger siblings and the dates at which index children were diagnosed (on the horizontal axis). Parents are 'informed' if this difference is positive because younger siblings were born after their index siblings were diagnosed. If this difference is negative, parents were 'uninformed'. Therefore, the shadow of ASD increases to the right of 0 on the horizontal axis, and the veil of ignorance increases to the left. The baseline for recurrence risk is 4.5 percent as in the data because logit models replicate sample means. Notice that the origin for the shadow of ASD is 2.91 percent because informed parents have lower odds ratios according to Table 7.2.

Figure 7.2 shows that recurrence risk varies directly with the gap between dates of birth and dates of diagnosis. It also shows that recurrence risk varies inversely with the shadow of ASD and the veil of ignorance. At one year, the veil of ignorance reduces recurrence risk from 4.5 percent to 3.87 percent and to 2.03 percent after 5 years. At one year, the shadow of ASD reduces recurrence risk from 4.5 percent to 2.71 percent and to 2.09 after 5 years. The results in Table 7.2 refer to 'informed' at birth. Since the results are similar for informed at conception, we do not present them here.

Discussion

The opening quotation from Rutter, made in 2010, applies also today. In this chapter, we respond to Rutter's challenge by reporting empirical evidence of three behavioral phenomena in the determination of recurrence risk. Our interpretation of these phenomena in terms of empowerment and imperilment theory, and self-selectivity into reproductive stoppage is less important than their statistical salience. Perhaps other interpretations exist. However, behavioral theory provides axioms, which predicted these effects. By contrast neurodevelopmental theory does not. On the contrary, neurodevelopmental theory specifically rules out these behavioral results.

The result that recurrence risk is smaller among informed parents is consistent with them being more resilient. This does not mean that they are better parents. It simply means that parents who knowingly or consciously decided against reproductive stoppage are different to parents who conceived before their index child was diagnosed. Nor do we claim that the neurodevelopmental model is false. Indeed, our results are consistent with this model. However, they are not exclusively so. We find that the three behavioral parental phenomena significantly improve predictions of recurrence risk when they are added to the neurodevelopmental model.

However, standard neurodevelopmental covariates such as birth gaps and birth orders continue to be statistically significant; they are not superseded by the three behavioral parental phenomena.

Can this putative behavioral evidence be confounded by neurodevelopmental effects? This would be the case if the difference between the dates of diagnosis of elder siblings and the dates of conception or birth of younger siblings happened to be correlated with neurodevelopmental phenomena. This difference is positive for uninformed families and negative for informed families. This difference also equals age at diagnosis minus sibling age gaps. There is no reason to suspect that sibling age gaps are directly or indirectly correlated with neurodevelopmental genotypes. However, age at diagnosis might be negatively correlated, if severer cases of ASD are diagnosed more quickly. If so, recurrence risk should vary inversely with age at diagnosis, and birth gaps should have no effect on recurrence risk. Since our results reject both of these predictions, we do not think that they are an artefact of confounding.

Standard neurodevelopmental covariates, such as birth order, might also bear behavioral interpretations. The neurodevelopmental interpretation is that birth order is naturally larger in families that have produced more regular children. These families are presumed to be genetically less susceptible to ASD recurrence. A behavioral interpretation might be that parents who have had more experience in raising children are more resilient, which is why recurrence risk varies inversely with birth order. The same applies to covariates such as the ages of parents, which have behavioral as well as neurodevelopmental interpretations. In observational studies results are inevitably ambiguous. On the other hand, whereas most neurodevelopmental covariates have behavioral interpretations, the three behavioral phenomena studied here do not have obvious neurodevelopmental interpretations.

We make a methodological contribution by exploiting the randomness in the timing of diagnoses as a source of natural experimentation. Randomized trials are obviously not feasible because parents cannot be assigned into treatment groups who are informed and controls who are uninformed. By contrast, natural experimentation induced by the timing of diagnosis most probably reveals the same information with greater reliability provided recurrence risk is sufficiently independent of the timing of diagnosis.

In summary, the Bettelheim Affair blighted behavioral research into the etiology of ASD. However, the distinction should be made between discredited psychoanalytical theories and untested psychopathological theories that are behavioral. We close with some further quotations from Rutter. "At first sight, it might seem that autism is the diagnostic category least likely to require a developmental psychopathology perspective." (Rutter and Sroufe 2000). However, in reference to grand discredited theories they add, "There is a continuing need to remain skeptical about the new evangelisms that have come to take their place, but equally the imperative must be to replace doubt with programmatic research that truly tests competing hypotheses." (Rutter and Sroufe 2000). Hopefully, the perhaps controversial results presented here will be judged in this enlightened light.

'New Evangelism' arises in all scientific disciplines (Kuhn 1970). The dominant paradigm marginalizes the alternatives. Indeed, vested interests may even conspire to delegitimize nonconformism. Kuhn's analysis of the structure of scientific revolutions relates how dominant paradigms go through crises before they are replaced. In the present context, the concern is not to overthrow the dominant paradigm, but to challenge its exclusivity. If recurrence risk of ASD has a behavioral etiology maybe ASD in the general population has a similar etiology.

Chapter 8

SELECTION BIAS IN ESTIMATES OF RECURRENCE RISK

"Among epidemiologists, the impact of endogenous selection bias has not appeared to be a concern of equal importance to that of confounding. This probably reflects the fact that it is more difficult to understand the impact of selection bias on internal validity than that of confounding."

Infante-Rivard and Cusson (*International Journal of Epidemiology*, 2018 p 1721)

Selection bias is a common problem in epidemiological studies because observational data may not be representative of the general population (Infante-Rivard and Cusson 2018). For example, estimates of recurrence risk in autism spectrum disorder are informed by parents who refrained from reproductive stoppage. If stoppage is not random, and if recurrence risk among parents who stopped is less than among parents who refrained from stoppage, standard estimates of recurrence risk in which stoppage is assumed to be random would be biased upwards.

Investigators have attempted to adjust estimates of recurrence risk for potential sample selection bias using the 'singles' method (Hoffmann et al. 2014), the 'later sib' method (Wood et al. 2014) the 'firstborn – older sibling' method (Hansen et al. 2019), and by assuming that the incidence of ASD is independent of birth order (Grønborg et al. 2015). The latter might be reasonable for second-borns if firstborns do not have ASD (although below we show that this is empirically invalid), but it is clearly unreasonable if firstborns have ASD. Indeed, it implicitly makes the contradictory assumption that recurrence risk is the same as it is in the general population.

These unorthodox methods are incompatible with two canonical methods for testing and correcting sample selection bias such as those proposed by Infante-Rivard and Cusson (2018). In the first of these methods, selection is assumed to be endogenous (Heckman 1976) in the sense that it is not independent of the outcome of interest (ASD recurrence). The second is the inverse probability weighting method (Rosenbaum 2002) in which selection is hypothesized to depend on exogenous variables, which are independent of the outcome of interest. A central purpose is to introduce these methods to investigators of recurrence risk using population cohort data for Israel described in chapter 5.

Selection bias is induced in estimates of recurrence risk if parents of children with ASD who do not engage in reproductive stoppage are not representative of the parents of children with ASD who engage in stoppage. The two orthodox methods are therefore concerned with *within-group* comparisons between parents of ASD children; between those who stop and those who did not. By contrast, the unorthodox methods do not focus on within-group comparisons but on various *between-group* comparisons. For example, they compare parents in the general population with parents of children with ASD (Hoffmann et al. 2014). Or the firstborn – older siblings method ignores selection bias induced by the fact some firstborns have older siblings while others do not. Hopefully, the confusion about what generates selection bias will be clarified below.

There is a modest literature on between - group studies of reproductive stoppage which is reviewed in chapter 6, but which does not concern us here. By contrast there are no empirical studies of within – group reproductive stoppage, except for the results in chapter 6. Studies of recurrence risk, including the present, typically focus on the younger siblings of index children. A separate genre attaches no importance to birth-order or seniority; younger siblings may be diagnosed first (Wood et al. 2014, Hansen et al. 2019). Implicitly these studies do not attach importance to the ascertainment of ASD on diagnosis. They assume instead that parents know in advance that their index child has ASD, which is formally confirmed on diagnosis, as discussed in chapter 4. Since selection bias in this genre is more complex, its analysis is not covered here.

METHODS

To set the scene methodologically, we apply the anatomy of the selection problem to the recurrent risk of ASD in terms of 'Manski's bounds', described in chapter 3, which in the present context bound the probability of ASD recurrence without making any ancillary assumptions. As it were, the data alone speak for themselves.

We follow the notation in Grønborg et al. (2013). Let X_j be a binary variable equal to 1 if child j has ASD and equals 0 otherwise, where j denotes birth order. By Bayes' rule recurrence risk for the first two children is:

$$P(X_2 = 1|X_1 = 1) = P(X_2 = 1|\, X_1 = 1, A)P(A|X_1 = 1) + P(X_2 = 1|\, X_1 = 1, A^c)P(A^C|\, X_1 = 1 \qquad (8.1)$$

where $A = 1$ if parents did not engage in stoppage and $A^c = 1$ otherwise. In words, recurrence risk unconditional on selection equals the probability that child 2 has ASD given that his elder sibling has ASD and his parents did not engage in stoppage multiplied by their probability of refraining from stoppage, plus the counterfactual probability that child 2 would have had ASD given that his elder sibling has ASD multiplied by his parents' probability of stoppage.

Suppose $P(X_2 = 1| X_1 = 1, A) = 0.045$ in equation (8.1), i.e. the observed probability of recurrence risk is 0.045, and that the proportion of parents refraining from stoppage is 0.54, hence $P(A|X_1 = 1) = 0.46$. The counterfactual probability of recurrence, $P(X_2 = 1| X_1 = 1, A^c)$ in equation (8.1), refers to recurrence risk among parents who stopped, had they not stopped. This counterfactual is naturally bounded between 0 (zero recurrence risk) and 1 (recurrence risk is 1). Studies of recurrence risk, which ignore selection bias implicitly assume that the counterfactual probability is 0.045. Equation (8.1) implies that the unconditional recurrence risk, which by definition is free of potential selection bias, cannot be less than 0.024, when the counterfactual probability of recurrence is 0, or greater than 0.484 when the counterfactual probability is 1.

Although these bounds are wide, they are informative especially regarding the lower bound. Without empirical data, recurrence risk may take any value between 0 and 1. The data enable us to narrow the ambiguity; recurrence risk cannot be greater than 0.424 or smaller than 0.024 when self-selectivity is taken into consideration. These bounds may be narrowed by making various untestable assumptions (Manski 1995). By making further assumptions these bounds may be narrowed to a point, as we now discuss.

Endogenous Selection: Incidental Truncation Method (ITM)

ITM was described in chapter 3. For convenience its main features are recalled, starting with equation (3.21) in chapter 3 and updated by equation (6.1) in chapter 6:

$$C_{it}^* = X_i\beta - \delta D_i + z_i \tag{8.2}$$

where C_{it}^* is a latent variable, which expresses the desire of parents in family i to have a further child when their index child is aged t, D is a dummy variable equal to 1 if parents are informed in the sense of chapter

6 and is zero otherwise, β and δ are parameters to be estimated, and z comprises the unobservables upon which C* depends. C is a dummy variable equal to 1 if stoppage does not occur and C = 0 otherwise. Stoppage is hypothesized to occur when C* is less than some threshold (assumed to be zero) in which event C = 0, otherwise stoppage does not occur, and C = 1.

This simple model implies that observationally similar parents of ASD children (parents with the same X) may have different rates of stoppage because they differ by z, which is unobservable. If z is assumed to have a logistical distribution, β and δ may be estimated by a logit model using data for C. If z is normally distributed, β and δ may be estimated by a probit model.

Let S* denote a latent variable for recurrence risk, which is hypothesized to depend on observables (Z) and unobservable s as in equation (3.22) in chapter 3:

$$S_i^* = Z\gamma + s_i \tag{8.3}$$

where γ is a vector of coefficients to be estimated. Let S be a binary variable, which equals 1 in the event that ASD recurs among younger siblings and is zero otherwise. S = 1 when S* is positive and is zero otherwise. If z and s are uncorrelated, probit or logit estimates of the probability of ASD recurrence are unbiased because what investigators don't observe about stoppage (z) is unrelated to what they don't observe about recurrence risk (s). Matters are different if z and s happen to be correlated because what they don't observe about stoppage is related to what they don't observe about recurrence risk.

If z and s are correlated with correlation ρ, estimates of recurrence risk may be corrected for selection bias. For example, ρ is positive if more resilient and pronatal parents are less likely to engage in reproductive stoppage, and if for behavioral reasons discussed in chapter 2 their children are less likely to develop ASD. According to equation (3.23) in chapter 3, the recurrence risk for family i conditional on no stoppage is:

$$P(S_i = 1 | C_i = 1, X_i, Z_i) = \Phi\left[\frac{Z_i\gamma + \rho X_i\beta}{\sqrt{1-\rho^2}}\right] \quad (8.4)$$

where Φ(.) denotes the standard normal cumulative density, and the correlation between z and s (ρ) is used to correct for selection out of stoppage. Note that when ρ = 0 recurrence risk reverts to Φ(Zγ), i.e., sample selectivity is ignorable; the probit models for stoppage and recurrence risk are independent of one another.

In summary, ITM assumes that for given observables, such as the age of parents and the birth orders of their children (X and Z), what we do not observe about parents (s and z) may be exploited to test for the presence of selection bias, provided that we are prepared to make parametric assumptions about their distribution, e.g., they are bivariate normal. If s and z happen to be correlated, i.e., ρ is statistically significantly different from zero, selection bias must be present, because what is not observed about parents' stoppage behavior is not independent of what is not observed about their recurrence risk. Estimates of s and z are obtained by jointly estimating the models for stoppage and recurrence risk. Then the estimate of ρ is used to remove selection bias from the estimates of γ, β and δ.

Exogenous Selection: Inverse Probability Weighting (IPW)

IPW was introduced in chapter 3. For convenience its main features are recalled. Whereas econometricians developed ITM and nonparametric bounds, statisticians developed the method of inverse probability weighting (IPW) for handling sample selection bias (Rosenbaum 2002). Let $\hat{p}_i$ denote the probability that parents from family i refrain from reproductive stoppage according to the selection model in equation (8.2). IPW maximizes the likelihood function weighted by the inverse of these probabilities:

$$lnL_{IPW} = \sum_{i=1}^{n} \frac{S_i}{\hat{p}_i} lnL_i \quad (8.5)$$

where, as in ITM, S = 1 in the event of non-stoppage, and L refers to the likelihood of ASD recurrence, i.e., S = 1. Since $C_i = 1$ for all parents who had further children by refraining from reproductive stoppage, the IPW likelihood attributes more weight to parents who are less likely to have further children, i.e., more likely to stop. The estimator is based on the assumption that P(C = 1| S, X, Z) = P(C = 1| X, Z), i.e., the probability of selection does not depend on recurrence risk once X and Z are taken into account. This is equivalent to assuming that $\rho = 0$, i.e., potential hidden confounders such as c (pronatality), which is a component of z in selection, are uncorrelated with randomness (s) in recurrence risk.

In short, IPW involves two steps. In the first, equation (8.2) is estimated as a regular probit model using the Z covariates. In the second, equation (8.3) is estimated as a separate probit model using the X covariates, by weighting its likelihoods as in equation (8.5) using the estimated probabilities of non-stoppage obtained from step 1. Under its maintained assumptions IPW corrects estimates of γ in equation (8.3) for potential sample selection bias under the crucial assumption that Z is independent of s and c.

Tests have been proposed to determine whether IPW estimates are sensitive to potential hidden confounders (Rosenbaum 2002), which induce dependence between X and s and z. Hidden confounders are observable and unobservable variables, which for one reason or another are omitted from X. These sensitivity analyses are based on the idea that if families have the same values for X, their results for recurrence risk should not be significantly different if they also have the same values for Z. If the results from IPW are insensitive, all is well. However, matters are different if they do not; they suggest that the Z variables specified in equation (8.3) are incomplete. The trouble is that 'sensitivity' is defined subjectively rather than objectively. There are also different proposals for conducting sensitivity analyses. Here we use the sensitivity analysis proposed by Zhao, Small and Bhattacharya (2019).

Whereas IPW assumes that $\rho = 0$ and carries out sensitivity tests to determine whether this assumption is plausible, ITM does not make this restriction and estimates ρ as a parameter in its own right. This sounds as if IPW is a special case of ITM in which $\rho = 0$. However, this is not so, because if $\rho = 0$ ITM implies that equation (8.3) for recurrence risk may be estimated by a regular probit model whereas IPW does not. In short, IPW and ITM are non-nested methods; neither method is a special case of its rival. In principle, non-nested tests may be used to determine whether IPW is preferable empirically to ITM (Santos Silva 2002). As is well known, non-nested tests may be inconclusive since neither ITM nor IPW may turn out to be mutually preferable.

In summary, IPW assumes that the observables, which determine stoppage (Z) may be used to neutralize selection bias among parents who do not engage in stoppage, because they are assumed to be independent of what is not observed about recurrence risk (s). The predicted probability of non-stoppage ($\hat{p}$) is used as a 'propensity score' for correcting for selection bias in the recurrence risk model.

RESULTS

Bringing Theory to Data

Population cohort data for Israel are used once again, this time to test for sample selection bias in recurrence risk using ITM and IPW. Since these data have been detailed at length in chapter 5, we turn directly to the results.

The study of recurrence risk has typically focused on immediate younger siblings. In the present study, we also attach importance to higher order siblings. ASD may not recur among immediate younger siblings, but it may recur among higher order siblings. Estimates of recurrence risk will be biased downwards if higher order siblings are ignored because families supply more than one observation for estimating recurrence risk. This bias will be smaller where fertility is low. The bias would be zero if parents limited their fertility to two children. Matters are different in our empirical application for Israel where fertility is high.

The use of data for all younger siblings and not just immediate younger siblings raises statistical concerns because the outcomes of younger siblings from the same family are likely to be dependent. Their ASD status certainly cannot be treated as the independent outcomes of younger siblings from different families. They share the same parents, the same index child, and they share each other. Consequently, we cluster standard errors of parameter estimates by family (chapter 3).

Another difference is that we use censoring methods instead of discarding observations, which are potentially censored. In chapter 6 the fertility of women was censored. In this chapter there are two types of censoring; apart from the fertility of women, the ascertainment of recurrence risk is censored. Our data are obtained from administrative records from 1985 up to December 2012. Younger siblings born, for example, in 2009 might not have been diagnosed with ASD by December 2012, when the study period ends. Their contribution to recurrence risk estimates is censored since they might have been diagnosed with ASD in 2013 and beyond. Some investigators assume that it takes 8 years for ASDs to be diagnosed (Raz et al. 2014, Nevison et al. 2018), and would exclude younger siblings born after 2003. In our data 15 percent were diagnosed with ASD after they were 8 years old. This radical solution to censoring typically discards numerous observations. Instead of discarding data, we assume that the probability of censoring varies inversely with younger siblings' age in December 2012.

Apart from censoring there are several other covariates that are related to time, including age of mothers, age at diagnosis, and year of diagnosis. These time related variables are not expected to be linear. For example, mothers' fecundity at age 40 is naturally less than at age 30. Also, the probability of censoring is expected to vary nonlinearly with the age of younger siblings in December 2012. Therefore, we estimate these relationships as splines as in chapters 6 and 7.

Rates of recurrence risk are reported in Table 8.1. Overall recurrence risk is 4.53%. However, for diagnoses of index children made prior to 2001 recurrence risk was lower (3.8%). Recurrence risk among ultra-orthodox Jews is smaller (3.2%). Recurrence risk also depends on gender mixes. The largest risk (8.62%) occurs among brothers of girls. The smallest risk (1.85%) occurs among sisters of boys. These differences may reflect the fact that the incidence of ASD is lower for girls, but the severity of ASD may be greater among girls (Ratto et al. 2018, Beenstock et al. 2020).

Table 8.1. Rates of recurrence risk

	Younger siblings	**Recurrence risk %**
All	8205	4.53 (CI: 4.03 – 5.03)
Before 2002	1655	3.83 (CI: 2.91 - 4.76)
Ultra-orthodox	1641	3.20 (CI: 2.35 - 4.0)
Boy - boy	3296	6.42 (CI: 5.58 - 7.26)
Girl –girl	822	3.21 (CI:2.00 - 4.42)
Girl - boy	806	8.62 (CI: 6.69 – 10.55)
Boy- girl	3281	1.85 (CI: 1.39 – 2.31)

Notes: Events of recurrence risk occur when younger siblings are diagnosed after older siblings. In 84 cases older siblings were diagnosed after their younger siblings, suggesting that older siblings were diagnosed as a consequence of their younger siblings' diagnosis. These siblings are removed from the study group. 95% confidence intervals in parentheses.

Recurrence Risk Models

The main results are reported in Table 8.2 where γ refers to the maximum likelihood estimates of the probit coefficients for the Z covariates specified in the recurrence risk model, and β refers to the probit coefficients of the X covariates specified in the selection model into fertility (non-stoppage). P-values refer to their clustered standard errors, which on the whole were slightly larger than their unclustered counterparts. There is an overlap between the Z and X covariates. For example, the probability of selection into fertility varies inversely with the birth order of the index (stoppage varies directly with birth order), and recurrence risk varies inversely with birth order. Several variables that feature in the recurrence risk model (gender, birth gap etc.) do not feature in the selection model, and some variables that feature in the selection model do not feature in the recurrence risk model (age of mother, twins etc.).

Table 8.2. Incidentally truncated bivariate probit model for recurrence risk

	Recurrence Risk			Selection into Fertility		
	Estimate γ	**SD-cluster**	**P-value**	**Estimate β**	**SD-cluster**	**P-value**
Intercept	-1.4151	0.0946	< 0.0001	5.7536	0.1569	<0.0001
Female sibling	-0.5541	0.0555	< 0.0001			
Birth order after index	-0.0810	0.0320	0.0114			
Index birth order	-0.0454	0.0233	0.0517	-0.1143	0.0171	<0.0001
Birth gap < 2 years	0.1699	0.0730	0.0199			
Index female	0.2158	0.0623	0.0005			
Mother disability	0.2529	0.1091	0.0205			
Ultra-Orthodox	-0.0547	0.0898	0.5420	1.0149	0.0655	<0.0001
Non-Jew	-0.5902	0.1712	0.0006	0.3469	0.0741	<0.0001
Diagnosis prior to birth	-0.0887	0.0591	0.1332			
Censor sibling	Spline +/0		< 0.0001			
Censor mother				Spline +		<0.0001
Age of mother	Spline +/-		0.0248	-0.1726	0.0053	<0.0001
Twins				-0.6229	0.0714	<0.0001
Age at diagnosis				Spline +		<0.0001
Log likelihood	-7061					
ρ	0.257 CI: -0.096 to 0.552					
Observations	Incidentally truncated 4219			Younger siblings 8205		

Estimated by maximum likelihood. Younger siblings diagnosed before their older siblings are removed from the study group. See notes to Tables 8.1 and 8.2. The probit model for recurrence risk is estimated using data for 8188 younger siblings of which 369 were diagnosed with ASD by December 31, 2012. The probit model for selection into fertility is estimated using data for 9117 families of which 4219 (46%) engaged in stoppage. SD-cluster refers to standard errors clustered by family since all younger siblings are included. Spline +: the sign of the variable is monotone positive. Spline +/-: the sign is positive then negative. The estimated correlation between the residuals from the selection and recurrence risk is denoted by ρ. If ρ is positive parents who did not engage in reproductive stoppage are negatively selected because their recurrence risk is larger. Note that unlike logit models, the parameter estimates from probit models cannot be expressed as odd-ratios. Also, whereas in logit models predicted recurrence risk equals the its counterpart in the data, the same does not apply to probit models. Source: Beenstock (2021b).

Intuitively, separate probit models are estimated for stoppage (equation 8.2) and recurrence risk (equation 8.3) to generate initial estimates of the parameters (β, γ and δ) as well as initial estimates of z and s, which are used to generate an initial estimate of ρ. The data for C and S are bias-corrected using the initial estimate of ρ, which are then used to re-estimate the parameters (β, γ, δ, and ρ). This iterative routine is repeated until the parameters converge on their maximum likelihood estimates as in Table 8.2.

The specification of the selection model into fertility is based on the results in chapter 6 for within-group stoppage. Here we concentrate on the recurrence risk model, which takes account of potential selection bias induced by reproductive stoppage, i.e., the selection model for non-stoppage and the recurrence risk model are estimated jointly by the method of maximum likelihood. Because of this, the stoppage model estimated in chapter 6 and its counterpart in Table 8.2 are not strictly comparable, although they have a family resemblance.

The specification choice in Table 8.2 reflects two considerations, theoretical and statistical. First, several variables such as the gender of siblings and their birth order are irrelevant to decisions about fertility, but have been reported as recurrence risk factors where they are relevant. Also, in the selection model what matters is the censoring of mothers, whereas the censoring of siblings matters for recurrence risk. Second, some variables, which on *a priori* grounds might be associated with recurrence risk and selection, are specified in the recurrence risk model but not in the selection model. For example, mothers with disabilities might have been expected to curtail their fertility. However, this variable was not statistically significant in the selection model, but recurrence risk is larger if mothers are disabled.

All the X covariates in the selection model are highly statistically significant, as they are in chapter 6. Selection into non-stoppage is greater among non-Jews and especially ultra-orthodox Jews, and it varies inversely with the age of mothers (when their index child was born), the birth order of index children, and if the index is a twin. Selection varies directly with the age at diagnosis because parents are more likely to conceive further children if they are unaware of the ASD status of their index children.

Recurrence risk is greater if the index child is female, but smaller if further siblings are girls. The latter result reflects the smaller incidence of ASD among girls in the general population, and the former may reflect the greater severity of ASD among girls. Recurrence risk also varies inversely with the number of regular children as reflected in the birth orders of the index and his or her younger siblings. ASD is more likely to recur among the children of disabled mothers, and it is less likely to recur if parents knew about the diagnosis prior to having a further child. Finally, recurrence risk has an inverted U-shaped relation with mothers' age increasing until age 35 and decreasing thereafter.

The estimate of ρ is 0.257 suggesting that parents who had further children are more likely to incur recurrence risk. This means that had parents who engaged in reproductive stoppage had children, their counterfactual recurrence risk would have been smaller than for parents who refrained from stoppage. Indeed, the model in Table 8.2 implies that average recurrence risk would have been 3.83 percent instead of 4.53 percent, i.e., the selection bias is positive in conventional estimates of recurrence risk, informed exclusively by parents who refrained from reproductive stoppage. Although ρ is positive, it is imprecisely estimated, but is significantly different from zero at $p = 0.082$.

In Table 8.3 we report robustness checks for the results in Table 8.2, which are estimated under the parametric assumption that the disturbance terms, z and s in equations (8.2) and (8.3), have bivariate normal distributions. Model 2 assumes that z and s have a bivariate logit distribution instead of a bivariate normal distribution. The estimate of ρ, its confidence interval and implications for sample selection bias are similar to Table 8.2. The same applies to model 4 in which the bivariate probit models for recurrence risk and selection when the relation between c and s is specified using the Frank copula (equation 3.28 in chapter 3). The only exception arises in model 3 where the t-copula estimates ρ at zero. We have not experimented with other copulas because they either restrict the sign of ρ or its range. Models 5 and 6 focus on the robustness of the estimate of ρ to the specification of the covariates and specific family effects. Model 5 shows that the addition of X covariates to Table 8.2 does not alter the results.

Table 8.3. Robustness checks for Table 8.2

	Risk Model	Selection model	ρ	Confidence interval for ρ	Unbiased recurrence risk
1 (Table 8.2)	Normal	normal	0.257	-0.096 – 0.552	0.0383
2	Logit	logit	0.268	-0.112 – 0.584	0.0382
3	Normal	t- copula	0.01	-0.347 – 0.356	0.0478
4	Normal	Frank copula	0.219	-0.158 – 0.497	0.0380
5	Model 1 with extra X covariates		0.296	-0.157 – 0.639	0.0376

See notes to Table 8.2. Model 1 is reproduced from Table 8.2. For models 3-4 ρ refers to Spearman (rank) correlations since Pearson correlations are undefined for copulas. 95% confidence intervals are bootstrapped and may not be symmetric. Biased recurrence risk is 4.53% obtained by estimating a standard probit model for recurrence i.e., ignoring sample selectivity. Source: Beenstock (2021b).

Table 8.4. Recurrence risk: inverse probability weighting

	Table 8.2 Incidental Truncation Method		Inverse Probability Weighting	
	Estimate γ	p-value	Estimate γ	p-value
Intercept	-1.4151	< 0.0001	-2.4457	<0.0001
Female sibling	-0.5541	< 0.0001	-1.3097	<0.0001
Birth order after index	-0.0810	0.0114	-0.2263	0.0009
Index birth order	-0.0454	0.0517	-0.0469	0.0907
Birth gap < 2 years	0.1699	0.0199	0.7030	<0.0001
Index female	0.2158	0.0005	0.7468	<0.0001
Mother disability	0.2529	0.0205	0.6179	0.0003
Ultra-Orthodox	-0.0547	0.5420	-0.3656	0.0183
Non-Jew	-0.5902	0.0006	-1.8027	<0.0001
Diagnosis prior to birth	-0.0887	0.1332	-0.1178	0.0126
Censor sibling	Spline +/0	< 0.0001	Spline +/0	<0.0001
Age of mother	Spline +/-	0.0248	Spline +/-	0.0027

lnL = -5663.7 for IPW estimated by probit. Results for the recurrence risk model in Table 8.2 are provided for convenience. The results for IPW are obtained by dividing the likelihoods for each observation by their probabilities generated by the selection model in Table 8.2. Source: Beenstock (2021b).

Table 8.4 compares ITM estimates of recurrence risk in Table 8.2 with IPW estimates. Although the signs of parameter estimates are similar, the IPW estimates tend to be larger in absolute size and their significance levels are on the whole greater (smaller p-values). We used a sensitivity test procedure (Zhao et al. 2019), which shows that these IPW results are very sensitive to hidden confounders. Intuitively this test checks whether parents with the same or similar X and Z variables have similar estimates of recurrence risk.

The estimates of recurrence risk according to IPW are correlated 0.937 with their ITM counterparts from Table 8.2. The main difference is that the IPW estimates have a longer right-hand tail. Since, as noted, IPW and ITM are based on mutually exclusive assumptions, they are non-nested methodologies. Hence it is not possible at this stage to declare which method provides more reliable estimates of recurrence risk. However, since the IPW model is sensitive to hidden confounders, which are explicitly taken into consideration in ITM, the results in Table 8.2 are preferable. These hidden confounders include the resilience of parents in raising children, their fear of having further children with ASD, and their fertility preferences.

DISCUSSION

This main motivation behind this chapter is methodological. Epidemiologists use observational data, which may not be representative of the relevant population due to self-selection. Estimates of recurrence risk for autism spectrum disorder are informed by parents who did not engage in reproductive stoppage. If recurrence risk among parents who engaged in reproductive stoppage was putatively different to recurrence risk among parents who refrained from stoppage, standard estimates of recurrence risk would be biased. Correcting for selection bias delivers unbiased estimates of recurrence risk faced by parents, which includes parents who engaged in reproductive stoppage.

As noted in the headline quotation, epidemiologists have attached disproportionate attention to confounding than they have to endogenous selection. This is also true of epidemiological studies of recurrence risk of ASD. We have cited three studies of recurrence risk, which sought to take account of sample selection bias, two of which used unorthodox methods not mentioned by the headline authors, while the third (Grønborg et al. 2015) was based on a technical error. This is the first study to use canonical methods recommended by the headline authors for attaching importance to endogenous selection as well as to confounding.

Parents of children on the spectrum seeking professional advice about having further children obviously should be informed about unbiased estimates of recurrence risk conditional on their risk group in terms of their demographics, birth gaps, ethnicity etc. If recurrence risk is over-estimated, they might be unnecessarily deterred from having further children. If it is under-estimated, they might be induced in undertaking risks of ASD recurrence against their wishes. It should go without saying, therefore, that failure to test for sample selection bias in estimates of recurrence risk, and if it is found to be present, failure to correct for it, would constitute a methodological error of the same order of importance as failure to take account of confounding.

In this chapter we illustrated two canonical methods for handling potential sample selection bias with an application to the recurrence risk of autism spectrum disorder. These are the incidental truncation method and the inverse probability weighting method. We used population cohort data for Israel for some 9000 families observed between 1985 and 2013. The central issue in selection involves reproductive stoppage by parents.

Our main result is that standard estimates of recurrence risk for ASD, which ignore sample selectivity, are over-estimated because recurrence risk in families that engaged in reproductive stoppage would have been smaller than in families that refrained from stoppage. Correcting for selection bias by the incidental truncation method delivers an estimate of recurrence risk of 3.83 percent instead of 4.53 percent, a difference with p-value 0.082. Indeed, this estimate is robust with respect to alternative parametric specifications. Furthermore, tests for sensitivity to hidden confounders in estimates of recurrence risk by inverse probability weighting support the need for incidental truncation in estimating recurrence risk. If these results for Israel apply elsewhere, standard estimates of recurrence risk would be too pessimistic.

Since the estimated selection bias for Israel in recurrence risk is small in absolute terms with p-value 0.082, the results may not matter for clinicians. However, if elsewhere selection bias is larger than in Israel, clinicians would be concerned. This is a call for epidemiologists of recurrence risk to check their results for selection bias. On the other hand, clinicians might be interested in the result that recurrence risk for brothers of sisters is many times larger (8.62 percent) than for sisters of brothers (1.85 percent).

Correcting for sample selection bias did not affect the statistical significance of covariates in recurrence risk models, which were estimated ignoring sample selectivity. However, it may affect their sizes. For example, recurrence risk among ultra-orthodox Jews is relatively small. This may be explained by their high fertility when recurrence risk varies inversely with the birth orders of index children and their younger siblings. Correcting for sample selection bias does not change this result. Nor does it change the negative association between birth gaps a recurrence risk.

Since during the study period the risk of ASD in the general population in Israel averaged approximately 0.5 percent (chapter 5), the relative risk of recurrence (RRR) according to our estimates is 7.7, which is 15 percent smaller than a recent estimate (Davidovitch et al 2013). The latter does not control for selection bias, and refers to one of Israel's four major MHOs for which membership is itself selective. Consequently, it is difficult to compare the estimate of the present study with RRR reported in by Davidovitch et al because they do not control for selection bias, do not use population cohort data, and attach no importance to birth-order.

The empirical evidence of potential selection bias in estimates of recurrence risk constitutes further evidence of behavioral influences in the etiology of ASD. According to the neurodevelopmental paradigm, selection bias induced by reproductive stoppage should not arise because the etiology of ASD, recurrent and otherwise, should be entirely genetic or biological. Therefore, the results presented in this chapter join the results reported in chapter 7, which showed that recurrence risk is not exclusively neurodevelopmental, and exhibits behavioral influences.

Limitations

We wish to mention reservations as well as counter-reservations. First, the probability (p-value) for the estimate of ρ, which tests for sample selection bias, exceeds 0.05. The same applies to several robustness checks, which use different parametric assumptions. Since our central purpose is to illustrate how investigators of recurrence risk might test for sample selection bias, we are not concerned by the fact that the results for Israel are not significant at conventional levels, although they are at slightly more lenient levels. Second, the main method identifies selection bias assuming bivariate normality. It is well known that this assumption might be invalid. On the other hand, we obtained the same result using unrelated alternatives to bivariate normality, suggesting that bivariate normality is not at issue. In any case, identification of bias is also based on instrumental variables, which feature in the selection model but not in the recurrence risk model and vice-versa. We draw particular attention to age at which elder siblings were diagnosed, which serves to randomize reproductive stoppage as in a natural experiment when there is no reason to believe that this variable is directly correlated with recurrence risk. Third, incidental truncation and inverse probability weighting are dependent on the specification of the selection model. In these respects, we have used covariates in standard models of stoppage. If these models are inadequate, so might be our results. On the other hand, experiments with alternative selection models does not support this.

Chapter 9

What Have We Learned About Recurrence Risk?

In chapter 1 we pointed out that this monograph has three audiences, academic and professional epidemiologists, parents concerned about recurrence risk of ASD, and practitioners. Since the monograph is an academic study, it has largely been concerned with academic epidemiologists who study the etiology of ASD in general, and recurrence risk in particular. However, the monograph is also relevant to parents and practitioners. And, it has some relevance to policy makers.

Recently, a new trend has emerged in which especially politicians refer to what 'the science' has to say about such matters as global warming and Covid-19. This expression creates the misleading impression that science is homogeneous, unambiguous and hard. The truth is that scientists disagree especially over issues where experimentation is not feasible, and they have to use instead observational data, such as atmospheric hydro-carbon concentrations, morbidity for Covid-19, and ASD recurrence. By contrast, the experimental sciences have been much more successful. Scientists carry out controlled experiments in their laboratories to test their hypotheses.

Even in the experimental sciences, we may distinguish between physical experiments and experiments involving human beings. Results from the latter are less unambiguous than results from the former because human beings are intelligent whereas physical matter is (presumably) inert. Take, for example, recent arguments about efficiency results from randomized trials of vaccines for Covid-19. See also, the discussion in chapter 3 about natural experimentation versus randomized trials in experiments involving human beings.

'The science' does not say, but scientists do. What they have to say is inherently ambiguous especially when it is based on observational data, and even more so when these data involve human beings, as in the case of recurrence risk for ASD.

Politicians do not use the expression 'the social science says'. They are, of course right, but for the wrong reasons. What lies behind this differentiation is that social science is 'soft' whereas natural science is 'hard'. This is a false dichotomy. The valid dichotomy is between experimental inference and inference using observational data. In this, astrophysicists and epidemiologists studying recurrence risk are the same; neither can experiment, both have to use observational data. These false and valid dichotomies data back, of course, to David Hume (1748). Experimental inference may be 'hard' and inference based on observational data may be 'soft'. In this sense there are natural sciences which are 'hard' and 'soft'. However, social sciences are 'soft' in the sense that they are largely observational. 'Hard' social science would require laboratories in which human beings participate in compulsory (to avoid self-selection) randomized trials rather like rats in experiments.

The dominance of the neurodevelopmental paradigm has 'elevated' the study of ASD into the natural sciences from its humble origins in the social sciences, especially psychology. Although this monograph is not concerned with the etiology of ASD in the general population, the results from this transition have not been very successful. "…despite the progress made in the discovery of a few genes that are well established as having important associations with autism, it does not explain the majority of cases of autism or ASD, and many unknown genetic factors remain to be discovered, thus hampering the progress of clinical testing as a diagnostic test for autism." (Waye and Cheng 2018). The genetic basis for ASD remains a mystery today as when first mooted by Rimland and Rutter 50 years ago. Like many other diseases, medical cures for ASD have yet to be discovered. It is ironical, therefore, that because recurrence risk is greater than in the general population, this has strengthened the belief that ASD must be genetic. It no more establishes this than, for example, does juvenile crime among siblings establish that crime must be genetic.

This disappointing progress is largely concerned with the methodology of GWAS (genome wide association studies), in which the human genome is data-mined for correlation between ASD and genetic markers. Since the number of genes (billions) vastly exceeds the typical number of observations for whom genetic mapping data are available, there is a fundamental problem of inference, which requires more observations than parameters to be estimated (Beenstock 2012, chapter 7). More recently machine learning has been introduced into GWAS to assist in searching the data for correlations. The basic epistemological problem is that genetic theory does not predict which genes are salient for ASD. Instead, GWAS is inductive rather than deductive; it expects the data to reveal the truth for us. But it cannot for reasons given long ago by David Hume (1748) and more recently by Karl Popper (1963).

This monograph argues that recurrence risk of ASD may have behavioral origins. It is not intended to overthrow the neurodevelopmental paradigm, but to challenge its exclusivity. In fact, it is not clear how neurodevelopmental theory might be falsified empirically. A requirement for falsification is a clear prediction based on theory, which may be investigated empirically. Until there are such predictions it is not possible to corroborate neurodevelopmental theory. What has transpired instead is the interpretation of empirical data as evidence supporting the neurodevelopmental paradigm. See for example, the interpretation of the role of short interpregnancy gaps in recurrence risk in Beenstock, Raz and Levine (2015) and the literature on pollution and the prevalence of ASD (Chun et al. 2020). The latter does not take account of the fact that house prices vary inversely with pollution (Nourse 1967), as a result of which poorer parents live where there is more pollution. This behavioral interpretation is not considered by Chun at al. By contrast, four predictions for recurrence risk based on behavioral theory are corroborated in chapters 7 and 8 using population cohort data for Israel.

More generally, this monograph calls for a level scientific playing field in which behavioral theory and neurodevelopmental theory are given equal consideration. It rejects what Rutter and Sroufe called 'New Evangelisms', which claim scientific exclusivity by ruling out alternative if not conflicting perspectives. It not only calls for theoretical pluralism, it also calls for methodological pluralism drawing upon ideas from statistics and econometrics. Indeed, the epidemiological study of recurrence risk has been impeded by methodological solipsism. As noted by Infante-Rivard and Cusson (2018), epidemiologists have been concerned with confounding to the exclusion of other major issues such as selection bias. We may add to this the treatment of causality, or lack of it.

Take for example, the issue of air pollution mentioned above. Weisskopf, Kioumourtzoglu and Roberts (2015) test for causality by checking for residual confounders. Suppose there happen to be none. This does not mean that air pollution has a causal effect on ASD. If the location of mothers during pregnancy happens to be endogenous through house prices, the location of mothers is just as endogenous as the incidence of ASD. Hence, the causal effect of pollution is not identified. To identify the causal effect, it is necessary to use an instrumental variable for the location of mothers, which is independent of house prices (chapter 3). This is equivalent to a natural experiment which randomizes the location of mothers.

Recurrence risk is inherently different to the risk of ASD in the general population. Parents in the general population are naturally concerned that their baby should be healthy. They are aware of the risks in general, but they do not focus on some specific risk, such as deafness, blindness or Down Syndrome. Typically, they push these risks to the back of their mind, and look forward to the safe arrival of their child. Matters are entirely different in the case of recurrence risk. Parents of children on the spectrum are anxious about the risk of ASD because it has become common knowledge that ASD is genetic. Matters would have been different but for this common knowledge. Presumably, prior to the rise of the neurodevelopmental paradigm in the 1950s and 1960s parents of children on the spectrum did seek genetic counselling regarding reproductive stoppage. Maybe it is no coincidence that reproductive stoppage became an issue for study (Jones and Szatmari 1988) after the neurodevelopmental ascendancy.

It is not inconceivable that this common knowledge is without foundation. This is not an argument about whether recurrence risk is elevated or not, but about why it is elevated. Suppose that in truth the reason is not genetic, but the public has been persuaded otherwise. Suppose futher that the reason is behavioral; as predicted by Thomas' theorem, anxious parents imperil the development of the younger siblings of children on the spectrum because they mistakenly believe the false common knowledge to be true. Parents would have needlessly engaged in reproductive stoppage. Challenging the paramountcy of the neurodevelopmental paradigm has enormous implications.

Parents

Parents are naturally interested in recurrence risk because they fear that having further children on the spectrum might be too heavy a burden for them. In the absence of elevated recurrence risk, they would not consider the option of reproductive stoppage. If parents thought that recurrence risk was prohibitively large, their fertility would be lower. If they all thought that recurrence risk was prohibitively large there would be no younger siblings of index children left to study.

Suppose these parents tried to inform themselves by accessing the scientific literature on recurrence risk, which features in Table 4.1 of chapter 4. Or they might refer directly to chapter 4 of this monograph. What would they conclude apart from the fact that recurrence risk is elevated? Here are a few suggestions.

1. Check the reference period for recurrence risk. For example, the estimate of Ozonoff et al. (2011) refers to recurrence risk within

three years. This will not be useful to parents who are naturally concerned with the probability that their child will eventually develop ASD. Unfortunately, some studies are vague about the reference period. Other studies provide estimates of recurrence risk for flexible reference periods up to 15 years.

2. Check for conditional recurrence risk. Suppose that recurrence risk is 18 percent as in Ozonoff et al (2011). This does not mean that this risk is faced by all parents. One size does not fit all. Conditional recurrence risk refers to parents with specific characteristics such as the ages of mothers and fathers, birth order and birth gaps, ethnicity etc. In chapter 4 it was noted that although recurrence risk until age 15 in Israel is 4.5 percent. Conditional recurrence risk ranges between 1 percent and 10 percent. Indeed, the range for conditional recurrence risk within studies exceeds the range of unconditional recurrence risk between studies. Unfortunately, the majority if studies do not refer to conditional recurrence risk, including Ozonoff et al (2011). These studies are most probably not useful to parents because conditional recurrence risk ranges so widely.
3. Check the source of data. Clinical samples are unlikely to be representative of the population of parents with children on the spectrum. Some samples, such as Ozonoff et al (2011) are conscripted through a consortium, which makes it difficult assess their representability. The gold standard is population cohort data for which there are a number of examples in Table 4.1 of chapter 4.
4. Check for sample selection bias. This is a different issue to suggestion 3, and refers to bias induced by reproductive stoppage. None of the studies in Table 4.1 of chapter 4 have allowed for sample selection bias. However, see chapter 8 and Beenstock (2021b) for results. Hopefully, future studies will attach importance to this issue.
5. Check for your country. There have been no studies of recurrence risk for most countries, such as France and Germany. May parents

in France and Germany rely on studies for California, Sweden, Denmark and Israel where population cohort data are available? Although estimates of recurrence risk differ between these countries (chapter 4), these differences are not large. So, French and German parents might usefully refer to these studies.

6. This is not a blame game; don't be defensive. Just because recurrence risk might have something to do with the family does not mean that parents are to blame. The behavioral risk factors identified in this study are largely driven by when index children are diagnosed, which is outside the control of parents.
7. Empower where possible. According to the neurodevelopmental paradigm, parents cannot mitigate recurrence risk because it is genetically predetermined; they are powerless. According to the behavioral paradigm they might be able to mitigate recurrence risk through experience; they are empowered. The results reported in chapter 7 indicated that parents may be imperiled rather than empowered. If so, they may be assisted to cope with their fears through psychological counselling.

PRACTITIONERS

Parents frequently turn to clinicians and counsellors for advice, especially concerning the prospects of having further children on the spectrum. Hence, the check list for parents applies equally to practitioners. Practitioners draw on their cumulative experience and they may also keep up with the scientific literature. Here are some suggestions.

1. The first obvious suggestion is that they should keep abreast of the scientific literature, which fortunately for them, but sadly for parents, is not fast moving.
2. They need to be aware that their experience may not be representative of the population of parents of children on the spectrum.

3. They should be aware that one size does not fit all. The unconditional, or average recurrence risk does not apply to specific families. Instead, they should counsel families according to their conditional recurrence risk prospects as in suggestion 2 for parents. They may do so by referring to studies of recurrence risk, which control for risk factors. They may even install these multivariate risk models on their computers.
4. They should consider attaching importance to behavioral phenomena, such as whether parents were informed or not when they conceived their next child, as well as the durations of the veil of ignorance and the shadow of ASD.
5. Behavioral theory suggests that parents might be helped to mitigated recurrence risk through psychological counselling. See suggestion 7 for parents.
6. Since recurrence risk is in many respects a separate subject from ASD in general, practitioners might usefully attend seminars and day courses dedicated to recurrence risk.

EPIDEMIOLOGY: THEORY

The main theoretical contribution has been to introduce behavioral theory into the study of recurrence risk in particular, and epidemiology more generally. We wish to stress that this is not specifically related to recurrence risk, but to epidemiology more generally. For example, the SIR (susceptible-infective-removal) model and its variants has dominated the epidemiology of infectious disease for almost a century. SIR involves mechanical equations for contagion and recovery, which imply that human beings do not learn from the spread of the disease. If susceptibles wish to protect themselves from infection, they will self-quarantine through voluntary social distancing if the rate of reproduction (R) is expected to increase, and they will relax self-quarantine when they expect R to decrease. What happens to R itself is therefore affected by two related behavioral effects. The first is induced by endogenous social distancing.

The second is induced by rational expectations of R. See Chudik, Pesaran and Rebucci (2021) for an application to Covid-19. The epidemiology of Covid-19 primarily involves social science as well as virology.

Social distancing naturally calls for a social science approach to its analysis. Mechanical SIR-type models of contagion are therefore unlikely to be adequate in the case of Covid-19 and other infectious diseases because the key parameter concerns social distancing, which is obviously endogenous. If social distancing was absolute, infectious diseases could not spread.

Since ASD is not infectious, the contribution of social science assumes another form. In this case the contribution refers to parenting theory and rational selection as described in chapter 2. We highlight a number of key issues in behavioral theory:

1. Parents of children on the spectrum cannot be compared with parents in the general population. Their 'resilience' matters for reproductive stoppage.
2. Parents of children on the spectrum who have had the status of their index children ascertained through diagnosis differ from parents whose children have yet to be diagnosed.
3. Parents who consciously refrain from reproductive stoppage differ from parents had further children before their index child is diagnosed.
4. Busy parents allocate their time efficiently between their children according to their needs.
5. Parents learn from their experience in raising children on the spectrum, which may mitigate recurrence risk.
6. Parents who raise younger siblings before their index children are diagnosed may benefit from their ignorance.

These six phenomena are alien to neurodevelopmental theory, which treats parents and younger siblings as mechanical automatons.

Behavioral genetics has exerted a major influence on the rise of the neurodevelopmental paradigm. In chapter 2 it was demonstrated that just because identical twins have more correlated outcomes than fraternal twins, this does not mean that the elevated correlation for identical twins must be genetic. Indeed, the difference might be behavioral. When Folstein and Rutter (1977) observed that recurrence risk was larger among (a handful) of identical twins, they fell into the behavioral genetics trap despite the fact that by 1977 this criticism of behavioral genetics was well known. The 'equal environments assumption' and the assumption that environments are independent of genotypes arbitrarily rule out behavioral interpretations of the higher correlation for identical twins.

They also rule out behavioral interpretations of recurrence risk. On the contrary, because recurrence risk is greater than it is in the general population, and because siblings are related genetically, neurodevelopmentalists have jumped to the behavioral genetic conclusion that recurrence risk must be genetic.

It is no surprise, therefore, that the critique of the neurodevelopmental paradigm regarding recurrence risk has much in common with the critique of behavioral genetics upon which it is based. Theory needs to be tested by failing to falsify its empirical predictions. Proponents of neurodevelopmental theory need to make empirical predictions regarding recurrence risk to corroborate it. However, this is not how they have proceeded. Instead, they interpret empirical phenomena in recurrence risk through neurodevelopmental spectacles. By contrast in chapters 6 – 8 four behavioral predictions regarding recurrence risk are corroborated using population cohort data for Israel.

EPIDEMIOLOGY: METHODOLOGY

There is a tradition in empirical papers in epidemiology to include a discussion of 'reservations', which is a form of self-criticism, and even confession. Two popular reservations are:

1. The results may not be causal.
2. The data may not be representative of the population.

If the data happen to be representative of the population, but the results are not causal, why do the research in the first place? The same applies in the unlikely combination that despite the fact that the data are not presentative of the population, the results are not causal. The same applies *a fortiori* if both confessions apply.

The meaning of non-causal results is unclear. If the relation between y and x is non-causal, does this mean that y might cause x (reverse causality) or y and x are spuriously correlated? Or does it mean that the relation may be confounded (there is a causal relation between y and z, but x and z happen to be correlated)? As Tolstoy might have put it "Every causal relation is similar, but every non-causal relation is non-causal in its own way."

The first confession is more serious than the second because it reflects a flakey understanding about what causality means, and how to test for it. In chapter 3 we defined causality in observational cross-section data, by introducing the instrumental variables estimator (IVE) developed in the 1930s and 1940s, which since 1982 has been improved by the generalized method of moments (GMM). These methods seem to be unfamiliar to epidemiologists despite the fact that they are not new. They are certainly unfamiliar to investigators of recurrence risk and ASD prevalence. Indeed, in chapter 3 it was pointed out that tests for confounding confound causality with model misspecification.

Another example of methodological isolationism in epidemiology concerns sample selection bias, which is especially relevant to the second confession. We saw in chapter 4 that clinical data for recurrence risk is unlikely to be representative of its relevant population. See also chapter 3. On the other hand, several investigators understood that reproductive stoppage might induce sample selection bias in estimates of recurrence risk. These investigators proposed unorthodox methods for handling sample selection bias. In doing so, they did not seem to be aware of canonical methods or orthodox methods for handling sample selection bias. Indeed, Infante-Rivard and Cusson (2018) tried to draw the attention of epidemiologists to these methods, despite the fact that inverse probability weighting (IPW) dates back to the 1950s and incidental truncation method (ITM) dates back to the 1970s.

A further example of isolationism concerns data censoring, which in the study of recurrence risk arises for two reasons. First, mother' fertility is censored if, when the data stop (2013 in chapters 5 – 8), their completed fertility is not ascertained. Second, ASD recurrence is censored if younger siblings were not diagnosed by 2013. A common procedure is to remove the censored observations from the data. For example, in the case of recurrence risk, younger siblings aged less than 8 years in 2013 would have been dropped from the data. Apart from the wholesale loss of data induced by this radical treatment of censoring, many diagnoses occur after 8 years. Also, this radical policy throws away information on recurrence risk; younger siblings aged 7 years who were still undiagnosed in 2013 were not diagnosed positive beforehand. Investigators of recurrence risk seem to be unaware of non-radical methods for handling data censoring (chapter 3).

In chapter 3 other concepts were introduced, which do not appear to be in the statistical tool box of investigators of recurrence risk. In larger families, index children have several younger siblings. Since they belong to the same family their observations are unlikely to be independent; they share the same parents, they share each other, and they share common environments. A radical solution is to sample one dyad per family. Apart from throwing away observations, how are the dyads to be sampled? The sensible alternative is to take account of sibling dependence by specifying family specific effects and by clustering the standard errors of parameters.

A more general issue concerns the natural history of recurrence risk, or rather the lack of it. The natural history of fertility among humans is observed if parents do not interfere with their fertility. However, parents have interfered with their fertility since time immemorial. In modern times technological advances have given parents greater control over their fertility to the point that in some countries, such as South Korea, Spain, Italy and Japan, the rate of reproduction (R) is close to 1. The more fertility is controlled, the more the natural history of fertility becomes truncated.

The growing truncation of the natural history of fertility creates methodological problems for investigators of recurrence risk. If R = 1 (parents have only one child) it would be impossible to study recurrence risk because there are no sibling dyads. There would be little point to investigating recurrence risk in South Korea. The key studies of recurrence risk have been carried out in locations where R is small, such as California (1.6), Denmark (1.73) and Sweden (1.76). Recall that if R is less than 2.1 the population does not replace itself. It is inevitable that one learns more about recurrence risk the larger is R. What makes the data for Israel particularly interesting and informative is that R is 3.1; the natural history of fertility is heavily truncated in California, Sweden and Denmark, but for all practical purposes it is not truncated in Israel.

If fertility continues to decline, it will become increasingly more difficult to study recurrence risk. One would have to turn to countries such as Egypt and Pakistan where R exceeds 3, but these countries are unlikely to have population cohort data, or even any data at all. Hence the prospects for the empirical study of recurrence risk are getting slimmer.

POLICY MAKERS

Policy makers have been concerned by the growing prevalence of ASD. CDC estimates for prevalence in the US have increased from 1/150 in 2000 to 1/68 in 2010 and to 1/54 by 2016. In chapter 5 we showed that prevalence in Israel has increased too, although by 2016 prevalence in Israel was less than half its US counterpart. More generally, prevalence seems to be growing globally. Despite the fact that ASD is not contagious, is there a pandemic in ASD induced by some global factor, such as air pollution, which should be of public concern? So far nobody has mentioned climate change. Or is it the case that diagnostic standards have simply become more liberal with the transition between DSM III and DSM V, with the result that children who would not have been diagnosed with ASD 20 years ago, are so diagnosed today?

To answer this question, data are required for severity of ASD. If the prevalence of severity-adjusted ASD has remained unchanged, the answer to the question is the latter; the relaxation of diagnostic standards is to blame for the trend in prevalence. Unfortunately, diagnostic data on severity are not systematically available. In chapter 5 we used data for Israel on severity at age 18 to test whether they vary inversely with age at diagnosis controlling for year-of-birth. The results reject the pandemic theory of ASD prevalence, and suggest instead that children diagnosed more recently (notice not when they were older) had lower severity when they were aged 18.

This important result implies that future cohorts of young adults on the spectrum are expected to have greater ability in making the transition into regular adulthood than previous cohorts. This means that adults on the spectrum are expected to be a lighter socioeconomic burden in the future than they might have been in the past. This implication is positive news for public health planners and providers of social services. It is also welcome news for those concerned with the pandemic theory of ASD prevalence.

The next chapter establishes empirically for Israel that severity metrics at age 18 predict the transition into adulthood for outcomes such as employment and tertiary education.

Chapter 10

The Transition into Adulthood with Autism Spectrum Disorders

This chapter is not about recurrence risk of ASD, so it does not strictly belong to this monograph. On the other hand, it exploits the same population cohort data for Israel that are used in chapters 5 – 8 to study a relatively neglected issue in the literature on autism spectrum disorder, which is concerned with the transition into adulthood by individuals with ASD. In chapter 5 it was mentioned that the benefit supplied by the National Insurance Institute (NII) to the parents of children with ASD expires when they are 18 years old. In fact, this deadline is flexible especially if those concerned happen to be in some educational program, or something similar. The NII assesses these 18 year-olds for invalidity benefit as adults by undertaking various tests including an ADL test to assess their ability to look after themselves (dressing, washing etc.), and a test to assess their communication and sociability skills as well as their employability. Based on these data a panel of experts at NII then deems their eligibility to invalidity benefit as adults.

Their personal IDs are used to track what happens to individuals in the study group after they are 18 years old. Because NII contributions depend on status, we are able to follow four outcomes. First, because there is compulsory military conscription we may ascertain service on a monthly basis in IDF (Israel Defense Forces) and National Service. The latter is a non-military alternative to service in IDF. Although individuals with ASD are exempt from conscription, many volunteer, and their service is recorded electronically in NII records. Second, so is their attendance at institutes of tertiary education recorded. Third, so is their participation in the regular labor market recorded through their NII contributions and those of their employers. These data include earnings and economic sector of employment. Finally, marital status is recorded including children, if any.

These records are longitudinal on a monthly basis. They provide a rare if not unique opportunity to study the transition into young-adulthood by individuals on the spectrum. Moreover, the test scores at age 18 may be used to see if they predict success and failure in the transition into adulthood. About 1500 individuals in the study-group described in chapter 5 were identified in NII records when they were aged between 19 and 31 in 2015, which is why the transition is into *young* adulthood. By 2025 it will be possible to extend the study into mature adulthood, and in the fullness of time over their entire life-cycle. Since these are population cohort data, they are not vulnerable to sample selection bias. Also, compared to other studies the number of observations is large.

Although study of children and adolescents with autism spectrum disorders (ASD) has expanded enormously, research on their transition into adulthood is sparse (Levy and Perry, 2011; Wehman et al., 2014). Such studies have tended to focus on one or two inter-related outcome measures, primarily symptomatology and communication skills (Schall and McDonough, 2010), or on the relation between ASD symptoms and employment placement (Holwerda et al., 2012; Taylor et al., 2012). We are unaware of studies that track the relation between multiple functional measures, such as social and communication skills and/or activities daily living (ADL), and multiple outcomes, such as engagement in social activities, tertiary education and employment.

The traditional model used in disability studies has been primarily medical, assuming that successful transition into adulthood is sequential, if not necessarily linear (Marks 1977). Accordingly, the completion of earlier developmental milestones lays the foundations for the successful passage of subsequent milestones. This medical model has been challenged by the social-functional model (WHO 2001), according to which 'successful participation' in adult life is not necessarily sequential but interfaced with activities, and personal and environmental opportunities, such as leisure or employment programs (Orsmond et al., 2013). Whereas the traditional model hypothesizes causal effects between type and severity of impairment and functioning, the social-functional model offers an alternative transactional approach. In the case of the transition into adulthood, the lack of consensus about developmental milestones is even greater, especially compared to children with other developmental disabilities (Matson et al. 2012). Investigation of both models in the context of ASD is naturally more complicated than it is with other developmental disabilities, which are easier to assess at an early age.

We offer a new methodology for studying the transition into adulthood of individuals with ASD using longitudinal population cohort data for Israel. Specifically, we investigate whether subsequent outcomes, such as participation in tertiary education, depend on the successful passage of earlier outcomes, such as civic participation, as predicted by the traditional medical model. We also investigate whether this association is induced by social functioning as predicted by the social-functional model. We use measures of activities in daily living (ADL) and social functioning at age 18 as potential predictors of outcomes in adulthood. In addition, controls include demographic and background variables such as gender, ethnicity, and parents' income, as well as controls for socioeconomic environments in terms of their socioeconomic scores (SES) and the peripherality of their localities. Because we focus on several outcomes, we are able to estimate the roles of differential ability in achieving them. Indeed, these measures facilitate the identification of the causal effects hypothesized by the medical sequential model. In this paper, we focus on these theoretical models, and are not concerned with specific practices designed to help youth with disabilities find work (Leucking, 2009).

Diagnosis of pervasive developmental disability (PDD) or ASD begins at about 30 months and has a long tail extending into teenage years (Beenstock et al., 2015; Raz et al., 2014). Importantly, diagnostic criteria have changed over time. Until 1995 ASD was defined by DSM 3 as a pervasive lack of responsiveness to other people, gross deficits in language development, and bizarre responses to various aspects of the environment (DeMyer, 1979). Subsequently, the definition was broadened in DSM 4, DSM 4R and DSM 5. In Israel, the clinical assessment of ASD was based on the traditional medical model. In recent years, there has been a shift to the social functional model. Although Matson et al. (2011) found differences in expressions of symptoms among people with ASD in Israel, US, UK and Korea, they found no significant differences in social relationships.

Studies of the transition into adulthood have almost exclusively been informed by sample data for the US with occasional exceptions. Historically, ASD outcome data were mainly clinical, and measured functioning in communication skills and dependency by the severity of symptoms. Studies focused primarily on adolescents and adults living with their parents, and enrolled in educational or rehabilitation settings (Rumsey et al. 1984, Szatmari et al. 1989). It was assumed that individuals with better communication and ADL skills did better than their less skilled counterparts (Kanner, 1971).

Lockyer and Rutter (1970) were the first to propose non-clinical outcome measures, including educational attainment, employment history, degree of independent living and social relationship skills. The most salient measures related to performance in educational and employment settings, and ability to live independently (Magiati et al., 2013). Studies of severity utilized subjective measures, primarily professional observation-based assessments, or parents' ratings of their children's symptoms and behavior. Standardized studies report improvement in behavioral problems in late adolescence, which are attributed to the maturation processes (Byrd, 2002; Howlin & Moss, 2012; Matson & Horovitz, 2010). Some studies report improvements particularly among individuals who function better, participating in educational or habilitation programs (Byrd, 2002; Howlin & Moss, 2012; Shattuck et al., 2007; Shea & Mesibov, 2005). Interestingly, they fail to track changes in severity over time (Billstedt et al., 2007; Larsen & Mouridsen, 1997), noting that early adolescence is the most difficult phase, which plateaus in mid-to-late adolescence (Larsen & Mouridsen, 1997; Venter et al., 1992).

The most common social outcome that is linked to independence, used in adult ASD research, is employment followed by educational attainment, social participation and family support (Chen et al., 2015; Orsmond et al., 2013). Individuals with ASD may be able to work, but are impeded from doing so (Hendricks, 2010). Indeed, employment cannot be separated from functioning and social participation (Roux et al., 2015). Investigating social participation and social engagement in community activities among young adults with ASD is important given the incidence of detachment from social contact. According to Orsmond et al. (2013), almost 40 percent of youth with ASD had never got together with friends, and almost 50 percent of young adults never received phone calls from friends or were invited to social activities. However, engagement in volunteering and activities after graduating high school promotes success in life (Carter et al., 2013).

About 50 percent of students with ASD drop-out from school (Chung et al., 1990), and even fewer complete college or university (Eaves & Ho, 2008; Howlin & Moss, 2012). These individuals under-achieve and demonstrate high job separation rates (Barnhill et al., 2007; Eaves & Ho, 2008). The most important predictors of success in the workplace are lack of disadvantages in the labor market and substantial support received from employers and co-workers (Baldwin et al., 2014). Most young adults with ASD are highly dependent on their families, and about half of those who functioned better live with their parents (Eaves & Ho, 2008). The socio-economic status (SES) of parents plays an important role in helping children with ASD. Pickard and Ingersoll (2015) report that educated middle and upper middle-class parents tend to be more aware of their children's needs and are better at accessing services. By contrast, parents with lower SES find it more difficult to cope with their children, and are more in need of information and in-home services.

In their review of the transition into adulthood, Anderson et al. (2018) have drawn attention to the lack of research into the roles of social capital, including family systems, social networks, communities, neighborhoods, delivery systems for services, and the role of public policy. The present study touches upon some of these issues through its focus on parents, neighborhoods, ethnic groups, the peripherality of communities, and policy towards civic volunteering in Israel.

In summary, our study involves several inter-related research questions.

i. What are the prevalence rates in employment, tertiary education and civic volunteering of young adults with ASD?
ii. Do assessments of social and functional severity at age 18 years predict these outcomes?
iii. Is there a causal effect of the successful transaction of earlier outcomes on later outcomes as predicted by the medical model?
iv. Do earnings vary directly with employment experience as in the general population?
v. How do these outcomes shed light on the medical and social-functional models of disability?
vi. Has the broadening of diagnostic standards in ASD meant that later diagnostic cohorts have easier transitions into adulthood?

We use longitudinal population cohort data for Israel to answer these questions. This is the first study of the transition into adulthood using population cohort data, and is one of the few studies for a country other than the United States.

THE STUDY GROUP

Characteristics of the study group, compared to the Israel population born between 1995 and 2005, are reported in Table 10.1. As expected, males and more recent birth cohorts are disproportionately represented. The correlation between 'functional severity' and 'social severity' is 0.67, however this correlation weakens with severity. Table 10.1 also records that the study group is over-represented in the higher socioeconomic and peripheral clusters localities.

It comes as no surprise that the vast majority of the study group were never employed. On the other hand, perhaps the most surprising statistic in Table 10.1 is that as many as 28.4 percent of the study group had been in competitive employment. Unfortunately, data on sheltered employment are not available. Another surprise is that 20 percent of the study group had been participated in National Service and had even served in the IDF. On the other hand, only 8 percent participated in tertiary education, including vocational training, and only 16 had married of which 5 had children.

Table 10.2 reports the coincidence ratios for positive outcomes. For example, 49.8 percent of the study group who participated in IDF and National Service also participated in employment, while 35.1 percent of participants in employment also participated in IDF and National Service. 44.8 percent of participants in tertiary study also did military or national service, whereas 18.4 percent of participants in military or national service participated in tertiary study.

Figure 10.1 reports the distribution of multiple participation in the four activities by gender and ethnicity. The majority of the sub-groups did not participate in any of these activities, especially ultra-orthodox Jews and Non-Jews (Arabs). Since the latter serve in the army voluntarily (especially Druze and Bedouins) they may at most participate in three activities. Only a tiny percentage of Jews participated in more than two activities.

'High performers' are defined as study group members who completed their army service, acquired higher education, worked for more than 50% of the time and married. In fact, there was only one such high performer since only 16 out of 1599 happened to marry. Dropping family status from the outcomes increases the number of high performers to 40 of which 37 were men and 3 were women. At the other end of the scale, the number of 'low performers' is 1027 (people who never worked, did not serve in the army and did not study), of which 832 were men and 195 were women.

Table 10.1. Characteristics of the study group (N = 1599) (percentages)

		Study group	Israel population at the same age
Male		81.1	50.8
Born in Israel		87.3	88.0
Ethnic group	Other Jews	88.1	61.8
	Ultra-orthodox Jews	9.2	14.1
	Arabs	2.8	24.1
Living with parents at age 18		93.1	69.9
Social severity			na
	mild	11.1	
	moderate	19.3	
	substantial	42.8	
	severe	15.2	
highest	severest	11.7	
Functional severity			na
	independent	11.1	
	not dependent on others	64.3	
	dependent for most ADL	9.3	
	dependent all ADL	8.2	
	totally dependent	7.1	
Socio-economic cluster			
lowest	1-3	6.6	22.2
	4	14.6	19.0
	5	27.3	24.6
	6	15.5	12.0
	7	12.8	7.9
	8	20.4	13.4
highest	9-10	2.4	1.1
Periphery cluster			
lowest	1-3	3.6	4.4
	4-5	14.5	24.3
	6-7	31.4	31.3
highest	8-10	50.6	40.0

		Study group	Israel population at the same age
Year of birth			
	1984 – 5	1.8	14.9
	1986	2.2	7.6
	1987	3.1	7.5
	1988	4.3	7.6
	1989	4.7	7.6
	1990	6.5	7.7
	1991	7.6	7.8
	1992	9.7	7.8
	1993	12.5	7.8
	1994	15.6	7.8
	1995	19.9	7.8
	1996	12.1	8.0
Age at diagnosis			na
	0-2	7.8	
	3-4	25.7	
	5-8	21.2	
	9-17	45.3	
Months employed since 18 years %			
	0	71.6	47.2
	25	18.0	4.3
	More than 25%	10.4	48,5
IDF & National Service (months)			
	0	80.1	35.0
	1-12	7.3	65
	12 +	12.7	10
Tertiary education (months)			
	0	91.7	63.9
	1-12	2.1	0.1
	12 +	6.2	35.9
Family status			
	single	98.8	
	married no children	0.8 (11)	
	married with children	0.4 (5)	

Source: Beenstock, Pinto and Rimmerman (2020).

Table 10.2. Co-incidence ratios between positive outcomes

	Military/national service	Employment	Tertiary study	Marriage
Military/national service		0.498	0.184	0.018
Employment	0.351		0.204	0.020
Tertiary study	0.448			0.052
Marriage	0.312	0.500	0.375	

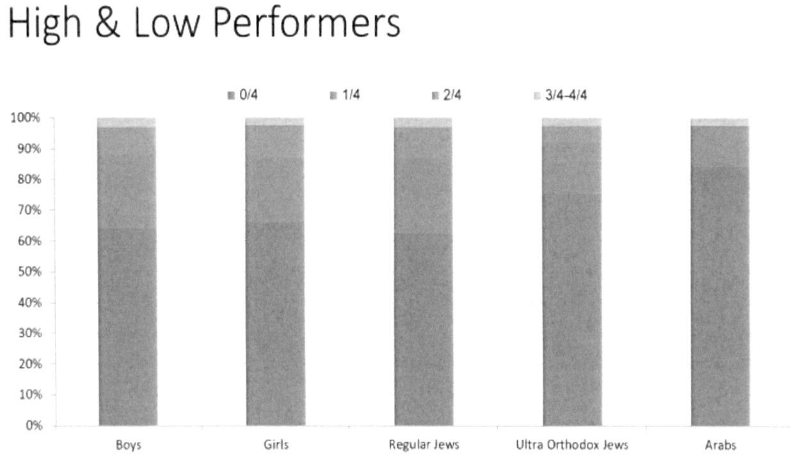

Figure 10.1. Participation in multiple activities.

Table 10.3. Outcome rates and severity

			Severity			
			1	2	3	4
Number		1,405	156	904	131	214
Military & National service %	Partial	14	18	17	3	0
	Full	7	31	5	.	.
Tertiary Studies %	Vocational	3	1	4	2	.
	Academic	5	10	6	1	.
Family %	Married	1	1	1	.	.
	with children	0	2	0	.	.
Employment %	up to 25%	27	38	32	15	4
	more than 25%	11	21	13	5	0

Table 10.3 shows that outcome rates are inversely related to severity as assessed at age 18 years. Outcome rates were zero for all activities except employment for study group members with highest severity (4). Table 10.3 omits the birth cohort of 1996 because, with the exception of employment, none of them had positive outcomes. Although all study group members were assessed for incapacity for work, many in fact worked, and some even earned well.

Figure 10.2 reports non-participation rates in the four activities in 2013 by birth cohort. The earliest birth cohort refers to members of the study group who were born during 1984 – 1986. The latest birth cohort refers to 1996, who would have been 18 years old in 2013. Non-participation rates tend to increase, as expected, the more recent the birth cohort, especially for employment and to some extent for tertiary studies. Note that the more recent birth cohorts' participation in IDF and National Service is censored; they might have participated in this activity after 2013.

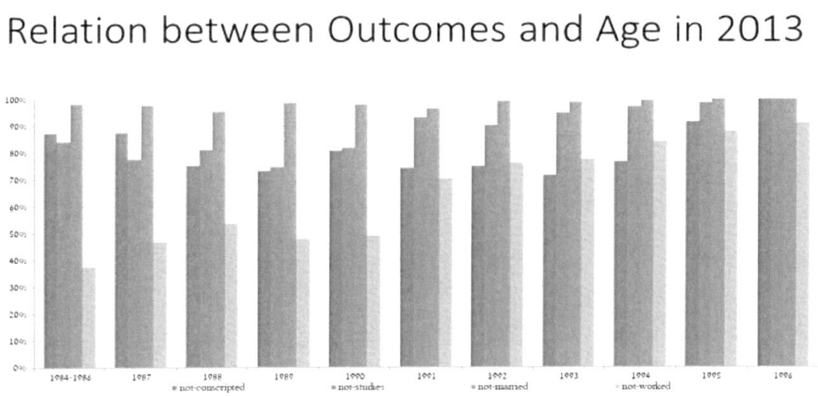

Figure 10.2. Outcomes and Age

Earnings

For the 349 study group members who worked, an unbalanced panel regression with fixed effects was estimated to quantify the return to labor market experience for the study group, where experience is defined as the number of months worked. The fixed effects control for measured and unmeasured differences between members of the study group, including severity, ability, education, birth cohort etc. as well as selectivity.

The regression model is:

$$ln(earnings) = fixed\ effects + \underset{(<0.0001)}{0.0161}\ experience - \underset{(0.0051)}{0.00005}\ experience^2 \quad (10.1)$$

with p-values reported below their parameters and adjusted $R^2 = 0.81$. Both terms in experience are statistically significant, and the negative coefficient on the square of experience means that the effect of experience on earnings is convergent. The marginal return to a month's experience is initially 1.6 percent falling to 1 percent after 5 years and to 0.5 percent after 10 years. Labor economists will recognize equation (10.1) as a 'Mincer model', according to which earnings vary directly with human capital, which accumulates with work experience (Ehrenberg and Smith 2018). Hence, earnings are initially low but increase over time as human capital accumulates. In these respects, equation (10.1) suggests that workers on the spectrum are no different to workers in general.

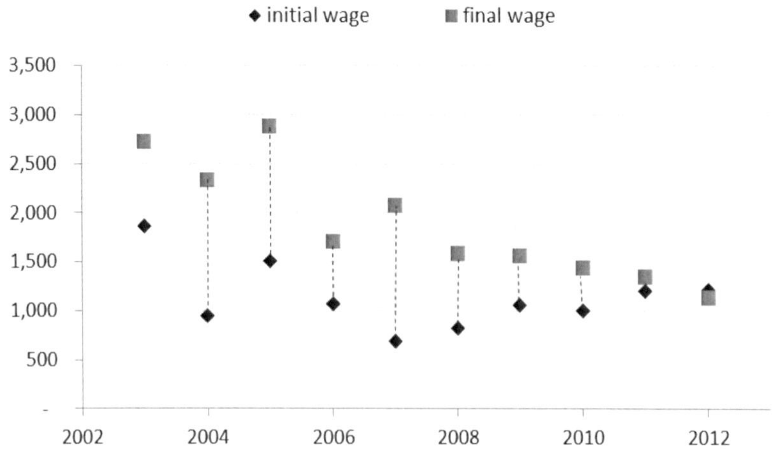

Figure 10.3. Initial and Final Earnings by Initial Year of Employment.

In Figure 10.3 the vertical axis records average earnings in shekels per month at 2012 prices. The horizontal axis refers to the year in which members of the study group first joined the labor market. Diamonds denote initial earnings (when they first joined) and squares (final) refer to the earnings of these labor force cohorts in 2014. For example, members of the study group who entered the labor force in 2003 initially earned, on average 1,900 shekels per month. By 2014 their cohort average earnings increased to 2,750 shekels. For some cohorts, such as 2004, 2005 and 2007, the increase was much larger. The difference between initial and final earnings naturally decreases in Figure 10.3 with cohort years because, for example, the cohort of 2012 had only two years to accumulate human capital by 2014.

Multivariate Analysis of the Transition into Adulthood

In this section we seek to explain participation in three main activities; employment, tertiary study and military/national service. Family status is omitted because almost all the members of the study group are single. Participation in these activities is unlikely to be independent; study group members who participated more in one activity may be expected to participate more in others because they are higher functioning. Also, there may be a hierarchical relationship between these activities. For example, the successful participation in e.g., military and national service might pave the way as a 'stepping stone' to successful participation in employment and tertiary studies.

Note that just because there happens to be a sequential relation between the activities does not mean that participation in an earlier activity has a beneficial causal effect on a later activity. It might simply mean that higher functioning members of the study group happened to undertake more than one activity, and they chose the first before the second. This phenomenon is known by 'spurious state dependence'. We cook before we eat, but this does not mean that cooking causes eating. Hunger causes both cooking and eating, but cooking naturally precedes eating.

Since the majority did not participate, and those who did, participated more or less, we distinguish between the external and internal margins, where the former concerns the decision to participate at all, and the latter is concerned with the amount or degree of participation.

Methodology

Most of the study group did not participate in any outcome. Therefore, to test hypotheses about the determination of these outcomes a statistical methodology is required, which recognizes that the outcome data are neither continuous, a requirement for linear regression, nor dichotomous, a requirement for e.g., logistical regression. We therefore use the incidentally truncated regression method (ITR Heckman, 1976), which hypothesizes two populations: one that does not participate in the outcome of interest, hence $y = 0$, and another that participates for which the outcome is positive. ITR is the same as ITM described in chapter 3 and applied in chapter 8, except whereas ITM involved two probit models (one for selection and the other for recurrence risk), ITR involves a probit model for the extensive margin ($y = 0$) or self-selection into participation, and a regression model for the intensive margin ($y > 0$). In short, ITM is for two binary outcomes while ITR is for a binary outcome and a continuous outcome.

ITR involves the joint estimation by maximum likelihood of equations (10.2), for participation, and equation (10.3) for positive outcomes

$$y_i^* = \alpha + \beta Z_i + e_i \tag{10.2}$$

$$y_i > 0 = \gamma + \delta X_i + \rho\sigma_u\lambda_i + u_i \tag{10.3}$$

$$\lambda_i = \frac{\phi(\alpha+\beta Z_i)}{\Phi(\alpha+\beta Z_i)} \tag{10.4}$$

where ϕ( ) and Φ( ) are the density and cumulative density of the standard normal distribution, i labels individuals, Z is a vector of covariates hypothesized to affect the probability of participation, X is a vector of covariates hypothesized to affect y if it is positive, and r denotes the correlation between e and u. Equation (10.3) is a regression model, controlling for participation in the outcome through λ_i, which measures the incidence of participation relative to its prevalence (hazard). In summary, ITR estimates the probability of participation, and the outcome conditional on participation. ITR was used, for example, by Benito et al. (2016) to study the effect of disability on earnings.

Since there are three key outcomes in the study, ITR generates estimates of residuals e and u for each outcome. These estimates measure unobserved functional abilities, which are likely to be correlated within individuals. We specify estimates obtained for one outcome in the ITR models for the other two outcomes. For example, if individuals more likely to study are also more likely to work, e for tertiary education is specified as a 'generated regressor' (Pagan, 1984) in the ITR model for employment. Whereas in single outcome studies these unobserved characteristics are concealed, in multiple outcome studies, such as ours, they are revealed. There are two natural stages to the generated regressor methodology. In the first, the three ITR models are estimated without generated regressors. In the second stage the ITR models are re-estimated using the residuals obtained from the first stage, as generated regressors in the second. Because the residuals from the first stage are used as generated regressors in the second, there is no order in which the residuals are estimated and incorporated.

There are several time related effects. First, individuals who happened to be younger in December 2013 had more opportunity to participate than their older counterparts; they are more censored. Second, there may be birth-cohort effects, which affect participation and outcomes. Third, if diagnostic criteria broaden over time, year-of-diagnosis is expected to have a positive effect on outcomes because individuals diagnosed more recently are likely to be higher up the spectrum. Fourth, if severer cases are diagnosed when younger, outcomes are expected to vary directly with age-at-diagnosis. Because year-of-diagnosis equals year-of-birth plus age-at-diagnosis, it is impossible to distinguish these three phenomena. Also, year-of-birth is perfectly negatively correlated with age in 2013.

The first effect is hypothesized to depend on the reciprocal of age in 2013 because younger individuals in 2013 are disproportionately more censored than their older counterparts. Since the reciprocal of age in 2013 is imperfectly correlated with year of birth, the first two effects may be identified parametrically. Because we are able to control for severity at age 18, the need to distinguish between the other effects is less crucial, as we comment in discussing the results.

A general-to-specific (GTS) search procedure (Hendry 1995) has been used to select the final model specifications reported in Table 10.4. GTS initially includes X and Z variables suggested by theory and previous research. Subsequently, variables that are not statistically significant are excluded. However, GTS differs from a backward stepwise procedure because variables omitted at an earlier stage are subsequently respecified to check whether their previous exclusion was path-dependent.

We also use a recursive bivariate probit methodology (RBP, Greene, 2012 pp 785-9) to test whether there is a causal effect of earlier outcomes on subsequent outcomes. RBP involves the joint estimation of equations (10.5) and (10.6) by maximum likelihood:

$$y_{1i}^* = \alpha_1 + \beta_1 Z_{1i} + e_{1i} \tag{10.5}$$

$$y_{2i}^* = \alpha_2 + \beta_2 Z_{2i} + \theta Y_{1i} + e_{2i} \tag{10.6}$$

where y_1 occurs before y_2, disturbances e_1 and e_2 are correlated within individuals, and Y_1 is a dummy variable if y_1 is positive. If θ is positive and statistically significant, participation in outcome 1 has a beneficial causal effect on participation in outcome 2, i.e., it does not constitute spurious state dependence. If θ is not statistically significant, participation in outcome 1 merely predicts participation in outcome 2, just as cooking predicts eating.

Results

The upper part of Table 10.4 reports the results for equation (10.3) in which the dependent variable refers to the number of months spent in military and national service, months of tertiary education, and employment measured by the fraction of time since age 18 spent in employment. The lower part (selection) reports the results for equation (10.2), which refers to the probability that the number of months is non-zero, i.e., participation. Hence, the lower part refers to the external margin and the upper part refers to the internal margin.

Initial and interim specifications show that the salient variables in Table 10.4 were salient in the initial and interim GTS specifications. Some variables, such as socio-economic cluster and DSM regime, do not feature in Table 10.4 because they were not statistically significant. Other variables, such as demographic group, feature in some outcome models but not others, or they feature in the selection models but not the regression models, or vice-versa.

The statistical significance of the variables retained in Table 10.4 is naturally high because of GTS; the largest p-value is 0.0837. Variables were either clearly significant, as in Table 10.4, or their p-values were prohibitively large. 'Functional severity' and 'social severity' were statistically significant in all three selection models. However, 'functional severity' matters for months employed but not for other outcomes, and 'social severity' mattered for months of military and national service, but not for other outcomes. Year of birth or the reciprocal of age in 2014 mattered for all selection models and for months of civic volunteering, but not concurrently. Age-at-diagnosis mattered for selection into civic volunteering and employment but not for these outcomes in months. Some variables, such as periphery cluster, born in Israel, or living with parents (at age 18) only mattered for selection with respect to single outcomes.

Table 10.4. ITR models for outcomes

	Military & national service		Tertiary studies		Employment	
	b	P value	b	P value	b	P value
Arab					0.2862	0.077
Haredi	8.2025	0.0024			-0.1161	0.0837
Severity						
Functional					-0.0506	0.0631
Social	-1.6789	0.0279				
1/age in 2014	-700.86	< 0.0001				
GR: emp			-12.128	0.0129		
GR: M&NS					0.0690	0.0168
SELECTION						
Arab			0.7573	0.0207		
Haredi	-0.7143	0.0002			-0.3076	0.0394
Born in Israel	0.3633	.0145				
Year of birth					-0.1710	< 0.0001
1/age in 2014	-39.24	< 0.0001	-111.1	< 0.0001		
Age diagnosis	0.0186	0.045			0.0286	0.0016
Live with parent	0.7040	0.0008				
Earning mother	0.0155	0.005			0.0058	0.0102
Earning father	0.0054	0.0450	0.0069	0.0025	0.0158	0.0016
Severity Function	-0.5604	< 0.0001	-0.2369	0.0025	-0.2130	0.0001
Cluster periphery					0.0514	< 0.0001
GR: M&NS			0.2365	0.0651	0.4932	< 0.0001
GR: tertiary study					0.6140	< 0.0001
GR: employment	0.5248	< 0.0001	0.5196	< 0.0001		
r	-0.3599	0.0293	-0.4766	0.0011	-0.0087	0.9467
Ln likelihood	-1512		-812.1		-654.63	

Notes: Dependent variable: months in activity. GR: generalized residual. Source: Beenstock, Pinto and Rimmerman (2020).

Finally, the generalized residuals used to represent e in equation (10.2) were statistically significant especially for employment. Individuals with a greater susceptibility for employment as measured by its generalized residual, were more likely to engage in civic volunteering and tertiary education, but were also more likely to drop-out of studying. Individuals with a greater susceptibility to participate in military and national service were more likely to work and study, and to work more if they do. These correlated effects are not causal because they express the unobserved functional abilities of members of the study group.

The estimates of ρ were negative in the cases of military and national service and tertiary education and ρ was not statistically significantly different from zero in the case of employment. The former mean that individuals with a greater susceptibility to engage in civic volunteering and tertiary education, volunteered and studied less if they did (negative selection). The latter means that the ever-employed and the never-employed stratified into distinct population subgroups. Indeed, because ρ is zero, the probit model for employment could have been estimated independently of its selection model.

Table 10.5. Size effects on outcomes

	Employment		Military & national service		Tertiary studies	
Margin	**External**	**Internal**	**External**	**Internal**	**External**	**Internal**
Severity Functional	-0.165	-0.051	-0.156	-1.307	-0.051	-3.407
Severity social	-0.072	0	-0.104	-2.394	-0.051	-2.166
Age at diagnosis	0.010	0	0.005	0.043	0	0
Year of birth	-0.058	0	-0.018	-1.184	-0.028	-1.625
Earnings mother	0.002	0	0.004	0.037	0	0
Earnings father	0.005	0	0.002	0.013	0.001	0.063

Source: Beenstock, Pinto and Rimmerman (2020). External margin: change in probability of participation. Internal margin: months.

Size effects of these variables for the three outcomes are calculated for the external and internal margins in Table 10.5. We begin with the probability of participation (external margin). The size effects of 'functional severity' and 'social severity' on all probabilities were large. For example, moving to a higher group of 'functional severity' (e.g., from low to medium, or medium to high) reduces the probability of employment by 0.165 and the probability of studying by 0.051. Because 'functional severity' and 'social severity' comprise the same number of categories (five), Table 10.5 shows that the size effects for 'functional severity' are larger (more negative) than for 'social severity'. For example, in the case of employment the size effect is twice as large for 'functional severity' than for 'social severity'.

The marginal size effect of age-at-diagnosis is 0.01 in the case of employment, i.e., the probability of employment is almost a percentage point higher. This effect is almost twice as large as the size effect for military and national service. The size effect for tertiary education is zero because age-at-diagnosis does not feature in Table 10.4 for tertiary education. The marginal size effect of year-of-birth is -0.058 in the case of employment, i.e., individuals who were younger in 2014 are less likely to be employed because they are more censored. This censoring effect is strongest for employment and weakest, as expected, for military and national service. The implicit size effects for year-of-diagnosis are obtained by summing these two effects, which are negative in all three cases, e.g., the size effect of year-of-diagnosis on the probability of employment is -0.0483; year-of-diagnosis reduced the probability of employment by almost 5 percentage points. Because earnings are measured in 1,000s of shekels (about $250), the size effects for parents' earnings are small. For example, if mothers earned an extra 1,000 shekels, the probability of employment increased by only a fifth of a percentage point. In the case of fathers, this effect was about half a percentage point.

Size effects for internal margins refer to months engaged in the outcomes conditional on participation. For example, the marginal effect of a category of 'functional severity' reduced tertiary education and military and national service by 3.4 and 1.3 respectively. The effect of 'functional severity' on the proportion of months employed was small (5 percentage points).

Causality v Spurious State Dependence

Table 10.4 shows that individuals who were more likely to engage in military and national service were also more likely to engage in tertiary education. These effects do not necessarily have a causal interpretation; they might result from spurious state dependence. Because military and national service is the only outcome to precede another, the recursive bivariate probit (RBP) model tests whether military and national service has a causal gateway effect on tertiary education. Hence, y_1 in equation (10.5) refers to military and national service, and y_2 in equation (10.6) refers to tertiary education.

Table 10.6. Recursive bivariate probit model: military and national service and tertiary study

	Military and national service		Tertiary study	
	b_1	P value	b_2	P value
Arab			0.7217	0.0166
Haredi	-0.6485	0.004		
Born in Israel	0.3411	0.019		
Severity social	-0.2419	< 0.0001		
Severity functional	-0.5315	< 0.0001	-0.4476	< 0.0001
Living with parents	0.6017	0.0026		
Earnings father	0.0071	0.0014	0.0075	0.0038
Earnings mother	0.0179	0.0006	0.0126	0.0437
Cluster periphery			0.0640	0.0273
θ			-0.0757	0.8114
ρ	0.3264 p value 0.0741			
Log likelihood	-927.3			

Source: Beenstock, Pinto and Rimmerman (2020).

Table 10.6 reports results. As in Table 10.4 the probabilities of engaging in civic volunteering and tertiary education vary inversely with ‘functional severity’ and ‘social severity’, and there are other similarities. Table 10.6 shows that θ in equation (10.6) is almost zero and is not statistically significant. Therefore, civic volunteering does not have a causal effect on subsequent engagement in tertiary education. The spurious state dependence is induced by the positive correlation ($\rho = 0.326$) between e_1 in equation (10.5) and e_2 in equation (10.6) with p-value 0.0741; members of the study group who are more likely to do military and national service because they are more high functioning are also more likely to participate in tertiary studies.

DISCUSSION

Three outcomes were used to study the transition into young adulthood by individuals with autism spectrum disorders in Israel: civic volunteering, tertiary education and employment. Although the majority (62 percent of males and 62 percent of females) did not engage in any of these outcomes, a substantial minority were engaged in one or more. Almost 30 percent were engaged in regular (unsheltered) employment.

These results, which are informed by longitudinal population cohort data, tend to support the social-functioning model of transition rather than the traditional sequential model in several respects. First, sequencing does not imply causality. Although earlier milestones such as civic volunteering precede subsequent ones, such as tertiary education, this does not mean that civic volunteering helped individuals with ASD to enter the regular labor market through schooling. Indeed, statistical tests clearly reject this causal pathway. Instead, sequencing is induced by self-selection; higher functioning individuals happen to engage in both earlier and later milestones. Second, the correlations between these outcomes are small. This means that just because someone does not participate in one outcome does not mean that he or she will not participate in another. For example, failure to participate in military and national service and tertiary education does not mean that the individuals concerned are less likely to enter the regular labor market. Consequently, we do not think that the classification of young adults with ASD into 'high' or 'low functioning is helpful. Third, 'functional severity' measured at age 18 predicts all three outcomes, and 'social severity' predicts two (tertiary education and military and national service), regardless of their sequencing. This result is consistent with the social-functioning model.

These results conflict with longitudinal studies, which typically find that measures of adult adaptive functioning serve as better predictors of outcomes than do measures of social communication abilities and skills (Gillespie-Lynch et al., 2012; Howlin et al., 2000; Szatmari et al., 2009). One reason for this difference may be that measures of functional severity are less subjective than measures of social severity (Magiati et al., 2014). Another is that adaptive functioning among children higher up the spectrum tends to improve with the transition into adolescence and adulthood more than do communication and social abilities (Gillespie-Lynch et al., 2012; Szatmari et al., 2009).

Our results show that what matters is the immediate family environment, as represented by parents' income, although these effects are small. The children of Arab families are more likely to engage in tertiary education and spend more time in employment than the children of Jewish families. The children of ultra-orthodox families are less likely to engage in civic volunteering but if they do, they volunteer for longer. Also, they are less likely to have been employed, and work less otherwise. These results suggest that social capital in terms of family capacity and social networks (Anderson et al. 2018) matters for some, but not all outcomes. On the other hand, the fact that outcomes do not depend on the socioeconomic status of locations suggests that social capital beyond the family does not seem to be important. The same applies to the finding that peripheral status of locations does not matter. The transition into adulthood is the same for ASDs raised in Tel Aviv where socioeconomic status is high as it is in Jerusalem where socioeconomic status is low, and it is the same in Tel Aviv where services are plentiful as it is in the periphery where they are not. These results do not conform to the expectations of Anderson et al. (2018).

The earnings of workers with ASD increase more rapidly with their employment experience than they do for the general population (Ehrenberg and Smith, 2018). These returns are four times larger than for the general population in Israel (Dahan, 2001), implying that although the earnings of workers with ASD are initially low, the gap with respect to the general population narrows over time, but does not close. Our results suggest that because employers expect the productivity of ASD workers to be low, their wages are initially low. Subsequently, their rapid wage growth results from employers' realization that, on average, the productivity of ASD workers is higher than initially expected.

Complete stratification arises when the probability of participating in an outcome is independent of the intensity of participation, measured by its duration. In this case, the population that participates and the population that does not do not overlap. Complete stratification arises between the never-employed and ever-employed because the duration of employment is independent of the probability of employment. Hence, the ever-employed and the never-employed constitute non-overlapping populations. Incomplete, or negative, stratification arises in civic participation and tertiary education, where we find that individuals more likely to participate do so for less time. This suggests that participants over-estimate their ability to persist in the activity, or that less able children are pushed into activities beyond their ability.

This study has several implications for policy regarding the transition of individuals with ASD into young adulthood. Just because there is no causal effect of military and national service on subsequent outcomes such as studies, does not mean that the policy to encourage national service in particular is not justified. National service may improve the quality of life, and is justified in its own right regardless of the implications for employment. In this context, negative stratification in national service and tertiary education suggests that participants need help in remaining engaged these activities. Complete stratification in employment implies that programs based on the experience of the employed aimed at increasing the employment prospects of the non-employed are unlikely to be successful, because the never-employed and ever-employed constitute separate populations.

These results are relevant to recent attempts to estimate the economic burden of ASD (Buescher et al., 2014; Leigh and Du 2015). Growing prevalence in ASD implies that the economic burden is likely to increase in the future. This would be true if the degree of disability among the population with ASD remained stable. However, in chapter 5 we reported that severity assessments at age 18 years varied inversely with year-of-diagnosis, suggesting that diagnostic criteria have broadened over time. This implies that the prospective economic burden is likely to decrease, and that employment rates among young adults with ASD are likely to be greater in the future than they have been in the past.

Limitations

Since the study is limited to young adults in their 20s, it may be too early for forming judgments about their transition into mature adulthood. Data deficiencies include whether individuals attended special or regular schools, their residential status after age 18, including hostels and sheltered accommodation, and their participation in protected employment. Finally, the statistical methodology used assumes that what we don't observe about selection into an outcome, and its intensity have bivariate normal distributions. Although the normal distribution enjoys a central place in hypothesis testing, the results might be sensitive to alternative parametric assumptions.

References

Akabayashi, H. (2006). An equilibrium model of child maltreatment. *Journal of Economic Dynamics and Control*, 30: 993-1025.

Anderson, E. A., Roux, A. M., Kuo, A. and Shattuck, P. T. (2018). Social-ecological correlates in adult autism outcome studies. *Pediatrics*, doi.org/10.1542/peds.2016-4300H.

Angrist, J., Lavy, V. and Schlosser, A. (2012). Multiple experiments for the causal link between the quantity and quality of children. *Journal of Labor Economics*, 28: 773-824.

Baldwin, S., Costley, D., and Warren, A. (2014). Employment activities and experiences of adults with high-functioning autism and Asperger's disorder. *Journal of Autism and Developmental Disorders*, *44*(10), 2440.

Barnhill, H. N., Claudel-Gillet, S., Ziessel, R., Charbonnière, L. J., and Wang, Q. (2007). Prototype protein assembly as scaffold for time-resolved fluoroimmuno assays. *Journal of the American Chemical Society*, *129*(25), 7799-7806.

Becker, G. S. (1992). *Treatise in the Family,* 2nd edition, Harvard University Press.

Beenstock, M. and Rahav, G. (2004). Immunity and susceptibility in illicit drug use, *Journal of Quantitative Criminology*, 20: 117-142.

Beenstock, M. (2007). Do abler parents have fewer children? *Oxford Economic Papers*, 59: 430-457.

Beenstock, M. (2012). *Heredity, Family and Inequality*, MIT Press.

Beenstock, M., Raz, R. and Levine, H. (2015). Birth gap and the recurrence risk of autism spectrum disorders: a population-based cohort study. *Research in Autism Spectrum Disorders*, 17: 86-94.

Beenstock, M., Pinto, O. and Rimmerman, A. (2020). Transition into adulthood with autism spectrum disorder: a longitudinal population cohort study of socioeconomic outcomes. *Journal of Disability Policy Studies*, https//doi.org/10.1177/1044207320943590.

Beenstock, M. (2021a). Parenting and reproductive stoppage in the psychopathology of recurrence risk in autism spectrum disorder. *Autism – Heterogeneity, Etiological Core and Outcome*. M. Fitzgerald (ed.), Intechopen, London. 2021.

Beenstock, M. (2021b). Selection bias induced by reproductive stoppage in estimates of recurrence risk for autism spectrum disorders. *Research in Autism Spectrum Disorders*, forthcoming. DOI: 10.1016/j.rasd.2021.101863

Benito, S. G., Glassman, T. S. and Hiedemann, B. G. (2016). Disability and labor market earnings: hearing earnings gaps in the United States. *Journal of Disability Policy Studies*, *27*(3), 178-188.

Bettelheim, B. (1967). *The Empty Fortress: Infantile Autism and the Birth of the Self*. New York, Free Press.

Billstedt, E., Carina, Gillberg, I. and Gillberg, C. (2007). Autism in adults: symptom patterns and early childhood predictors. Use of the DISCO in a community sample followed from childhood. *Journal of Child Psychology and Psychiatry*, *48*(11), 1102-1110.

Bolton, P. et al. (1984). A case-control family history study of autism. *Journal of Child Psychology and Psychiatry*, 35: 877-900.

Bouchard, T. J. and McGue, M. (1981). Familial studies of intelligence: a review. *Science*, 212: 1055-1059.

Buescher, A. V., Cidav, Z., Knapp, M. and Mandell, D. S. (2014). Costs of autism spectrum disorders in the United Kingdom and the United States. *JAMA Pediatrics*, *168*(8), 721-728.

Bushman, B. J., Baumeister, R. F. Stack, A. D. (1999). Catharsis, aggression and persuasive influence: self-fulfilling or self-defeating prophecies? *Journal of Personal Social Psychology*. 1999; 76: 367-376.

Byrd, R. S. (2002). The epidemiology of autism in California: a comprehensive pilot study. MIND Institute, University of California, Davies.

Cameron, C. and Trivedi, P. (1998). *Regression Analysis of Count Data*. Cambridge: Cambridge University Press.

Carter, E. W., Harvey, M. N., Taylor, J. L. and Gotham, K. (2013). Connecting youth and young adults with autism spectrum disorders to community life. *Psychology in the Schools*, *50*(9), 888-898.

Central Bureau of Statistics, (2003). Characterizing local authorities by socio-economic clustering (Hebrew), Jerusalem, ISSN 1565-2743.

Chen, J. L. Leader, G. et al. (2015). Trends in employment for individuals with Autism Spectrum Disorders: A review of the research literature. *Review Journal of Autism and Developmental Disorders*, 2, 115-127.

Cheslack-Postava, K., Lui, K. and Bearman, P. S. (2011). Closely spaced pregnancies are associated with increased odds of autism in Californian sibling births. *Pediatrics*, 127, 246-253.

Chiarotti, F. and Venerosi, A. (2020). Epidemiology of autism spectrum disorder: a review of worldwide prevalence estimates since 2014. *Brain Science*, 10: 274.

Chudik, A., Pesaran, M. H. and Rebucci, A. (2021). Covid-19 time-varying reproduction numbers worldwide: an empirical analysis of mandatory and voluntary social distancing. *National Bureau of Economic Research*, working paper 28629.

Chudley, A. E. et al. (1998). Outcomes of genetic evaluation in children with pervasive development disorder. *Journal of Developmental and Behavioral Pediatrics,* 19: 321-325.

Chun, H., Leung, C., Wen, S. W. et al. (2020). Maternal exposure to air pollution and risk of autism in children: a systematic review and meta-analysis. *Environmental Pollution*, 256: 113307.

Chung, S. Y., Luk, S. L. and Lee, P. W. (1990). A follow-up study of infantile autism in Hong Kong. *Journal of Autism and Developmental Disorders*, 20(2), 221-232.

Constantino, J. N., Zhang, Y., Frazier, T., Abbacchi, A. M. and Law P. (2010). Sibling recurrence and genetic epidemiology of autism. *American Journal of Psychiatry*, 167, 1349-1356.

Constantino, J. N. et al. (2013). Autism recurrence in half siblings: strong support for the genetic mechanism of transmission in autism spectrum disorders. *Molecular Psychiatry*, 18: 137-138.

Cox, D. and Oakes, D. (1985). *Analysis of Survival Data.* Chapman and Hall, New York.

Dahan, M. (2001). The growth in inequality. *The Israeli Economy 1985 – 1998: From Government Intervention to Market Economics.* A. Ben Bassat (ed.), 610 – 656, Am Oved, Tel Aviv.

Davidovitch, M., Hemo, B., Manning-Courtney, P. and Fombonne, E. (2013). Prevalence and incidence of autism spectrum disorder in an Israeli population. *Journal of Autism and Developmental Disorders*, 43(4), 785-793.

DeMyer, M. K. (1979). *Parents and Children in Autism*. VH Winston.

Dunning, T. (2012). *Natural Experiments in the Social Sciences: A Design-based Approach.* Cambridge: Cambridge University Press.

Eaves, L. C. and Ho, H. H. (2008). Young adult outcome of autism spectrum disorders. *Journal of Autism and Developmental Disorders*, 38(4), 739-747.

Egeland, B., Carlson, E. and Sroufe, L. A. (1993). Resilience as process. *Development and Psychopathology,* 5: 517-528.

Ehrenberg, R. G. and Smith, R. S. (2018). *Modern Labor Economics: Theory and Public Policy*. 13th edition, Routledge.

Engström, I., Ekström, L. and Emilsson, B. (2003). Psychosocial functioning in a group of Swedish adults with Asperger syndrome or high-functioning autism. *Autism*, 7(1), 99-110.

Eyal, G., Hart, B., Onculer, E., Oren, N. and Rossi, N. (2010). *The Autism Matrix: the Social Origins of the Autism Epidemic*. Cambridge, Polity Press.

Feinstein, A. A. (2010). *History of Autism: Conversations with the Pioneers*. Oxford: Blackwell.

Folstein, S. and Rutter, M. (1977). Infantile autism: a genetic study of 21 twin pairs. *Journal of Child Psychology and Psychiatry, and Allied Disciplines*, 18: 297-321.

Galton, F. (1875). The history of twins, as a criterion for the relative powers of nature and nurture. *Journal of the Anthropological Institute*, 5: 391-406.

Gillespie-Lynch, K., Sepeta, L., Wang, Y., Marshall, S., Gomez, L., Sigman, M. and Hutman, T. (2012). Early childhood predictors of the social competence of adults with autism. *Journal of Autism and Developmental Disorders*, *42*(2), 161-174.

Goldberger, A. S. (1977). Twin methods: a skeptical view. *Kinometrics: Determinants of Socioeconomic Success within and between Families*. P. Taubman (ed), Amserdam, North Holland.

Goldberger, A. S. (1979). Heritability, *Economica*, 46: 327-347.

Goldberger, A. S. (2005). Structural equation models in human behavioral genetics, *Identification and Inference for Econometric Models: Essays in Honor of Thomas Rothenberg*. D. Andrews and J. Stocks (eds), Cambridge University Press.

Goodman, L. A. (1961). Snowball sampling. *Annals of Mathematical Statistics*, 32: 147-170.

Greene, W. A. (2012). *Econometric Analysis*, 7th edition, Prentice Hall.

Grønborg, T. K., Schendel, D. E. and Parner, E. T. (2013). Recurrence of autism spectrum disorders in full and half siblings, and trends over time: a population-based cohort study. *JAMA Pediatrics*, 167: 947-953.

Grønborg, T. K., Hansen, S. N., Nielsen, S. V. et al. (2015). Stoppage in autism spectrum disorders. *Journal of Autism and Developmental Disorders*, 45: 3509-3519.

Gunnes, N., Suren, P., Bresnahan, M. et al. (2013). Interpregnancy interval and risk of autistic disorder. *Epidemiology*. 24, 906-912.

Hallmayer, J. et al. (2011). Genetic heritability and shared environmental factors among twin pairs with autism. *JAMA Psychiatry*, 68:

Hansen, S. N. et al. (2019). Recurrence risk of autism in siblings and cousins: a multinational population-based study. *Journal of the American Academy of Child and Adolescent Psychiatry*, 58: 866-875.

Hausman, J. (1978). Specification tests in econometrics. *Econometrica*, 46: 1251-1271.

Heckman, J. (1976). The common structure of statistical models of truncation, sample selection, and limited dependent variables, and a simple estimator for such models. *Annals of Economic and Social Measurement*, 5: 475-492.

Hendricks, D. (2010). Employment and adults with autism spectrum disorders: Challenges and strategies for success. *Journal of Vocational Rehabilitation*, *32*(2), 125-134.

Hendry, D. F. (1995). *Dynamic Econometrics*. Oxford University Press.

Hoffmann, T. J., Windham, G., Andersen, M. et al. (2014). Evidence of reproductive stoppage in families with autism spectrum disorders. *JAMA Psychiatry*, 71(8): 943-951.

Holwerda, A., van der Klink, J. J., Groothoff, J. W. and Brouwer, S. (2012). Predictors for work participation in individuals with an autism spectrum disorder: A systematic review. *Journal of Occupational Rehabilitation*, *22*(3), 333-352.

Howlin, P., Mawhood, L. and Rutter, M. (2000). Autism and developmental receptive language disorder—A follow-up comparison in early adult life. II: Social, behavioural, and psychiatric outcomes. *The Journal of Child Psychology and Psychiatry and Allied Disciplines*, *41*(5), 561-578.

Hume, D. (1748). *An Enquiry Concerning Human Understanding*. A. Millar, London.

Infante-Rivard, C. and Cusson, A. (2018). Reflection on modern methods: selection bias - a review of recent developments. *International Journal of Epidemiology*, 1714-1722.

Jencks, C. (1972). *Inequality: A Reassessment of the Family and Schooling in America*. Harper and Row, New York.

Jones, M. B. and Szatmari, P. (1988). Stoppage rules and genetic studies of autism. *Journal of Autism and Developmental Disorders*, 18: 31-40.

Jorde, L. B. et al. (1991). Complex segregation analysis of autism. *American Journal of Human Genetics*, 49: 932-938.

Kalbfleisch, J. and Prentice, R. (2002). *The Statistical Analysis of Failure Time Data*. 2nd edition, John Wiley & Sons, New York.

Kaplan, E. and Meier, P. (1958). Nonparametric estimation from incomplete observations. *Journal of the American Statistical Association*, 53: 457-481.

Kanner, L. (1943). Autistic disturbances of affective contact. *Nervous Child.* 2: 217-250.

Kanner, L. Problems of nosology and psychodynamics in early childhood autism. *American Journal of Orthopsychiatry*. 1949; 19: 416-426.

Kanner, L. Infantile autism and the schizophrenias. *Psychiatric Digest*. 1968; 29: 17-28.

Kanner, L. (1971). Follow-up study of eleven autistic children originally reported in 1943. *Journal of Autism and Developmental Disorders*, *1*(2), 119-145.

Kuhn, T. S. (1970). *The Structure of Scientific Revolutions*. 2nd edition, University of Chicago Press, Chicago. Illinois.

Kuja-Halkola, R., Larrson, H., Lundström, S. et al. (2019). Reproductive stoppage in autism spectrum disorders in a population of 2.5 million individuals. *Molecular Autism*, 10: 45.

Lambert, D. (1992). Zero-inflated Poisson regression, with an application to defects in manufacturing. *Technometrics*, 34: 1-14.

Landrigan, P. J. (2010). What causes autism? Exploring the environmental contribution. *Current Opinion in Pediatrics*, 22: 219-225.

Larsen, F. W., and Mouridsen, S. E. (1997). The outcome in children with childhood autism and Asperger syndrome originally diagnosed as psychotic. A 30-year follow-up study of subjects hospitalized as children. *European Child & Adolescent Psychiatry*, *6*(4), 181-190.

Lauritsen, M. B., Pedersen, C. B. and Mortensen, P. B. (2005). Effects of familial risk factors and place of birth on the risk of autism: a nationwide register-based study. *Journal of Child Psychology and Psychiatry*, 46: 963-971.

Lauritsen, M. B., Jørgensen, M., Madsen, K. M. et al. (2010). Validity of childhood autism in the Danish Psychiatric Central Register: findings from a cohort sample born 1990–1999. *Journal of Autism and Developmental Disorders*. 40, 139-148.

Leigh, J. P. and Du, J. (2015). Brief report: Forecasting the economic burden of autism in 2015 and 2025 in the United States. *Journal of Autism and Developmental Disorders*, *45*(12), 4135.

Levy, A. and Perry, A. (2011). Outcomes in adolescents and adults with autism: A review of the literature. *Research in Autism Spectrum Disorders*, *5*(4), 1271-1282.

Lizzeri, A. and Siniscalchi, M. (2008). Parental guidance and supervised leaning. *Quarterly Journal of Economics*, 123: 1161-1195.

Lockyer, L. and Rutter, M. (1970). A five to fifteen year follow-up study of infantile psychosis: IV. Patterns of cognitive ability. *British Journal of Clinical Psychology*, *9*(2), 152-163.

Luecking, R. G. (2009). *The Way to Work: How to Facilitate Work Experiences for Youth in Transition*. Brookes Publishing Company. PO Box 10624, Baltimore, MD 21285.

Loehlin, J. C. (1992). *Genes and Environment in Personality Development*. Sage.

Madalla, G. S. (1983). *Limited Dependent Variables and Qualitative Variables in Econometrics*. Cambridge University Press.

Magiati, I., Tay, X. W. and Howlin, P. (2014). Cognitive, language, social and behavioural outcomes in adults with autism spectrum disorders: a systematic review of longitudinal follow-up studies in adulthood. *Clinical Psychology Review*, *34*(1), 73-86.

Maller, R. and Zhou, X. (1997). *Survival Analysis with Long-term Survivors*. Wiley.

Manski, C. H. (1995). *Identification Problems in the Social Sciences*, Harvard University Press.

Marks, D. (1997). Models of disability. *Disability and Rehabilitation*, *19*(3), 85-91.

Matson, J. L. and Horovitz, M. (2010). Stability of autism spectrum disorders symptoms over time. *Journal of Developmental and Physical Disabilities*, *22*(4), 331-342.

Matson, J. L. and Kozlowski, A. M. (2011). The increasing prevalence of autism spectrum disorders. *Research in Autism Spectrum Disorders*, *5*(1), 418-425.

Matson, J. L., Worley, J. A., Fodstad, J. C. et al. (2011). A multinational study examining the cross-cultural differences in reported symptoms of autism spectrum disorders: Israel, South Korea, the United Kingdom, and the United States of America. *Research in Autism Spectrum Disorders*, *5*(4), 1598-1604.

Matson, J. L., Beighley, J. and Turygin, N. (2012). Autism diagnosis and screening: Factors to consider in differential diagnosis. *Research in Autism Spectrum Disorders*, *6*(1), 19-24.

Meyer, W. S. (2010). Bruno Bettelheim and his window to the soul. *Clinical Social Work Journal*. 38: 275–285.

Moffat, P. G. (2021). Experiments: a survey. *Foundations and Trends in Econometrics*, 11 1-152.

Nevison, C., Blaxill, M. and Zahorodny, W. (2018). California's autism prevalence trends from 1931 – 2014 and comparison to national ASD data from IDEA and ADDM. *Journal of Autism and Developmental Disorders*, 48: 4103–4117.

Nourse, H. O. (1967). The effect of air pollution on house values. *Land Economics*, 43: 181-189.

Orsmond, G. I., Shattuck, P. T., Cooper, B. P., Sterzing, P. R. and Anderson, K. A. (2013). Social participation among young adults with an autism spectrum disorder. *Journal of Autism and Developmental Disorders*, *43*(11), 2710-2719.

Ozonoff, S., Young, G. S., Carter, A. et al. (2011). Recurrence risk for autism spectrum disorders: a baby siblings research consortium study. *Pediatrics*, 128: e488-e495.

Pagan, A. (1984). Econometric issues in the analysis of regressions with generated regressors. *International Economic Review, 25:221-247.*

Pickard, K. E. and Ingersoll, B. R. (2015). Brief report: high and low level initiations of joint attention, and response to joint attention: differential relationships with language and imitation. *Journal of Autism and Developmental Disorders*, 45(1), 262.

Plomin R., DeFries, J., McLearn, G. E. and McGuffin, P. (2001). *Behavioral Genetics*, 4th edition, Worth.

Popper K. R. (1963). *Conjectures and Refutations: The Growth of Scientific Knowledge*. London: Routledge and Kegan Paul.

Ratto, A. B. et al. (2018). What about girls? Sex-based differences in autistic traits and adaptive skills. *Journal of Autism and Developmental Disorders*, 48: 1698-1311.

Raz, R., Weisskopf, M. G., Davidovitch, M., Pinto, O. and Levine, H. (2014). Differences in autism spectrum disorders incidence by sub-populations in Israel 1992-2009: a total population study. *Journal of Autism and Developmental Disorders*, doi 10.1007/s10803-014-2262-z.

Richardson, G. E. (2002). The metatheory of resilience and resiliency. *Journal of Clinical Psychology*, 58: 307-321.

Rimland B. (1964). *Infantile Autism: The Syndrome and its Implications for a Neural Theory of Behavior*. New Jersey: Prentice Hall.

Ritvo, E. R., Jorde, L. B., Mason-Brothers, A. et al. (1989). The UCLA-University of Utah epidemiological survey of autism: recurrence risk estimates and genetic counseling. *American Journal of Psychiatry*, 146, 1032-1036.

Robert, S. (2011). *Le Mur*, Youtube.

Roberts, E. M., English, P. B., Grether, J. K. et al. (2007). Maternal residence near agricultural pesticide applications and autism spectrum disorders among children in the California Central Valley. *Environmental Health Perspectives,* 115: 1482-1489.

Rosenbaum, P. M. (2002). *Observational Data*, 2nd edition, Springer.

Roux, A. M., Shattuck, P. T., Rast, J. E., Rava, J. A. and Anderson, K. A. (2015). National autism indicators report: Transition into young adulthood. *Life Course Outcomes Research Program,* AJ Drexel Autism Institute, Drexel University, Philadelphia, PA.

Rumsey, J. M., Rapoport, J. L. and Sceery, W. R. (1985). Autistic children as adults: psychiatric, social, and behavioral outcomes. *Journal of the American Academy of Child Psychiatry*, *24*(4), 465-473.

Rutter, M. (1967). Psychotic disorders in early childhood. In *Recent Developments in Schizophrenia*, Coppen A, and Walk A. (eds.). *British Journal of Psychiatry, Special Publication 1*.

Rutter M. (2010). Interview in Feinstein (2010).

Rutter, M. and Sroufe, L. A. (2000). Developmental psychopathology: concepts and challenges. *Development and Psychopathology*, 12: 265-296.

Sacerdote, B. (2007). How large are the effects from changes in family environment? A study of Korean – American adoptees. *Quarterly Journal of Economics*, 122: 119-157.

Sandin, S., Lichtenstein, P., Kuja-Haikola, R. et al. (2014). The familial risk of autism. *JAMA*, 311: 1770-1777.

Schall, C. M. and McDonough, J. T. (2010). Autism spectrum disorders in adolescence and early adulthood: Characteristics and issues. *Journal of Vocational Rehabilitation*, *32*(2), 81-88.

Segev, A., Weisskopf, M. G., Levine, H., Pinto, O. and Raz, R. (2019). Incidence time trends and socioeconomic factors in the observed incidence of autism spectrum disorders: a nationwide nested case control study. *Autism Research*, 12: 1870-1879.

Shattuck, P. T., Seltzer, M. M., Greenberg, J. S. et al. (2007). Change in autism symptoms and maladaptive behaviors in adolescents and adults with an autism spectrum disorder. *Journal of Autism and Developmental Disorders*, *37*(9), 1735-1747.

Shea, V. and Mesibov, G. B. (2005). Adolescents and adults with autism. *Handbook of Autism and Pervasive Developmental Disorders, Volume 1, (3rd ed.)*. 288-311.

Smith, M. D. (2003). Modeling sample selection using Archimedean copulas. *The Econometrics Journal,* 6: 99-123.

Sumi, S., Taniai, H., Miyachi, T. and Tanemura, M. (2006). Sibling risk of pervasive developmental disorder estimated by means of an epidemiologic survey in Nagoya, Japan. *Journal of Human Genetics*, 51: 518-522.

Sutton, N. (1996). *Bettelheim, a Life and Legacy*. New York: Basic Books.

Szatmari, P., Bartolucci, G., Bremner, R., Bond, S. and Rich, S. (1989). A follow-up study of high-functioning autistic children. *Journal of Autism and Developmental Disorders*, 19(2), 213-225.

Tick, B. et al. (2016). Heritability of autism spectrum disorders: a meta-analysis of twin studies. *Journal of Child Psychology and Psychiatry*, 57: 585-595.

Thomas, W. I. and Swain Thomas, D. (1928). *The Child in America: Behavior Problems and Programs*. New York: Knopf.

Venter, A., Lord, C. and Schopler, E. (1992). A follow-up study of high-functioning autistic children. *Journal of Child Psychology and Psychiatry*, *33*(3), 489-597.

Waye, M. M. Y. and Cheng, H. Y. (2018). Genetics and epigenetics of autism: a review. *Psychiatry and Clinic Neurosciences*, 72: 228-244.

Wehman, P., Schall, C., Carr, S. et al. (2014). Transition from school to adulthood for youth with autism spectrum disorder: What we know and what we need to know. *Journal of Disability Policy Studies*, *25*(1), 30-40.

Weisskopf, M. G., Kioumourtzoglu, M. and Roberts, A. L. (2015). Air pollution and autism spectrum disorders: causal or confounded? *Current Environmental Health Reports*, 2: 430-439.

Wood, C. L., Warnell, F., Johnson, M. et al. (2014). Evidence for ASD recurrence rates and reproductive stoppage from large UK ASD research family databases. *Autism Research,* 8:73-81.

World Health Organization. (2001). *International Classification of Functioning, Disability and Health: ICF*. World Health Organization.

Wynand, P. and van Praag, B. (1981). The demand for deductibles in private health insurance; a probit model with sample selection. *Journal of Econometrics*, 17: 229-252.

Yates, T., Egeland, B. and Sroufe L. A. (2002). Rethinking resilience: a developmental process perspective. In S. Luthar (ed.) *Resilience and*

Vulnerability: Adaptation in the Context of Childhood Adversities. (pp 243-266). Cambridge University Press.

Zhao, Q., Small, D. and Bhattacharya, B. (2019). Sensitivity analysis for Inverse Probability Weighting estimators via the percentile bootstrap. *Journal of the Royal Statistical Society, Series B*.

Author Contact Information

Michael Beenstock

Hebrew University of Jerusalem

Professor of Economics

Jerusalem, Israel

Michael.beenstock@mail.huji.ac.il

INDEX OF NAMES

H

I

J

K

L

M

O

P

R

S

T

V

W

Z

Index of Terms

D

E

F

G

H

I

M

N

O

P

R

S

T

U

V

W